Index / Inhaltsverzeichnis

Page / Seite

Vocabulary	English–German		3
Units			57
Wörterverzeichnis	Deutsch–Englisch		63
Einheiten			117

*****

Electric motors, generators, transformers
Elektromotoren, Generatoren, Transformatoren — egt 1 – 32

Conventional and alternative energy
Konventionelle und alternative Energie — kae 1 – 28

Machine parts and vehicle parts
Maschinen- und Fahrzeugelemente — mfe 1 – 31

Pumps, gates and valves
Pumpen, Schützen und Ventile — psv 1 – 28

Statics, strength
Statik, Festigkeit — stfe 1 – 19

Internal combustion engines
Verbrennungsmotoren — vbm 1 – 27

SV

Schnellmann Verlag
Widnau
Schweiz/Switzerland

ISBN 3-907972-48-1

a number of forces(pl	mehrere Kräfte(pl
ablative plastics	ablativer Kunststoff(m
ablative resin	Abschmelzkunstharz(m
abrader, abrading device	Schleifapparat(m
abrasion test	Abnutzungstest(m
abrasive finishing	Feinen(n mit Schleifmittel
abrasive wheel	Schleifscheibe(f
absolute error	absoluter Fehler(m
absolute permeability	magnetische Feldkonstante(f
absolute permittivity	elektrische Feldkonstante(f
absorber	Absortionsmittel(n
absorbing screen	Absorptionsschirm(m
absorption coefficient	Absorptionskoeffizient(m
AC, alternating current	Wechselstrom(m
accelerating	Beschleunigen(n
accelerating relay	Beschleunigungsrelais(n
accelerating torque	Beschleunigungsmoment(n
acceleration	Beschleunigung(f
acceleration time	Beschleunigungszeit(f
acceleration time	Anlaufzeit(f
accelerator, hardener	Beschleuniger(m, Härter(m
accetance tests	Abnahmeprüfungen(pl
accumulator box	Akkumulatorengefäss(n
accumulator group	Akkumulatorplattensatz(m
accumulator head	Speicherkopf(m
accumulator, store	Speicher(m, Akku(m
accuracy	Genauigkeit(f
accuracy grade, degree of accuracy	Genauigkeitsgrad(m
acid refractory	saurer feuerfester Stoff(m
acid-resisting paint	säurefeste Anstrichfarbe(f
acidproof	säurebeständig, säurefest
action potential	Aktionspotential(n
activation overvoltage	Aktivierungs(über)spannung(f
activation, sensitization	Aktivierung(f
activator, sensitizer	Aktivator(m, Aktivierungsmittel(n
active area	wirksame Oberfläche(f
active current, actual -	Wirkstrom(m
active power	Wirkleistung(f
actuator, spray gun	Sprühkopf(m
acyclic machine	azyklische Maschine(f
adamantine	diamantarti
adapter plate	Aufspannplatte(f
adapter ring	Passring(m
adapter, adaptor, adopter	Passstück(n
addendum	Kopfhöhe(f
adhesion coefficient	Reibungskoeffizient(m
adhesive bonding	Klebekaschieren(n
adhesive joint	Klebeverbindung(f

adhesive solution	Klebelösung(f
adhesive surface, adherend	Klebefläche(f
adhesive varnish	Klebelack(m
adhesive, glue	Klebstoff(m
adjustable capacitances	verstellbare Kapazitäten(pl
adjustable resistor	einstellbarer Widerstand(m
adjusting clip	Klemmplatte(f
adjusting screw	Regulierschraube(f
admission pipe	Einlassrohr(n
aerated plastic, foamed –	Schaumkunststoff(m
afterbodying, afterthickening	Nachdicken(n
aftercontraction	Nachschwinden(n
aftercooling	Nachkühlung(n
afterexpansion	Nachdehnung(f
aftertreatment	Nachbehandlung(f
age resistor, antioxidant	Alterungsschutzmittel(n
agitator	Rührtank(m, Agitator(m
air cleaner, – filter	Luftfilter(m, Luftreiniger(m
air conduit	Luftleitung(f
air filter	Luftfilter(m
air inlet	Lufteinlass(m
air lock	pneumatische Schleuse(f
air seal	Luftabdichtung(f
air valve	Luftventil(n
air-hydraulic press	lufthydraulische Presse(f
air-inflated cushion	Luftkissen(n
air-jet mill	Luftstrahlmühle(f
alarm switch	Alarmschalter(m
alkali hydrometer, alkalimeter	Alkalimeter(n, Laugenmesser(m
alloy diode	Legierdiode(f
alternating control, dual –	Wechselsteuerung(f
alternating current	Wechselstrom(m
alternating current motor	Wechselstrommotor(m
alternating field	Wechselfeld(n
alternating flux	Wechselfluss(m
alternating-current bridge	Wechselstrombrücke(f
alternating-current circuit	Wechselstromkreis(m
alumetization, alumizing	Aluminieren(n, Aluminisieren(n
aluminized screen	aluminisierter Schirm(m
ambient light	Umgebungsbeleuchtung(f
ammeter	Strommesser(m, Amperemeter(n
ammeter	Ampèremeter(n
amount of substance	Stoffmenge(f
ampere-conductors	Ampereleiter(pl
ampere-turns	Amperewindungen(pl
amplification factor	Verstärkungsfaktor(m
amplifier	Verstärker(m
anchor clamp	Abspannklemme(f

anchoring cable	Abspannkabel(n
angle bar, turning bar	Wendestange(f
angle of divergence	Streuungswinkel(m
angle of lead	Steigungswinkel(m (Gewinde-)
angle of twist	Verdrehwinkel(m
angle of Vee	Oeffnungswinkel(m
angle press	Winkelpresse(f
angle support	Winkelstütze(f
angular frequency	Kreisfrequenz(f
annealing range	Kühlstrecke(f
annular cross section	rinförmiger Querschnitt(m
anode strap	Anodenkoppelleitung(f
anode anchoring	Anodenverankerung(f
anode clamp	Anodenbügel(m
anode effect	Anodeneffekt(m
anode fin, plate fin	Anodenkühlrippe(f
anode neck	Anodenhals(m
anode protecting cap	Anodenschutzkappe(f
anode voltage, plate -	Anodenspannung(f
anode, plate	Anode(f
anomalous magnetic moment	anomales magnetisches Moment(n
anti-parallel coupling	Antiparallelschaltung(f
anti-vacuum	Gegenvakuum(n
anticorrosive paint	Korrosionsschutzfarbe(f
antirust agent	Rostschutzmittel(n
antiwear additive	verschleisshindernde Zugabe(f
aperiodic	aperiodisch
aperiodic time constant	aperiodische Zeitkonstante(f
apparent power	Scheinleistung(g
approach control	Annäherungssignal-System(n
approximate, approximative	angenähert
arbor, spindle	Achse(f, Welle(f, Spindel(m
arc crater	Schweissblase(f, Schweisskrater(m
arc of contact	Überdeckungsgrad(m
arching of a cylinder	Walzenwölbung(f
arcing contact	Abreisskontakt(m
arcing ring	Schutzring(m
area of contact, length - -	Eingriffsstrecke(f
armature	Anker(m
armature core	Ankerkern(m
armature current	Ankerstrom(m
armature hub	Ankernabe(f
armature pair	Anker(zweig)paar(n
armature reaction	Ankerrückwirkung(f
armature reed, armature spring	Ankerfeder(f
armature resistance	Ankerwiderstand(m
armature winding	Ankerwicklung(f
armo(u)red	bewehrt, gepanzert

artificial resin, synthetic –	Kunstharz(n
artificial rubber	synthetischer Gummi(m
ascending tube	Steigrohr(n
asphalt coating	Asphaltschicht(f
asphalt lining	Asphaltfutter(n
assembly adhesive, structural	– Montagekleber(m
astatic	astatisch
astatic element	astatisches Organ(n
asynchronous generator	Asynchrongenerator(m
asynchronous impedance	Asynchron-Impedanz(f
asynchronous machine	Asynchronmaschine(f
asynchronous operation	asynchroner Lauf(m
asynchronous reactance	Asynchronreaktanz(f
asynchronous resistance	Asynchronwiderstand(m
at rest	in Ruhe(f, ruhend
atomizer	Zerstäuber(m
attachment coefficient	Anlagerungskoeffizient(m
attemperation	Temperaturregelung(f
attemperator	Temperaturregulator(m
attrition test	Abriebdauerversuch(m
auto-transformer	Sparumspanner(m
auto-transformer starting	Anlauf(m mit Sparumspanner(m
automatic change-over switch	automatischer Umschalter(m
automatic control	selbsttätige Fernbedienung(f
automatic focusing	automatische Fokussierung(f
automatic release	Selbstauslösung(f
automatic scaler	selbsttätiger Teiler(m
automatic starter	Selbstanlasser(m
automatic switching on	selbsttätige Einschaltung(f
auxiliary contact	Hilfskontakt(m
auxiliary equipment	Folgeeinrichtungen(pl
auxiliary motor	Hilfsmotor(m
auxiliary resistor	Hilfswiderstand(m
auxiliary switch	Hilfsschalter(m
auxiliary winding	Anlauf-Hilfswicklung(f
average acceleration	mittlere Beschleunigung(f
average voltage	mittlere Spannung(f
axial (bearing) force	Axialkraft(f
axial head, straight head	Längskopf(m
axial spacing	Ach(sen)abstand(m
axial vector	axialer Vektor(m
axle-counter	Achszähleinrichtung(f
back contact	Ruhekontakt(m
back fire, arc-back	Rückzündung(f
back-pressure plate	Gegendruckplatte(f
backing roll, counter-pressure	– Gegendruckwalze(f
backlash	Gitterrückstrom(m
baffle	Trennblech(n

baking current	Formierungsstrom(m
balance control	Balanceregler(m
balanced-line system	erdsymmetrisches System(n
balancing, matching	Anpassung(f
ball cock	Kugelschieber(m, Kugelhahn(m
banana plug	Bananenstecker(m
band conveyer	Bandförderer(m
band feed, belt –	Bandzuführer(m
bank of capacitors	Kondensatorbatterie(f
bar screen	Stabrost(m, Stangenrost(m
bar suspension, yoke –	Gestängeaufhängung(f
bare electrode	blanke Elektrode(f
barrel electro-plating	Trommelgalvanisierung(f
barrier layer	Sperrschicht(f
barrier sheet	Abschirmschicht(f
base	Fuss(m, Fundament(n
base lip	Basisflansch(m
base load	Grundlast(f
base material	Ausgangsmaterial(n
base plate	Grundplatte(f, Fundament(n
basic equation	Grundgleichung(
basic time	Grundzeit(f
batcher	Dosiermaschine(f
bath lubrication	Tauchschmierung(f
battery charger	Batterieladegerät(n
beam	Träger(m
beam loading	Strahlbelastung(f
bearing friction	Lagerreibung(f
bed plate	Grundplatte(f
bell crank	Kniehebel(m
belt drive	Riementrieb(m
belt velocity	Riemengeschwindigkeit(f
bend	Bogen(m, Krümmer(m
bending	Verbiegung(f
bending	Biegung(f
bending due to heat	Wärme-Ausbiegung(f
bending stress	Biegespannung(f
bevel angle	Abschrägung(f
bevel gear	Kegelrad(n
bevelled edge	abgeschrägte Kante(f
bidirectional coupler	Zweirichtungskoppler(m
bifilar winding	bifilare Wicklung(f
bilateral	beid(er)seitig
bilateral transmission	beidseitiger Achsantrieb(m
bimetal fuse	Bimetallsicherung(f
bimetallic instrument	Bimetallinstrument(n
bimetallic wire	Bimetalldraht(m
binding band	Bandage(f

bipolar	zweipolig
bipolar machine	zweipolige Maschine (f
bituminous cement, - compound	Asphaltkitt (m
blade contact	Messerkontakt (m
blade latch	Messersperre (f
blanket	Mantel (m
blanking machine	Stanzmaschine (f
blanking, outline cutting	Ausstanzen (n, Fassonschnitt (m
blender, mixer	Mischer (m
block diagram	Blockschaltbild (n
blocking capacitor	Koppelkondensator (m
blocking period	Sperrzeit (f
blow air	Blasluft (f
blow head	Blaskopf (m
blow pressure	Blas(e)druck (m
blow-out coil	Blasspule (f
blower	Gebläse (n
bobbin winding	Spulenwicklung (f
bobbin, coil	Spule (f
body of the roll, roller body	Walzenkörper (m
bond testing	Haftfestigkeitsprüfung (f
bore	Bohrung (f
bored well, drilled roll	ausgebohrte Walze (f
boss	Nocken (m, Nocke (f
bottom block	Bodengestell (n
bottom discharge	Entleerung (f von unten
bottom feed	Beschickung (f unten
bottom force press, - ram -	Unterkolbenpresse (f
bottom plate	Bodenplatte (f, Grundplatte (f
bottom roll	Unterwalze (f
bow frame	Bügelgestell (n
bowl calender, roll -	Walzenkalander (m
bracket	Ausleger (m
brake dynamo	Bremsdynamo (m
braking magnet	Bremsmagnet (m
braking torque	Bremsmoment (n
branch	Abzweigung (f
braze welding	Schweisslöten (n
break spring	Unterbrechungsfeder (f
breakaway torque	Anzugsmoment (n
breakdown signal	Pannensignal (n
breast roll (air-knife coater)	Brustwalze (f
breathing cycle, degassing -	Entlüftungszyklus (m
bridge contact	Brückenkontakt (m
bridge hanger	Brückenausleger (m
briquet machine	Brikettiermaschine (f
bronze pigmented lacquer, -paint	Bronzelack (m
bronzing	Bronzieren (n

brush	Bürste(f
brush box	Bürstenkasten(m
brush holder	Bürstenhalter(m
brush rocker	Bürstenbrücke(f
brush spring	Bürstenfeder(f
brushless machine	**bürstenlose Maschine(f**
bucking circuit	Kompensationskreis(m
buckling	Knicken(n, Knickung(f
buckling stress	Knickspannung(f
buffing	Polieren(f), Schwabbeln(n)
built-on motor	Anbaumotor(m
bull ring	Abspannring(m
bundle of cables	Kabelbündel(n
burning time	Abschmelzzeit(f
burning, combustion	Verbrennung(f)
bus bar	Sammelschiene(f
butt joint	Stossfuge(f, Stossnaht(f
button	Stellknopf(m
button seal	Pressglasverschmelzung(f
buzzer	Summer(m
cab cable, car cable	Steuerleitung(f
cab signal, car signal	Führerstandsignal(n
cable drum, cable reel	Kabeltrommel(f
cable joint, splice	Kabelverbindungsstelle(f
calender	Kalander(m
calibration	Eichung(f
calibration, gauging	Kalibrierung(f
calorimeter	Kalorimeter(n
calorizing	Kalorisieren(n
cam controller	Nockenfahrschalter(m
caoutchouc, india rubber	Kautschuk(m, Rohgummi(m
cap nut, screwed cap	Überwurfmutter(f
capacitance	elektrische Kapazität(f
capacitance, capacity	Kapazität(f
capacitor	Kondensator(m
capacitor plate	Kondensatorplatte(f
capacitor-capacitance	Kondensatorkapazität(f
capsuling machine, sealing -	Verschlussmaschine(f
carbon arc	Kohlebogen(m
carbon compounds	Kohlenstoffverbindungen(pl
carbonaceous	kohlenstoffartig, -haltig
cardan drive	Kardanantrieb(m
cardiotachometer	Kardiotachometer(n
carrier plate	Trägerplatte(f
cascade agitator	Kaskadenrührwerk(n
case, jacket	Gehäuse(n, Hülse(f
casein glue	Kaseinleim(m
cast steel grate	Gussstahlrost(m

casting compound	Vergussmasse(f, Vergiessmasse(f
casting resin	Vergussharz(n, Gussharz(n
casting roll	Auftragwalze(f
catalyst	Katalysator(m
cathode	Katode(f
cathode bias	Katodenvorspannung(f
cathode current	Katodenstrom(m
cathode fall, potential fall	Katodenfall(m
cathode neck	Katodenhals(m
cathode tack	Katodennagel(m
cathode terminal	Katodenanschluss(m
cathode voltage	Katodenspannung(f
cathodic cleaning	katodische Reinigung(f
cathodic reaction	Kathodenreaktion(f
ceiling plate	Deckenplatte(f
cement, glue	Klebstoff(m, Leim(m
cementation	Aushärten(n, Härten(n
cemented socket joint	Klebmuffe(f
centering control	Zentrierungsregler(m
centigrade scale	Celsius-Skala(f
centre layer, center -	Mittelschicht(f
centre of gravity	Schwerpunkt(m
centrifugal compressor	Zentrifugalkompressor(m
centrifugal fan	Zentrifugalventilator(m
ceramic seal	Keramikabschmelzung(f
change of state	Zustandsveränderung(f
change-over time	Umstellzeit(f
change-over time	Übergangszeit(f
character reader	Zeichenleser(m
characteristic curve	Kennlinie(f
charge multiplication	Ladungsvervielfachung(f
charge neutralization	Ladungsausgleich(m
charging hole	Beschickungsöffnung(f
charging time	Ladezeit(f
checking circuit	Überwachungskreis(m
chemical diffusion	chemische Diffusion(f
chill roll, cooling cylinder	Kühlwalze(f, Kühlzylinder(m
chip thickness	Spandicke(f
choke coil	Drosselspule(f
choke coupling, choke joint	Drosselkupplung(f
choke piston	Drosselkolben(m
circuit	Kreis(m, Schaltung(f
circuit breaker	Schaltmechanismus(m
circuit, circulation	Kreislauf(m, Umlauf(m
circular	kreisförmig
circular pipe	kreisförmiges Rohr(n
circular tank	runder Tank(m, Kreisbehälter(m
circular windings(pl	Kreiswindungen(pl

circulating reflux	umlaufender Rücklauf(m
circulation cooling	Umlaufkühlung(f
circulation, magnetic potential	elektrische Durchflutung(f
circumferential components(pl	Umfangskomponenten(pl
circumferential winding	Umfangwickeln(n
clamp	Klemme(f
clamping force, locking –	Schliesskraft(f
clamping plate, mounting –	Aufspannplatte(f
clamping plunger	Schliesskolben(m
clamping pressure, locking –	Schliessdruck(m
clamping ring	Spannring(m
classical system	klassisches System(n
classifier	Klassierer(m, Klassifizierer(m
cleaning, dressing	Putzen(n, Reinigen(n
clear lacquer	Klarlack(m
cleat	Klampe(f, Klemmisolator(m
clip, loop-type clamp	Befestigungsschelle(f
closed filter	geschlossener Filter(m
closing cylinder	Schliesszylinder(m
closing time	Schliesszeit(f
closing travel	Schliessbewegung(f
closing unit	Schliesseinheit(f
coal tar dyes	Teerfarbstoffe(pl
coarse filter, roughing filter	Grobfilter(m
coating	Beschichten(n, Beschichtung(f
coating compound, – resin	Streichmasse(f, Überzugmasse(f
coating varnish	Überzugslack(m
coatingt activation	Überzugs-Aktivierung(f
coaxial cylinder	koaxialer Zylinder(m
code system	Codier(ungs)system(n
coefficient of elongation	Dehnungskoeffizient(m
coefficient of expansion	Ausdehnungskoeffizient(m
coefficient of friction	Reibungskoeffizient(m
coefficient of friction	Reibungszahl(f
coefficient of resistance	Widerstandsbeiwert(m
coefficient of shape	Formfaktor(m
coercive force	Koerzitiv-Feldstärke(f
cohesion	Kohäsion(f
cohesive force	Kohäsionskraft(f
coil cross section	Wicklungsquerschnitt(m
coil holder	Spulenhalter(m
coil, worm, spiral tube	Spirale(f, Rohrspirale(f
coiled spring	gewundene Feder(f
coiling, winding	Wicklung(f
cold setting	kalte Fixierung(f
cold setting adhesive, – – glue	kalthärtender Leim(m
collective control	Sammelsteuerung(f
collector efficiency	Kollektor-Wirkungsgrad(m

collision	Kollision(f, Stoss(m
color disk, colour disk	Farbenscheibe(f
color lake, colour lake	Farblack(m
coloring barrel, colouring drum	Einfärbetrommel(f, Farbtrommel(
column	Säule(f
common cathode	gemeinsame Katode(f
common collector	Gemeinschaftskollektor(m
commutating capacitor	Sperrkondensator(m
commutating pole	Wendepol(m
commutator	Kommutator(m, Stromwender(m
commutator spider	Kommutatortragvorrichtung(f
compacting, compression	Komprimieren(n, Verdichten(n
compartment dryer	Trockner(m mit Abteilen
compensating choke	Ausgleichsdrossel, Saugdrossel(f
component	Komponente(f
components	Komponenten(pl
composite braking	gemischte Bremsung(f
composite characteristic	zusammengesetzte Kennlinie(f
composite foam	Verbund-Schaumstoff(m
composite panel	Verbundplatte(f
composite stresses	zusammengesetzte Spannungen(pl
composites	Verbundstoffe(pl
compound	Verbindung(f
compound	Kompound(n, Compound(n
compound wound motor	Doppelschlussmotor(m
compressed air pipe	Hochdruckrohr(n
compression gland	Stopfbüchse(f
compression melting	Hochdruckplastifizierung(f
compression ratio	Verdichtungsverhältnis(n
compression ratio	Kompressionsverhältnis(n
compression zone	Verdichtungszone(f
compressive stress	Druckspannung(f
compressor jacket	Kompressormantel(m
concentrated load	Einzellast(f
concentrated winding	konzentrierte Wicklung(f
concentric cable, coaxial cable	Koaxialkabel(n
concrete shield	Betonpanzer(m
condensing coil, cooling -	Kühlschlange(f, -serpentine(f
condition of equilibrium	Gleichgewichtsbedingung(f
conductance	elektrischer Leitwert(m
conductivity	elektrische Leitfähigkeit(f
conductivity, admittance	Scheinleitwert(m
conductor	Leiter(m
conduit	Schutzrohr(n
conduit box	Abzweigdose(f
cone classifier	Kegelklassierer(m, Konuskl.(m
cone impeller mixer	Kegelkreiselmischer(m
conical rotor machine	Maschine(f mit konischem Läufer

connect to frame	mit dem Gehäuse verbinden
connection diagram	Anschlussschema(n
constant losses	konstante Verluste(pl
contact	Kontakt(m
contact adhesive, impact -	Kontaktkleber(m
contact clip	Kontaktklammer(f
contact electrode	Kontakt-Elektrode(f
contact member	Kontaktelement(n
contact rail, conductor rail	Stromschiene(f
contact spring, make spring	Kontaktfeder(f
continuity equation	Kontinuitätsgleichung(f
continuous belt mixer	Endlos-Bandmischer(m
continuous dyeing machine	kontinuierliche Färbmaschine(f
continuous furnace	Durchlaufofen(m
continuous output	Dauerleistung(f
continuous-flow calorimeter	Durchflusskalorimeter(n
contraction, shrinkage	Schrumpfen(n, Schwinden(n
contrast	Kontrast(m
control cable	Steuerkabel(n
control circuit	Steuerkreis(m
control desk	Steuerpult(n
control grid	Steuergitter(n
control line	Steuerleitung(f
control room	Schaltraum(m
control system	Regelungssystem(n
controlling section	Steuerabschnitt(m
conventional voltage	genormte Spannung(f
conversion loss	Umwandlungsverlust(m
conversion ratio	Umwandlungsgrad(m, -verhältnis(n
converter	Umformer(m
conveying belt	Förderband(n
coolant, cooling agent	Kühlmittel(n
cooling	Kühlung(f, Abkühlung(f
cooling air	Kühlluft(f
cooling coil	Kühlschlange, Kühlspirale(f
cooling fin	Kühlrippe(f
cooling jacket	Kühlmantel(m
cooling plate	Kühlplatte(f
cooling press	Kühlpresse(f
cooling roll	Kühlwalze(f
cooling trough	Kühlrinne(f
coordinates(pl	Koordinaten(pl
cop	Spule(f
copper	Kupfer(n
copper wire	Kupferdraht(m
core wire	Kerndraht(m
core-pin retainer plate	Lochstift-Halteplatte(f
cored carbon	Dochtkohle(f, Kernkohle(f

corkrubber sheet	Korkgummiplatte(f
corner joint	Eckstoss(m, Winkelstoss(m
corona discharge	Korona-Entladung(f
corona effect	Koronaerscheinung(f
corrosion	Korrosion(f
corrosion inhibitor	Korrosionsschutzmittel(n
corrugated sheet, - panel	Wellplatte(f
counter	Zähler(m
counter dead time	Zählertotzeit(f
counter electrode	Gegenelektrode(f
counter tome-lag	Zählerverzögerung(f
counterweight	Gegengewicht(n
counting rate	Zählgeschwindigkeit(f
couple	Paar(n, Kräftepaar(n
coupling agent	Haftmittel(n
coupling coefficient	Kopplungskoeffizient(m
coupling resistance	Kopplungswiderstand(m
covering film	Abdeckfolie(f
coverplate, faceplate	Abdeckplatte(f, Deckplatte(f
cpacitor power	Kondensatorleistung(f
cracker roll	Brechwalze(f
cramped construction	gedrängter Aufbau(m
Cremona method	Cremona-Verfahren(n
crest angle	Kopfwinkel(m
crest factor, peak value	Spitzenwert(m
critical dimension	kritische Abmessung(f
critical frequency	Grenzfrequenz(f
critical grid voltage	Gitterzündspannung(f
critical speed	kritische Geschwindigkeit(f
critical whirling speeds	biegekritische Drehzahlen(pl
cross	Kreuzstück(n
cross brace	Traverse(f, Querriegel(m
cross coil	Kreuzspule(f
cross section of wire	Drahtquerschnitt(m
cross-layers	kreuzweise Schichten(pl
crosslinking, interlacing	Vernetzung(f
crude metal	Rohmetall(n
crusher, breaker	Brecher(m
crushing roll	Brechwalze(f, Walzenbrecher(m
cube mixer	Würfelmischer(m
cubic expansion	Raumdehnung(f, räumliche Dehnung
cuff heater band, heater band	Erhitzungsband(n
cup-shaped base	tellerförmiger Halter(m
cuprous oxide	Kupferoxyd(n
curing temperature	Härtungstemperatur(f
current amplification	Stromverstärkung(f
current density	Stromdichte(f
current sensitivity	Stromempfindlichkeit(f

current supply	Stromzuführung(f
current, intensity of current	Stromstärke(f
curved surface	gekrümmte Fläche(f
cut-off relay	Trennrelais(n
cut-off voltage	Einsatzspannung(f
cut-out box	Ausschaltkasten(m
cutting device, chopper, cutter	Schneidvorrichtung(f
cutting drive	Schnittantrieb(m
cutting machine	Schneidmaschine(f
cutting speed	Schnittgeschwindigkeit(f
cutting time	Schnittzeit(f
cyclic impedance	Drehfeldimpedanz(f
cyclical load	zyklische Belastung(f
cylindrical counter	Zylinderzähler(m
cylindrical grader	Sortierzylinder(m
damp air blower	Feuchtluftgebläse(n
damper	Dämpfer(m
damping ratio	Dämpfungsgrad(m
daylight unit	Tageslichteinheit(f
de-aerator	Entlüfter(m
de-ionization grid	Entionisierungsgitter(n
dead time, insensitive time	Totzeit(f
dead zone	tote Zone(f
deceleration	Verzögerung(f
declared efficiency	Nennwirkungsgrad(m
dedendum	Fusshöhe(f
deep-etch testing	Tiefätzprobe(f
definite time	konstante Verzögerung(f
deflecting blades	Ableitbleche(pl
deflection yoke	Ablenkjoch(n
degassing	Entgasung(f
degreaser, cleaner	Entfettungsmittel(n
degree of lossening	Auflockerungsmass(n
delamination	Schichtentrennung(f
delay cable, delay line	Verzögerungskabel(n
delay time	Verzögerungszeit(f
delaying belt	Verzögerungsband(n
delivery chute	Ablaufrinne(f
delivery valve, head valve	Steuerventil(n
delta-circuit	Dreieckschaltung(f
demagnetize	entmagnetisieren
densimeter, densometer	Densimeter(n, Dichtemesser(m
density of heat flow	Wärmestromdichte(f
depolarization	Depolarisation(f
depth of teeth	Zahnhöhe(f
derivation	Abweichung(f
derivation action	differenzierendes Verhalten(n
desiccant, drying agent	Trocknungsmittel(n

detachable joint	lösbare Verbindung (f
dewing machine	Anfeuchtmaschine (f
diagonal member	Diagonalstab (m
diagram	Diagramm (n
diagram of forces	Kräfteplan (m
diameter of pipe	Rohrdurchmesser (m
diameter of the electrode	Elektroden-Durchmesser (m
dicer, cube dicer, cutter	Würfelschneider (m
die approach, die channel	Düsenkanal (m
die body, die base	Düsenplatte (f, Düsenhalter (m
die gap adjustment	Düsen(spalt)verstellung (f
dielectric constant	Dielektrizitätskonstante (f
dielectric displacement	elektrische Flussdichte (f
differential calorimeter	Differentialkalorimeter (n
differential current	Differenzstrom (m
differential phase section	Phasendifferenz-Abschnitt (m
diffusion coefficient	Diffusionskoeffizient (m
dilatometer	Dilatometer (n, Dehnungsmesser (m
dimmer lever	Hebelregler (m
dip coating, immersion –	Tauchlackierung (f
dip coating, impregnating	Tauchbeschichten (n, Tränken (n
dip roll	Tauchwalze (f
dip tube	Tauchröhrchen (n
dipped electrode	getauchte Elektrode (f
dipping barrel	Tauchzylinder (m
dipping bath, immersion bath	Tauchbad (n
dipping lacquer	Tauchlack (m
dipping tank	Tauchgefäss (n
direct coupling	direkte Kupplung (f
direct current	Gleichstrom (m
direct current motor	Gleichstrommotor (m
direct current relay	Gleichstromrelais (n
direct drive	direkter Antrieb (m
direct fired furnace	direkt geheizter Ofen (m
direct-current machine	Gleichstrommaschine (f
direct-on-line starting	Anlauf mit direktem Einschalten
direction of lay	Drallrichtung (f
directional relay	Richtungsrelais (n
disc impeller, disk –	Scheibenkreiselrührer (m
discharge valve	Druckventil (n, Ablassventil (n
discharge, unloading	Abnahme (f, Entladung (f
disconnect position	Ausschaltstellung (f
disk anode	Rundplattenanode (f
disk feeder	Verteilerscheibe (f
disk mixer	Scheibenmischer (m
disk seal	Scheibeneinschmelzung (f
disk wheel	Scheibenrad (n
disoperating time	Ausserbetriebsetzungszeit (f

dispersion resins	Dispersionsharze(pl
displacement flux	Verschiebungsfluss(m
disruptive voltage	Durchschlagspannung(f
dissipation of energy	Energieverlust(m
distorsion testing	Verformungstest(m
distribuited load	verteilte Last(f
distributed constant	verteilte Konstante(f
distribution function	Verteilungsfunktion(f
distribution point	Verteilungspunkt(m
distributor duct	Verteilungsrohr(n
distributor rolls, - rolls	Verteilerwalzen(pl
doctor blade, doctor knife	Dosierrakel(f, Dosiermesser(n
doser, dosing device	Dosiereinrichtung(f
dosing feeder, weight feeder	Gewichtsdosierer(m
double cone mixer, - - blender	Doppelkegelmischer(m
double force press, - ram -	Doppelkolbenpresse(f
double layer	Doppelschicht(f
double naben kneader	Fischschwanzkneter(m
double ventilation	Doppel-Achsialbelüftung(f
double walled tube	doppelwandiges Rohr(n
double-face coating	beidseitige Beschichtung(f
double-feeding	Doppelspeisung(f
down time	Ausfallzeit(f
drain valve	Ablassventil(n
drawing	Verstrecken(n
drill tip angle	Bohrer-Spitzenwinkel(m
drilled roll	gebohrte Walze(f
drip pan, catch pan	Auffanggefäss(n
drive belt	Antriebsriemen(m, Treibriemen(m
drive rating, power demand	Antriebsleistung(f
driven roll	angetriebene Walze(f
driving torque	Antriebsmoment(n
drum dryer	Trommeltrockner(m
drum mixer, barrel -, tumbler	Trommelmischer(m
drum reflux	Rücklaufbehälter(m
drum winding	Trommelwicklung(f
dry filler	Trockenfüllstoff(m
dryer	Trockner(m
drying chamber	Trockenkammer(f
duct entrance	Kabelrohreingang(m
dummy coil	blinde Spule(f
durometer, hardness tester	Härteprüfer(m, Durometer(n
dust collecting tube	Staubsammelrohr(n
dust filter	Staubfilter(m
duty cycle	Arbeitsphase(f, Arbeitszyklus(m
duty factor	Arbeitsphasenfaktor(m
duty-type	Betriebsart(f
dying-out time	Abklingzeit(f, Ausschwingdauer(f

dynamic resistance	dynamischer Widerstand(m
dynamic sensitivity	dynamische Empfindlichkeit(f
dynamo	Dynamo(n
dynamometer test	Dynamometer-Test(m
dynetric balancing	elektronische Auswuchtung(f
E bend	E-Bogen(m
E corner	E-Winkel(m
E plane Tee junction	E-Verzweiger(m
earth lead, work -, ground -	Masseleitung(f, Erdkabel(n
earthed circuit	geerdeter Kreis(m, Erdkreis(m
earthing cable, grounding -	Erdkabel(n
ebonite, hard rubber, vulcanite	Ebonit(m, Hartgummi(m
eccentric press	Exzenterpresse(f
eccentric tumbler	Taumelmischer(m
Eddy currents	Wirbelströme(pl
edge joint	Stirnstoss(m
edge trim roll	Kantenschneidwalze(f
Edison effect	Edison-Effekt(m
eduction pipe	Ablassrohr(n, Ausflussrohr(n
eduction valve	Abzugsventil(n, Auslassventil(n
effective length of a screw	wirksame Schneckenlänge(f
effective value	Effektivwert(m
efficiency	Wirkungsgrad(m
efficiency	Wirkungsgrad(m
ejecting blanking cutter	Stanzmesser(n mit Auswerfer
ejecting device, piece knockout	Auswurfvorrichtung(f
ejection pin, knockout -	Auswurfstift(m
ejection plate, ejector -	Drückplatte(f, Ausdrückplatte(f
ejection spring, ejector -	Auswurffeder(f
ejection tie bar	Ausdrücker-Stange(f
ejector (connecting) bar, - rod	Auswerferkolben(m
ejector (pin) plate	Auswurfplatte, Ausdrückplatte(f
ejector pin, knock-out pin	Ausdrückstift(m
ejector ram	Ausdrückbolzen(m
elastic aftereffect	elastische Nachwirkung(f
elastic limit	Elastizitätsgrenze(f
elastomer	Elastomer(n
elastomeric plastic	elastomerer Kunststoff(m
elastometer	Elastometer(n
elbow, knee	Winkel(m, Kniestück(n
elecronic processing	elektronische Verarbeitung(f
electric charge	elektrische Ladung(f
electric circuit	elektrischer Stromkreis(m
electric clutch	elektrische Kupplung(f
electric conduction	Elektrizitätsleitung(f
electric field	elektrisches Feld(n
electric field strength	elektrische Feldstärke(f
electric line	elektrische Leitung(f

electrical conductivity	elektrische Leitfähigkeit(f
electrical efficiency	elektrischer Wirkungsgrad(m
electrical interconnecting	Zusammenschalten(n
electrical work	elektrische Arbeit(f
electrical work	elektrische Leistung(f
electricity	Elektrizität(f
electrode support	Elektrodenhalter(m
electrodynamic	elektrodynamisch
electrodynamic relay	elektrodynamisches Relais(n
electrodynamics	Elektrodynamik(f
electromagnet	Elektromagnet(m
electromagnetic deflection	elektromagnetische Ablenkung(f
electromagnetic lens	elektromagnetische Linse(f
electron microscope	Elektronenmikroskop(n
electronegative element	elektronegtives Element(n
electronic	elektronisch
electronic air cleaner	elektronischer Luftfilter(m
electronic altimeter	elektronischer Höhenmesser(m
electronic clock	elektronische Uhr(f
electronic commutator	Elektronenschalter(m
electronic component	elektronisches Bauelement(n
electronic control	elektronische Steuerung(f
electronic controller	elektronischer Regler(m
electronic counter	elektronischer Zähler(m
electronic fathometer	elektronisches Echolot(n
electronic grey wedge	elektronischer Graukeil(m
electronic key	elektronischer Taster(m
electronic lung	elektronische Lunge(f
electronic micrometer	elektronisches Mikrometer(n
electronic multiplier	elektronischer Multiplikator(m
electronic profilometer	elektronischer Rauheitsmesser(m
electronic punch-card machine	elektronischer Locher(m
electronic scanning	elektronische Abtastung(f
electronic sewing	elektronisches Nähen(n
electronic tachometer	elektronisches Tachometer(n
electronic timer	elektronischer Zeitschalter(m
electronic voltmeter	elektronisches Voltmeter(n
electronic wattmeter	elektronisches Wattmeter(n
electronic weighing	elektronische Wägung(f
electronique calculator	elektronischer Rechner(m
electrostatic coating	elektrostatisches Beschichten(n
electrostatic pressure	elektrostatischer Druck(m
electrostatics	Elektrostatik(f
elektronegativity	Elektronegativität(f
elevator, lift	Aufzug(m, Fahrstuhl(m, Lift(m
embedding	Einbetten(n
embosser, embossing machine	Prägevorrichtung(f
embossing calender	Prägekalander(m

embossing plate	Prägeplatte(f
emergency stop switch	Notausschalter(m
emery	Schmirgel(m
emery grinder	Schmirgelmühle(f
emery roll	Schmirgelwalze(f
emitter bias	Emittervorspannung(f
emulsifying machine, coating –	Emulsionsauftragmaschine(f
enamel coating	Emailüberzug(m
encapsulating	Einkapselung(f, Kapselung(f
encapsulation	Einkapseln(n
end sealing	Endversiegeln(n
end shield, end hat	Abschlussschirm(m
endurance test, fatigue –	Dauerfestigkeitsprüfung(f
energy balance	Energiebilanz(f
enriching	Anreicherung(f
enriching section	Anreicherungszone(f
epicyclic gearing	Planetengetriebe(n
epicyclic screw mixer	epizyklischer Schneckenmischer
equalizing	Egalisieren(n
equalizing charge	Ausgleichsladung(f
equalizing connection	Ausgleichsverbinder(m
equation of moments	Momentengleichung(f
equation of state	Zustandsgleichung(f
equilibrium	Beharrungszustand, Gleichgewicht
equilibrium chamber	Gleichgewichtskammer(f
equilibrium force	Gleichgewichtskraft(f
equilibrium methode	Gleichgewichtsmethode(f
equipment	Ausrüstung(f
equipotential cathode	Äquipotentialkatode(f
equivalent charge	Äquivalentladung(f
equivalent stress	Vergleichsspannung(f
error in indication	Anzeigefehler(m
escalator	Rolltreppe(f
essiccator, dessiccator	Trockner(m, Exsikkator(m
etching	Ätzen(n
evacuating machine	Evakuiermaschine(f
evaporating plant	Verdampferanlage(f
evaporative cooling	Verdampfungskühlung(f
evaporator coil	Kühlschlangensystem(n
evaporator, vaporizer	Verdampfer(m
even speed	Gleichlauf(m
excess conduction	Überschussleitung(f
excess overflow, spew, spue	Überlauf(m
excess pressure	Überdruck(m
excess, excess material	Überschuss(m
exchange of energy	Energie-Austausch(m
exchanger	Austauscher(m
excitation	Erregung(f, Anregung(f

exciter	Erregermaschine(f
exciting current	Erregerstrom(m
exfoliation, flaking	Abblättern(n, Häuten(n
exhaust gas stack	Abluftkamin(m
exhaust gases, waste gases	Abgase(pl
exhaust tube, pumping tube	Entlüftungsrohr(n
exhausting fan, air exhauster	Entlüftungsgebläse(n
expandet sweep	kompensierte Abtastung(f
expansion	Ausdehnung(f
expansion joint	Dehnungsfuge(f
extender	Füllstoff(m, Streckmittel(n
extensometer	Dehnungsmesser(m
external diameter	Aussendurchmesser(m
external thread	Aussengewinde(n
extinction	Löschung(f
extra high tension, E.H.T.	Höchstspannung(f
extraction funnel, separating –	Scheidetrichter(m
extruder core, extrusion core	Spritzdorn(m
extruder head, extrusion –	Extruderkopf(m
extruder, extruding machine	Strangpresse(f, Spritzmaschine(f
extrusion	Extrudieren(n
extrusion coating	Extrusionsbeschichten(n
extrusion die	Extruderdüse(f
extrusion laminating	Extrusionsbeschichten(n
extrusion mandril	Spritzdorn(m
extrusion mo(u)lding	Strangpressen(n
extrusion plunger	Strangpresskolben(m
extrusion welding	Extrusionsschweissen(n
extrusion-lamination	Extrusionslaminieren(n
facing sand	Modellsand(m
factor of safety, safety factor	Sicherheitsfaktor(m
fading test	Lichtechtheitsprobe(f
falling characteristique	fallende Kennlinie(f
fat	Fett(n
feed	Vorschub(m
feed cylinder	Füllzylinder(m
feed dosing	Gewichtsdosierung(f
feed force	Vorschubkraft(f
feed funnel, – hopper	Beschickungstrichter(m
feed mill	Vorwärmwalze(f
feed roller	Speiserolle(f, Zufuhrrolle(f
feed slide	Dosierschieber(m
feed valve, filling valve	Füllventil(n
feed zone	Beschickungszone(f
feed, load, mo(u)ld charge	Beschickung(f, Ladung(f
feeding voltage	feeding voltage
felt	Filz(m
felt guide	Filzführung(f

figure mask, cipher mask	Ziffernmaske(f
filament delivery carriage	Fadenführungsschlitten(m
filament guide	Fadenführung(f
filament lamp	Glühlampe(f
filler	Füllstoff(m
filler metal	Füllmetall(n
filler plate, loading shoe	Füllplatte(f
fillet weld	Kehlnaht(f
filling machine	Abfüllmaschine(f
film	Film(m, Feinfolie(f
film glue	Leimfolie(f
filter felt	Filtrierfilz(m
filter mantle	Filtermantel(m
filter tube	Filterrohr(n
filtering	Filtrieren(n, Filterung(f
filtering medium	Filtermittel(n
filtering surface layer	Filterdeckschicht(f
final cleaning	Nachreinigung(f
fine grinding mill	Feinmühle(f
finishing agent	Nachbearbeitungsmittel(n
finishing plant	Aufbereitungsanlage(f
finned torpedo	Flügeltorpedo(n
finned tube	Rippenrohr(n
fire protecting paint	feuerabweisende Farbe(f
fireproof	feuerfest, feuersicher
fireproof paint	Feuerschutzanstrich(m
five roller mill	Fünfwalzenmühle(f
fixed coil	feste Spule(f
fixed conductor	fester Leiter(m
fixed expansion	konstante Expansion(f
fixed plate	feste Formplatte(f
fixed roll	Festrolle(f, Festwalze(f
fixed sheave	feste Rolle(f
fixed trip	bolckierte Auslösung(f
flame guard	Flammenschutz(m, Feuerschirm(m
flame hardening	Flammenhärtung(f
flame welding	Flammenschweissen(n
flange joint	Flanschverbindung(f
flange, elbow	Bord(n, Bördelprofil(n
flash chamber, overflow space	Überlaufkammer(f
flash land, - surface, - ridge	Abquetschrand(m, Abquetschfläch
flash lathe	Abgratbank(f
flash ring	Abquetschring(m
flasher relay	Blinkrelais(n
flat sheet	Flachfolie(f
flexible	flexibel, biegsam
flexible coupling	flexible Kupplung(f
flexible support	nachgiebige Stütze(f

float	Schwimmer (m
floating knife coater	Luftrakel-Streichmaschine (f
floating plate	Schwebeplatte (f, Schwebetisch (m
floating ring	schwebender Ring (m
flow control	Strömungsregelung (f
flow mixer, pipeline mixer	Durchflussmischer (m
flowability, fluidity	Fliessfähigkeit (f
flowmeter	Strömungsmesser (m
fluctuation voltage	schwankende Spannung (f
fluidification	Verflüssigung (f
fluorescent screen	Leuchtschirm (m
fluorescent screen	Fluoreszenzschirm (m
fluted filter, folded filter	Faltenfilter (m
flying shears	mitlaufende Schneidevorrichtung
foam glue	Schaumleim (m
foam laminate	Überschichtungs-Schaumstoff (m)
foamed plastics, expanded –	Schaumstoffe (pl
folding angle, creasing –	Abkantwinkel (m
foot switch, floor switch	Fussschalter (m
force	Kraft (f
force of repulsion	Abstossungskraft (f
force polygon	Krafteck (n
force side, movable side	Schliessseite (f
forced circulation, – flow	Zwangsumlauf (m
forecooler	Vorkühler (m
formula, formulation	Formel (f, Rezept (n
forward direction	Durchlassrichtung (f
forward voltage	Vorwärtsspannung (f
fouling	Verschmutzung (m, Verkrustung (f
foundation, footing	Fundament (n, Gründung (f
four-roll calender	Vierwalzenkalander (m
frame heater	rechteckiger Heizkörper (m
frame mounting	Rahmenmontage (f
frame press, strain plate press	Rahmenpresse (f
framework structure	Rahmenkonstruktion (f, Fachwerk (n
free opening, daylight –	lichte Weite (f
free sheave	lose Rolle (f
free-falling evaporator	Freifall-Verdampfer (m
free-falling mixer	Freifallmischer (m
free-running	freier Lauf (m
freeze resistance	Frostbeständigkeit (f
frequency	Frequenz (f
frequency change	Frequenzgleiten (n
frequency range	Frequenzbereich (m
frequency-dependent	frequenzabhängig
frequency-independent	frequenzunabhängig
friction calender	Friktionskalander (m
friction coefficient	Reibungsbeiwert (m

friction contact	Reibungskontakt(m
friction force	Reibungskraft(f
friction losses	Reibungsarbeit, Reibungsverlust
frosting	Mattieren(n
fuel	Brennstoff(m
fuel economy	Brenstoffwirtschaft(f
fundamental units	Grundeinheiten(pl
fuse	Sicherung, Schmelzsicherung(f
fusible covering	schmelzende Umhüllung(f
fusing current	Schmelzstrom(m
fusion point	Schmelzpunkt(m
fusion welding	Schmelzschweissen(n
fusion zone	Schmelzzone(f
ga(u)ge, manometer	Manometer(n
gage rolls, gauging rolls	Kalibrierwalzen(pl
galvanic cell	galvanisches Element(n
galvanomagnetric effect	galvanomagnetischer Effekt(m
gamma rays	Gammastrahlen(pl
gap-filling adhesive	Klebekitt(m
gas discharge	Gasentladung(f
gas layer	Gasschicht(f
gas pocket	Gaseinschluss(m
gas propellant	Treibgas(n
gaseous fuel	gasförmiger Brennstoff(m
gasket ring, joint - , packing	- Dichtungsring(m
gate switch, door switch	Türschalter(m
gate voltage	Steuerspannung(f
gear wheel	Zahnrad(n
gear, gearing	Getriebe(n
Geiger counter	Geiger-Zähler(m
gel coat	Gel-Coat(m, Gel-Feinschicht(f
generator	Generator(m
generator	Generator(m
Gill-Morell oscillator	Gill-Morell-Oszillator(m
girder on two supports	Träger(m auf 2 Stützen
glass fibre laminate, - fiber	- Glasfaserschichtstoff(m
glass fibre, - fiber, fiberglas	Glasfaser(f
glass plate	Glasplatte(f
glass wool, spun glass	Glaswolle(f
glass-to-metal seal	Glas-Metall-Verschmelzung(f
glasspaper	Glaspapier(n
glazing calender	Glättkalander(m, Glättwerk(n
glazing rolls, calender stack	Satinierkalander(m
gloss paint	Glanzlackfarbe(f
gloss-reducing agent, flatting	- Mattierungsmittel(n
glossmeter	Glanzmesseinrichtung(f
glow-bar test	Glutfestigkeitsprüfung(f
glue cooker	Leimsiedekessel(m

glue joint	Verleimung(f
glue layer	Leimschicht(f, Klebefläche(f
gold coating	Goldbeschichtung(f
graininess	Körnigkeit(f, Körnung(f
granulating mill, granulator	Granulator(m, Abfallmühle(f
graphical solution	**graphische Lösung(f**
graphite electrode	Graphitelektrode(fd
gravitational force	Gewichtskraft(f
gravity closing	Schwerkraftverschluss(m
gravure roll, print -	Rasterwalze(f, gravierte Walze
grease	Schmiermittel(n, Fett(n
grease gun	Fettspritze(f
greaseproof paint	fettfeste Farbe(f
grid stretcher	Gitterreckdorn(m
grid transformer	Gittertransformator(m
grid voltage	Gitterspannung(f
grindery	Schleiferei(f
grinding	Schleifen(n
grinding machine	Schleifmaschine(f
grinding wheel, polishing wheel	Polierscheibe(f
groove	Nut(f
grooved cylinder, - roll	Riffelwalze(f
ground plate, earth plate	Erdplatte(f
ground state, normal energy level	Grundzustand(m
grounding rod, earthing pole	Erdungsstange(f
guard ring	Führungsring(m
guide bracket	Führungsarm(m
guide bushing	Führungsbuchse(f
guide pin, aligning plug	Führungsstift(m, Suchstift(m
guide pin, dowel -, leader -	Führungsstift(m
guide roll	Leitwalze(f, Führungsrolle(f
gum	Gummi(n, m
gyrator	Gyrator(m
H bend, H corner	H-Bogen(m, H-Winkel(m
H plane lens	H-Flachlinse(f
hairlines	Haarrisse(pl
half-closed	halb geschlossen
hammer mill	Hammermühle(f
hand rule	Dreifingerregel(f
hanging filter, insertion -	Einsatzfilter(m
hardener	Härter(m, Härtungsmittel(n
heat absorption	Wärmeaufnahme(f
heat accumulation	Wärmespeicherung(f
heat accumulator	Wärmespeicher(m
heat exchange, - exchanging	Wärmeaustausch(m
heat flow, heat current	Wärmestrom(m
heat of compression	Kompressionswärme(f
heat of emission	Abstrahlungswärme(f

heat of fusion	Schmelzwärme(f
heat of sublimation	Sublimationswärme(f
heat of vapourisation	Verdampfungswärme(f
heat per unit mass	massebezogene Wärme(f
heat radiation	Wärmestrahlung(f
heat resistance	Hitzebeständigkeit(f
heat sealing	Warmschweissen(n
heat shield	Wärmeschutz(m
heat storage capacity	Wärme-Speichervermögen(n
heat, termal energy	Wärme(f, Wärmeenergie(f
heater battery	Heizbatterie(f
heater circuit	Heizkreis(m
heater plate	Heizplatte(f, Wärmeplatte(f
heater, heating element	Heizelement(n
heating bore, - passage	Heizkanal(m
heating cable	Heizkabel(n
heating jacket	Heizmantel(m
heating time	Anwärmzeit(f
helical conveyor, screw -, worm -	Förderschnecke(f
helically wound pipe	Spiralrohr(n
hermetic seal	luftdichter Verschluss(m
hermetic seal, hermetic closure	hermetischer Verschluss(m
heteropolar machine	Heteropolarmaschine, Wechselpolm.
high frequency generator	Hochfrequenzgenerator(m
high vacuum	Hochvakuum(n
high voltage	Hochspannung(f
high-pressure mo(u)lding	Hochdruckpressung(f
high-speed agitator	Schnellrührer(m
high-vacuum stopcock	Hochvakuumhahn(m
high-voltage accelerator	Hochspannungsbeschleuniger(m
hinge clamp	Scharnierklemme(f
hinged nose piece	Gelenkkopf(m
holding basin, storing basin	Speicherbecken(n
homopolar machine	Homopolarmaschine(f, Gleichpolm.
hook operation	Hakenbetätigung(f
horizontal axis	horizontale Achse(f
horizontal blanking	Horizontalaustastung(f
horizontal deflection	Horizontalablenkung(f
hot floor	Trockenboden(m
hot press mo(u)lding	Heisspressverfahren(n
hot probe	geheizte Sonde(f
hot spot	überheizte Stelle(f
hot-melt coater	Hotmelt-Beschichter(m
hour meter	Zeitzähler(m
housing	Gehäuse(n
hub diameter	Naben-Durchmesser(m
hub length	Nabenlänge(f
humidity controller	Feuchtigkeitsregler(m

hydraulic diameter	hydraulischer Durchmesser(m
hydraulic machine	hydraulische Maschine(f
hydraulic presse, hydropress	hydraulische Presse(f
hydraulic radius	hydraulischer Radius(m
hydrodynamics	Hydrodynamik(f
hydrostatics	Hydrostatik(f
hydrotometer	Hydrotometer(n
hysteresis motor	Hysteresismotor(m
idle run	Leerlauf(m
ignition magneto	Zündmagnet(m
ignition plug, sparking plug	Zündkerze(f
ignitor firing time	Zündintervall(n
ignitor rod	Zündstift(m
immersed roll	eingetauchte Walze(f
immersion lens	Immersionslinse(f
immersion thermostat	Eintauchthermostat(m
impact breaker, - crusher	Prallbrecher(m
impact mill	Prallmühle(f
impact strength	Schlagzähigkeit(f
impedance	Scheinwiderstand(m
imperveous	undurchdringlich
implosion	Implosion(f
impregnation pan	Imprägnierkessel(m
impulse current	Stossstrom(m
impulse excitation	Impulserregung(f
impulse meter	Impulszähler(m
in motion	in Bewegung(f
in-line die, straight through	Geradeaus-Düse(f
inclinable press, tilting press	Kipp-Presse(f
inclined plane	schiefe Ebene(f
incombustible	un(ver)brennbar
incremental induction	zusätzliche Induktion(f
independent contact	Einzelkreiskontakt(m
independent firing	unabhängige Zündung(f
indicator	Anzeiger(m, Signaltafel(f
indirect operation	indirekte Betätigung(f
indirect rotary drier	indirekte Trockenzentrifuge(f
individual drive	Einzelsteuerung(f
indoor apparatus	Innenraumgerät(n
induced voltage	induzierte Spannung(f
inductance	Induktivität(f
induction accelerator	induktiver Beschleuniger(m
induction effect	Induktionseffekt(m
induction law	Induktionsgesetzt(n
induction machine	Induktionsmaschine(f
induction motor	Induktionsmotor(m
induction motor	Asynchronmotor(m
inductive circuit	induktiver Stromkreis(m

inductor machine	Induktormaschine (f
inductor, jet agitator	Injektordüse (f
infeed	Zustellung (f
inflammable	entflammbar, feuergefährlich
infrared radiation	Infrarotstrahlung (f
infrared scanner	Infrarotabtaster (m
initial deflection	Vorhub (m
initial resistance	Anfangswiderstad (m
initial temperature	Anfangstemperatur (f
injection cylinder, feed –	Spritzzylinder, Füllzylinder (m
injection process	Einspritzverfahren (n
inlet opening	Zufuhröffnung (f
inlet, gate	Einlass (m, Zugang (m
inner cylinder	innerer Zylinder (m
inner grid	Innengitter (n
input capacitance	Eingangskapazität (f
input transformer	Eingangstransformator (m
input voltage	Eingangsspannung (f
insert pin, carrier pin	Haltestift (m, Fixierdorn (m
inserted winding	eingefügte Wicklung (f
inspection of a meter	Zählerprüfung (f
instantaneous release	Schnellauslösung (f
instrument lamp	Instrumentenlampe (f
insulated	isoliert
insulated joint	Isolierstoss (m
insulating grid, grid	Isolierrost (m
insulating layer	Isolierschicht (f
insulation current	Isolationsstrom (m
insulator	Isolator (m
integrated circuit	integrierte Schaltung (f
interaction time	Wechselwirkungszeit (f
interchangeable	austauschbar
interface	Grenzfläche (f, Zwischenfläche (f
interference	Unterschneidung (f
interlocking device	Verriegelungsvorrichtung (f
intermediate couting, – layer	Zwischenschicht (f
intermetallic compound	intertmetallische Verbindung (f
internal angle	innere Ecke (f), Innenwinkel (m)
internal lubricant	eingeschlossenes Gleitmittel (n)
internal power	innere Leistung (f
internal resistance	Innenwiderstand (m
internal thread, female –	Innengewinde (n)
interrupting time	Unterbrechungszeit (f
intrinsic mobility	Eigenbeweglichkeit (f
inverse blocking state	Rückwärtssperrstellung (f
inverse direction, reverse –	Gegenrichtung (f
involute-tooth system	Evolventen-Verzahnung (f
ion engine	Ionenmotor (m

ion flow	Ionenfluss(m
ion sheath	Ionenschicht(f)
ionic charge	Ionenladung(f
ionic semiconductor	Ionenhalbleiter(m
ionizing energy	Ionisationsenergie(f
iron length	Eisenlänge(f
iron losses	Eisenverlust(m
irradiation	Bestrahlung(f
irregular pattern	ungeordnete Anordnung(f
irreversible electrode	irreversible Elektrode(f
isoelectronic	isoelektronisch
isolating link	Trennlasche(f
jack-leg, overflow pipe	Überlaufrohr(n
jacket	Mantel(m, Gehäuse(n
jet, nozzle	Düse(f, Strahlrohr(f
jigging conveyor, shaking shoot	Schüttelrinne(f
joint	Verbindung(f, Verbindungsstück(n
Joule effect	Joule-Effekt(m
junction box	Verbindungsdose(f
Kelvin scale	Kelvin-Skala(f
key number	Kennzahl(f, Kennziffer
kinematic viscosity	kinematische Viskosität(f
kinetic momentum	kinetisches Moment(n
kiosk	Verteilerschrank(m
kneader	Innenmischer(m)
kneader-mixer	Mischkneter(m
knife-over-roll coater	Walzenrakelmaschine(f
known resistance	bekannter Widerstand(m
L/D ratio, length/diametre ratio	Verhältnis(n Länge/Durchmesser
lacquer, lake, lac	Lack(m, Farbstofflack(m
lacquering	Lackieren(n
laminar flow	laminare Strömung(f
laminated core	Blechpaket(n
laminated sheet, - board	Schichtplatte(f, Schichttafel(f
laminating, doubling	Beschichten(n, Laminieren(n
lamination layer	Blechlage(f
laminator, film laminator	Beschichtungsanlage(f
land area	Kontaktfläche(f
land, land area	Abquetschfläche(f
laser	Laser(m
latent heat	latente Wärme(f
lateral aperture	Seitenöffnung(f
lateral conductor	Seitenleitung(f
lattice girder	Fachwerkträger(m
layer lattice	Schichtgitter(n
lead paint	Bleifarbe(f
lead sleeve	Bleimuffe(f
lead spring	Bleifeder(f

leakage flux	magnetischer Streufluss(m
leakage transformer	Streutransformator(m
leather gasket, - packing	Lederpackung(f
leather wheel	Lederscheibe(f
length	Länge(f
length of a span, span length	Spannweite(f
length of the air gap	Luftspaltlänge(f
length of winding	Windungslänge(f
lens	Linse(f
level	Niveau(m, Pegel(m
lever switch	Hebelschalter(m
lift motor	Aufzugmotor(m
light resistant, lightfast	lichtecht
lightning conductor	Blitzableiter(m
limited proportionality	begrenzte Proportionalität(f
limiting density	Grenzdichte(f
limiting friction	Gleitgrenze(f
limiting values	Grenzwerte(pl
line current	Leiterstromstärke(f
line of application	Wirkungslinie(f
line, production line	Produktionsstrasse(f
linear accelerator	Linearbeschleuniger(m
linear expansion	Längenausdehnung(f
linear timebase	lineare Zeitbasis(f
liner	Scheider(m
lining, liner	Auskleidung(f
link polygon	Seileck(n
liquid body	flüssiger Körper(m
liquid level indicator	Flüssigkeitsstandanzeiger(m
load	Betriebszustand(m, Last(f
load impedance	Belastungsimpedanz(f
load on screw	Schrauben-Beanspruchung(f
load peak	Belastungsspitze(f
load test	Belastungsprobe(f
load-dependent	lastabhängig
loading	Belastungsart(f
loading device	Ladevorrichtung(f
loading funnel	Fülltrichter(m, Zuführöffnung(f
loading tray, charging tray	Füllplatte(f
local action	örtliche Einwirkung(f
local oscillator	Empfangsoszillator(m
locking contact	Verriegelungskontakt(m
locking ring	Klemmring(m, Schliessring(m
long duration test	Dauerprobe(f
long-stroke press	Presse(f mit hohem Hub
loss angle	Verlustwinkel(m
loss factor, damping factor	Verlustfaktor(m
loss tangent	Tangens(m des Verlustwinkels

losses	Verluste(pl
low speed	niedrige Geschwindigkeit(f
low vacuum	niedriges Vakuum(n
low voltage	niedrige Spannung(f
low-pressure vaporizer	Niederdruckverdampfer(m
lower boom	Untergurt(m
lower cross head, - traverse	unteres Querhaupt(n
lubricant	Gleitmittel(n, Schmiermittel(n
lubricating lacquer	Gleitlack(m
machine part	Maschinenelement(n
machine tool	Werkzeugmaschine(f
machining	Abspantechnik(f
magnet wheel	Polrad(n
magnet(izing) coil	Feldspule(f
magnetic circuit	magnetischer Kreis(m
magnetic conductance	magnetischer Leitwert(m
magnetic deflection	magnetische Ablenkung(f
magnetic field strength	magnetische Feldstärke(f
magnetic flux	magnetischer Fluss(m
magnetic flux density	magnetische Flussdichte(f
magnetic focusing	magnetische Fokussierung(f
magnetic needle	Magnetnadel(f
magnetic pole	Magnetpol(m
magnetic rules	magnetische Richtungsregeln(pl
magnetic screen, - shield	magnetische Abschirmung(f
magnetic voltage	magnetische Spannung(f
magnetism	Magnetismus(m
main axis	Hauptachse(f
main contact	Hauptkontakt(m
main protection	Hauptschutz(m
make contact	Arbeitskontakt, Schliesskontakt
mandrel carrier	Dornhalter(m
mandrel, mandril	Dorn(m
manifold	Verteiler(m, Abzweigung(f
mass of iron	Eisenmasse(f
master clock	Hauptuhr(f
master roll, control -	Leitwalze(f
master switch	Hauptschalter(m
masticator blade, kneader -	Mastikator-Schaufel(f
matching diaphragm	Anpass(ungs)blende(f
material testing	Materialprüfung(f
mathematical	rechnerisch
matrix, base material	Grundmaterial(n
matter	Materie(f, Stoff(m
maximum capacity	Höchstleistung(f
mean cathode loading	mittlere Katodenbelastung(f
mean free time	mittlere freie Zeit(f
measuring comparator	Messwertgeber(m

measuring cylinder, graduated	Messzylinder(m
measuring instrument	Messinstrument(n
mechanical efficiency	mechanischer Wirkungsgrad(m
mechanical flotation	mechanische Flotation(f
mechanical loss(es)	mechanische Verluste(pl
mechanical power	mechanische Leistung(f
mechanical properties	mechanische Eigenschaften(pl
mechanical test	mechanische Prüfung(f
medium speed	mittlere Geschwindigkeit(f
melting point	Schmelzpunkt(m
melting rate	Schmelzgeschwindigkeit(f
mercury column	Quecksilbersäule(f
mercury contact	Quecksilberkontakt(m
meshed network	Maschennetz(n
metadyne generator	Metadyngenerator(m
metal rectifier	Metallgleichrichter(m
metal spraying	Metallspritzverfahren(n
metal-ceramic, cermet	Metallkeramik(f
metallic bond	metallische Bindung(f
metallic coating	Metallüberzug(m
metallization, metal plating	Metallisieren(n
meter	Messer(m, Meter(n, Zähler(m
meter case	Zählergehäuse(n
metering rod, meter bar	Dosierstab(m, Dosierrakel(m
metering tank	Dosiergefäss(n
metering zone	Zumesszone(f
mica plate	Glimmerplatte(f
mica washer	Glimmerunterlagsscheibe(f
microalloy	Mikrolegierung(f
microbalance	Mikrowaage(f
microelectronics	Mikro-Elektronik(f
microwave filter	Mikrowellenfilter(n
middle wire	Mittelleiter(m
mill opening, bite	Spaltweite(f, Walzenspalt(m
milling width	Fräsbreite(f
missing operation	unterbliebenes Arbeiten(n
mixing blade	Mischarm(m
mixing cylinder	Mischzylinder(m
mixing drum	Mischtrommel(f
mixture	Gemisch(n, Mischung(f
mo(u)ld chase	Formrahmen(m
mo(u)ld release agent	Formentrennmittel(n
mo(u)ld with conical splits	Kegelform(f
mo(u)lding press	Formpresse(f
mo(u)lding pressure	Pressdruck(m
mobile transformer	fahrbarer Transformator(m
moderate accelerator	mittelstarker Beschleuniger(m
modified resin	modifiziertes Harz(n

modulus of elasticity	Elastizitätsmodul(m
moisture trap	Feuchtfänger(m
mold load, mould charge	Pressformbeschickung(f
molecular volume	molares Volumen(n
moment	Moment(n
moment constant	Momentenkonstante(f
moment of friction	Reibungsmoment(n
moment of inertia, second moment	Trägheitsmoment(n
moment theorem	Momentensatz(m
momentum equation	Impulssatz(m
motive power unit	Triebeinheit(f, Motoreinheit(f
motor equipment	Antriebsaggregat(n
motor vehicle	Triebfahrzeug(n
mounting position	Montagestellung(f
mouving element	bewegliches Organ(n
movable coil	bewegliche Spule(f
movable conductor	beweglicher Leiter(m
movable part	bewegliche Hälfte(f
multi-circuit winding	Mehrfachwicklung(f
multi-layer welding	Mehrlagen-Schweissung(f
multi-platen press, day-light	-Etagen-Plattenpresse(f
multilayered cathode	mehrschichtige Katode(f
multiple connection	Gruppenschaltung(f
multiple thread, multi-flighted	mehrgängige Schraube(f
multiple transmission	Mehrfachantrieb, Mehrachsantrieb
multiplication factor	Vervielfachungsfaktor(m
n equal resistances	n gleiche Widerstände(pl
natural characteristic	natürliche Kennlinie(f
neck insert, neck ring	Halseinsatz(m, Halsring(m
needle counter	Nadelzähler(m
needle lubricator	Nadelschmiergerät(n
needle-deflection	Nadelausschlag(m
negative charge	negative Ladung(f
negative conductor	negativer Leiter(m
neon lamp	Neonlampe(f, Neonröhre(f
neutral axis	neutrale Achse(f, - Faser(f
neutral conductor	Nulleiter(m
neutral zone	neutrale Zone(f
nickel layer	Nickelschicht(f
nip rolls, nipper rolls	Klemmwalzen(pl, Haltewalzen(pl
nitrocellulose	Nitrozellulose(f
non circular	nicht kreisförmig
non-critical dimension	nichtkritische Dimension(f
non-intermeshing	nicht ineinandergreifend
non-linear scale	nichtlineare Skala(f
non-lined construction	unverkleidete Konstruktion(f
normal band	Normalband(n
normal position	Grundstellung(f

normal state, ground state	Normalzustand(m
nozzle	Düsenmundstück(n
nucleation	Kernbildung(f
number of conductors	Leiterzahl(f
number of layers	Zahl(f der Lagen
number of pairs of poles	Polpaarzahl(f
number of spokes	Anzahl(f der Arme
numbre of turns	Windungszahl(f
oblique anode	Schräganode(f
oblique head	Schrägkopf(m, Winkelkopf(m
oblique structure	Schrägstellung(f, Schrägaufbau(m
observation pipe, – tube	Beobachtungsrohr(n
observation window, peep-window	Beobachtungsfenster(n
octal base	Achtersockel(m, Oktalsockel(m
off-position	Aus-Stellung(f, Ruhestellung(f
off-state	Sperrstellung(f
ohmic contact	Ohmscher Kontakt(m
Ohm's law	Ohmsches Gesetz(m
oil bath	Ölbad(n
oil channel	Ölkanal(m, Ölrinne(f
oil cooler	Ölkühler(m
oil filter	Ölfilter(m
oil jacket	Ölmantel(m
oil length	Ölgehalt(m
oil pump	Ölpumpe(f
oil resistant	ölbeständig
oil ring, scraper ring	Schmierrille(f, Ölring(m
oil separator	Ölabscheider(m
oil-feeding reservoir	Ölzufuhrgefäss(n
on-period	Arbeitszeit(f, Leitperiode(f
on-position	Arbeitsstellung, Ein-Stellung(f
on-state	Durchlassstellung(f
one-hour duty	Stundenbetrieb(m
one-screw mounting	Einschraubenmontage(f
open circuit	offener Kreis(m
open filter	offener Filter(m
open-circuited electrode	nichtangeschlossene Elektrode(f
opening surface	Öffnungsfläche(f
operating characteristics	Betriebsdaten(pl
operating conditions	Betriebsverhalten(n
operating device	Betätigungsorgan(n
operating platform, working –	Arbeitsbühne(f
operating point	Arbeitspunkt(m
operating voltage, working –	Betriebsspannung(f
optical pyrometer	optisches Pyrometer(n
orifice	Öffnung(f
oscillating conveyor	Schwingförderband(n
outdoor insulator	Aussenisolator(m

outer coating	Aussenbelag(m
outer cylinder	äusserer Zylinder(m
outlet hopper, discharge -	Überlauftrichter(m
outline	Umriss(m, Kontur(f
output	Ausgang(m
output capacitance	Ausgangskapazität(f
output power, power output	Ausgangsleistung(f
output, through-put	Ausstossleistung(f
outside circle	Kopfkreis(m
overall efficiency	Gesamtwirkungsgrad(m
overcompression	Überkompression(f
overcurrent factor	Überstromfaktor(m
overflow conduit	Überlaufleitung(f
overflow cone	Überlaufkonus(m
overflow trap	Überlaufauslass(m
overlap	Überlappung(f
overlap angle	Überlappungswinkel(m
overlap fillet weld	Überlappstoss(m mit Kehlnaht
overlap period	Überlappungszeit(f
overlapping blades	überlappende Knetschaufeln(pl
overload	Überlast(f, Überlastung(f
overvoltage	Überspannung(f
oxide covering	oxydierende Umhüllung(f
oxy-arc cutting	Elektro-Sauerstoffschneiden(n
oxygen cutting, lance -	Brennschneiden(n
paddle mixer, - agitator	Paddelrührer(m, Paddelmischer(m
paint	Farbe(f, Anstrichfarbe(f
paint film	Anstrichfilm(m
paint-spraying gun	Farbspritzpistole(f
pan, flat tank	Wanne(f)
panel, sheet	Platte(f), Tafel(f)
parallel conductor	paralleler Leiter(m
parallel connection	Parallelschaltung(f
parallel forces	parallele Kräfte(pl
parallel resonant circuit	Parallel-Schwingkreis(m
paralleling	Parallelschalten(n
paralysis circuit	Blockierschaltung(f
parametric amplifier	parametrischer Verstärker(m
paraxial	achsenparallel, paraxial
parent metal	Basismetall(n
particle size apparatus	Korngrössenbestimmungsapparat(m
parting agent	Trennmittel(n
path of force	Lastweg(m
path of load	Kraftweg(m
pattern	Testbild(n
pay-off drum	Zufuhrtrommel(f
peak load	Höchstbelastung(f
peak point	Gipfelpunkt(m, Höckerpunkt(m

peak point current	Gipfelstrom(m, Höckerstrom(m
peak point voltage	Gipfelspannung(f
peak value	Scheitelwert(m, Höchstwert(m
peep-hole, spy glass	Schauloch(n
pelleting machine, tablets press	Tablettenpresse(f
penetration depth	Eindringtiefe(f
penetrometer, quotimeter	Penetrometer(n
perforated bottom	Siebboden(m
perforated plate, slotted -	Siebblech(n
period	Periode(f, Periodendauer(f
periodic current	periodischer Strom(m
periodic duty	Aussetzbetrieb(m
periodic time	Zeitperiode(f
permanent fault	Dauerfehler(m
permanent joint	unlösbare Verbindung(f
permeability	Permeabilität(f
permissible stress	zulässige Spannung(f
permissible torsion stress	zulässige Verdrehspannung(f
pH-meter	pH-Messer(m
pH-recorder	pH-Registrierer(m
phase anlge	Phasenwinkel(m
phase changer	Phasenschieber(m
phase conductor	Phasenleiter(m
phase constant	Phasenkonstante(f
phase shift	Phasenverschiebung(f
phase voltage	Strangspannung(f
phase winding	Phasenwicklung(f
photoconductor	Photoleiter(m
photoelectric cell	lichtelektrische Zelle(f
photoelectric counter	lichtelektrischer Zähler(m
photoelectric timer	photoelektrischer Zeitschalter(
photosensitive, light sensitive	lichtempfindlich
pick-up value	Ansprechwert(m
pinch roll	Förderwalze(f
pipe bend	Rohrbogen(m
pipe bending	Biegen(n von Rohren
pipe clip, pipe clamp	Rohrschelle(f
pipe cooler	Röhrenkühler(m
pipe extruder	Rohrpresse(f
pipe flow	Rohrströmung(f
pipe joint, - connection	Rohrverbindung(f
pipe nipple	Rohrnippel(m
pipe support	Rohrhalter(m
pipe, tube	Rohr(n, Röhre(f
pipe-type cable	Rohrkabel(n
pipeline, closed conduit	geschlossene Leitung(f, Pipeline
piston manometer	Kolbendruckmesser(m
pitch	Teilung(f

pitch angle	Kantenwinkel(m
pitch circle	Teilkreis(m
pitched blade, inclined –	geneigter Flügel(m
planetary mixer	Planetenrührwerk(n
plastic (material)	Kunst(harz)stoff(m
plastic flow	elastisches Fliessen(n
plastic pipe, – tube	Kunstharzrohr(n
plastic piping	Kunststoffrohrleitung(f
plasticizer tank	Plastifizierbehälter(m
plastics welder	Kunststoffschlosser(m
plastics(pl	Kunststoffe(pl, Plaste(pl
plastification zone	Plastifizier(ungs)zone(f
plastimeter, plastometer	Plastometer(n
plate	Platte(f
plate anode	Plattenanode(f
plate area	Plattenfläche(f
plate block	Plattenblock(m
plate check	Blechkontrolle(f
plate cooler, surface cooler	Plattenkühler(m
plate current, anode current	Anodenstrom(m
plate input power	Anodeneingangsleistung(f
plate load, anode –	Anodenbelastung(f
plate support	Plattenhalter(m
plate support	Plattenstütze(f
plating rack	Einhängegestell(n
plug	Stecker(m
plug adaptor	Übergangsstecker(m
plug-in relay	Stecksockelrelais(n
plug-in unit	Einsteckblock(m
plunger	Kolben(m
ply, layer	Schicht(f, Lage(f
pneumatic dryer	pneumatischer Trockner(m
pneumatic drying	Presslufttrocknen(n
pneumatic structure	luftgestützte Konstruktion(f
pneumatic switch	pneumatischer Schalter(m
point cathode	Punktkatode(f
point contact	Punktkontakt(m
point motor, switch motor	Weichenmotor(m
point of application	Angriffspunkt(m
point of connection	Anschlussort(m
point of intersection	Schnittpunkt(m
pointer	Zeiger(m
pointer instrument	Zeigerinstrument(n
Poisson's equation	Poissonsche Gleichung(f
poke welding	Handpunktschweissen(n
polar contact	polarer Kontakt(m
polar port	polare Öffnung(f
polar wind(ing)	Polwicklung(f

polarity	Polarität (f
polarity indicator	Polprüfer (m
polarization current	Polarisationsstrom (m
polarized relay	Polarrelais (n
pole face	Polfläche (f
pole pair	Polpaar (n
pole pitch	Polteilung (f
pole reverser	Polumschalter (m, Umpoler (m
pole unit	Einzelpol (m
polishing barrel, - drum	Poliertrommel (f
polishing calender	Polierkalander (m
polishing machine	Poliermaschine (f
polishing roll(er), wheel roll	Putzwalze (f
polishing, brightening, ashing	Polieren (n
polyelectrode, multiple electrode	Mehrfachelektrode (f
polymerizing	Polymerisierung (f
polyphase	mehrphasig
polyphase machine	Mehrphasenmaschine (f
portable battery	transportable Batterie (f
position A	A-Stellung (f
positive charge	positive Ladung (f
positive conductor	positiver Leiter (m
post-acceleration	Nachbeschleunigung (f
postcuring	Nachbehandlung (f
pot core	Topfkern (m
pot press, oil press	Ölpresse (f
potential divider	Spannungsteiler (m
potential gradient	Potentialgradient (m
power	Kraft (f, Leistung (f
power amplification	Leistungsverstärkung (f
power divider	Leistungsteiler (m
power factor	Leistungsfaktor (m
power feeder	Kraftspeiseleitung (f
power transformer	Netztransformator (m
pre-drilled hole	Vorbohrung (f
precessing plant	Bearbeitungsanlage (f
precision balance	Präzisionswaage (f
precoating	Vorbeschichtung (f
precompressed	vorverdichtet
predrier	Votrockner (m
preheater	Vorwärmer (m
preheating	Vorwärmung (f
preheating time, warm-up time	Anheizzeit (f
preliminary dimensioning	Vor-Dimensionierung (f
press	Presse (f
press bonding	Leimen (n unter Druck
press plate	Pressplatte (f, Druckplatte (f
pressed-glass base	Pressglassockel (m

pressing mould, block mold	Pressform(f
pressure air, compressed air	Druckluft(f, Pressfluft(f
pressure angle	Eingriffswinkel(m
pressure boiler	Druckkessel(m
pressure bottle	Druckflasche(f
pressure build-up	Druckaufbau(m
pressure butt welding	Press-Stumpfschweissen(n
pressure converter	Druckwandler(m
pressure during heating time	Anwärmdruck(m
pressure nozzle	Druckdüse(f
pressure pad, forming	Presskissen(n
pressure relay	Druckrelais(n, pneumatisches R.
pressure roll	Anpresswalze(f
primary	primär
primary crusher	Vorbrecher(m, Grobbrecher(m
primary radiation	primäre Strahlung(f
priming speed	Aktivierungsgeschwindigkeit(f
principal mode	Grundmodus(m
printed circuit	gedruckte Schaltung(f
process computer	Prozessrechner(m
programmed heating	Temperaturprogrammierung(f
progressive ratio	Stufensprung(m
propagation	Ausbreitung(f, Fortpflanzung(f
propeller agitator, - stirrer	Propellerrührwerk(n, Schrauben-(n
proportional limit	Proportionalitätsgrenze(f
proportional region	Proportionalbereich(m
protected	geschützt
protection against corrosion	Korrosionsschutz(m
protection cap	Schutzgehäuse(n
protective coating	Schutzüberzug(m
protective gloves	Schutzhandschuhe(pl
protective system	Schutzsystem(n
proving circuit	Prüfstromkreis(m
pull box	Drahtziehdose(f
pull-back ram	Rückzugkolben(m
pulley block	Flaschenzug(m
pulling knob	Ziehknopf(m, Zuggriff(m
pulling out of synchronism	Aussertrittfallen(n
pulsator jig	Schüttelsiebmaschine(f
pulse number	Pulszahl(f
pulse transformer	Impulsübertrager(m
pumping frequency	Pumpfrequenz(f
punch-through, penetration	Durchdringung(f
punching	Stanzen(n
punching ridges	Stanzgrat(m
pushback	hydraulischer Auswerfer(m
pushbutton	Druckknopf(m
putty, stopper	Kitt(m

quality, figure of merit	Güte(f
quantity of electricity	Elektrizitätsmenge(f, Ladung(f
quantum number	Quantenzahl(f
quench hardening	Abschreckhärtung(f
quick-break switch	Schnellausschalter(m
quiescent value	Ruhewert(m
radar screen	Radarschirm(m
radial (bearing) force	Radialkraft
radial deflection	Radialablenkung(f
radial flow agitator	Rührwerk(n mit Radialströmung
radiating surface	Strahlungs(ober)fläche(f
radiation density	Strahlungsdichte(f
radiation intensity	Strahlungsintensität(f
radiation loss	Strahlungsverlust(m
radiation source	Strahlenquelle(f
radiator	Strahler(m
radiator	Radiator(m, Strahler(m
rail contact	Schienenkontakt(m
raised front roll	angehobene Vorderwalze(f
raising platform	Hebebühne(f
rake mixer	Rechenmischer(m
raking mechanism, rabbling -	Krählwerk(n
ram extruder	Kolbenstrangpresse(f
range of measurement	Messbereich(m
range-energy relation	Verhältnis(n Reichweite-Energie
rapid release, quick release	Schnellauslösung(f
rapid traverse speed	Eilganggeschwindigkeit(f
rated	Nenn-
rated current	Nennstrom(m
rated frequency	Nennfrequenz(f
rated quantity	Nennwert(m, Nenngrösse(f
rating	Nennbetrieb(m
rating chart	Belastungsdiagramm(n
ratio of current	Stromverhältnis(n
ratio of voltages	Spannungsverhältnis(n
reactance	Blindwiderstand(m
reaction force	Reaktionskraft(f
reactive power	Blindleistung(f
real iron volume	wirkliches Eisenvolumen(n
rear light, tail light	Rücklicht(n
receiver magnet	Empfängermagnet(m
reciprocating table	Schütteltisch(m
recirculating pump	kontinuierliche Umlaufpumpe(f
reclosing time	Wiedereinschaltzeit(f
recoil	Rückstoss(m
recombination coefficient	Rekombinationskoeffizient(m)
recovery time	Erholungszeit(f
recovery, recuperation	Rückgewinnung(f

rectangular cathode	Rechteckkatode(f
rectangular cross section	rechteckiger Querschitt(m
rectified current	gleichgerichteter Strom(m
rectified value	Gleichrichtwert(m
rectifier	Gleichrichter(m
rectifier anode	Gleichrichteranode(f
rectifying section	Rektifizierteil(m
recycling	Wiederverwendung(f
recycling air, recirculating -	Luftzirkulation(f
reducing fitting, reducer	Reduzierstück(n
reducing joint	Reduktionsmuffe(f
reduction gear	Untersetzungsgetriebe(n
reel change	Rollenwechsel(m
reference axis	Bezugsachse(f
reference coil	Eichspule(f
reference gage, master gauge	Kontrolllehre(f, Prüflehre(f
reference point	Bezugspunkt(m
refiner mill	Raffinierwalze(f
refractory coating	feuerfeste Auskleidung(f
refractory lining	feuerfestes Futter(n
refrigerant, coolant	Kühlmittel(n
refrigeration plant	Kühlanlage(f
regenerative braking	Nutzbremsung(f
region of operation	Arbeitsbereich(m
regulating tap	Regulierhahn(m
reignition voltage, restriking -	Wiederzündspannung(f
reinforced plastics	verstärkter Kunststoff(m
relative error	relativer Fehler(m
relative permeability	Permeabilitätszahl(f
relative permittivity	Dielektrizitätszahl(f
relative roughness	relative Rauhigkeit(f
relay	Relais(n, Schütz(n
release relay	Auslöserrelais(n
reliability	Betriebssicherheit(f
reluctance	magnetischer Widerstand(m
reluctance motor	Reluktanzmotor(m
remanence	Remanenz(f
remanent-flux density	Remanenz-Induktion(f
removable element	auswechselbares Element(n
renewal parts	Ersatzteile(pl
repeated solidification	wiederholte Erstarrung(f
repulsion motor	Repulsionsmotor(m
reset time	Rückstellzeit(f
resetting value	Rückgangswert(m
residual error	Restfehler(m
resistance	Widerstand(m
resistance	elektrischer Widerstand(m
resistance heating	Widerstandsheizung(f

resistance of conductor	Leiterwiderstand(m
resistance standard	Normalwiderstand(m
resistance welding	Widerstandsschweissen(n
resistivity	spezifischer Widerstand(m
resistor element	Widerstandselement(n
resolution of a force	Kraftzerlegung(f
resonance condition	Resonanzbedingung(f
resonant circuit	Schwingkreis(m
resonant frequency	Resonanzfrequenz(f
resonant mode	Resonanzmodus(m
resonant period	Schwingungsdauer(f
resting potential	Ruhepotential(n
resultant force	resultierende Kraft(f
retardation test	Auslaufversuch(m
retarder	Verzögerer(m
retarding force	Verzögerungskraft(f
retention tank	Speichertank(m
return pulley	Kehrrolle(f
reverse cylinder	Umkehrwalze(f
reverse grid current	Gittergegenstrom(m
reversed polarity	umgekehrte Polung(f
reversible converter	umkehrbarer Stromrichter(m
revolution counter	Tourenzähler(m
rhenium-tungsten alloy	Rhenium-Wolframlegierung(f
ribbed panel	Rippenplatte(f
ribbed surface	geriffelte Fläche(f
ribbon blender, - mixer	Bandmischer(m
ribbon cable	Bandkabel(n, Flachkabel(n
rigid	hart, spröde
ring circuit	Ringkreis(m
ring counter	Ringzähler(m
ring heater	Ringheizkörper(m
ring marking	Ringmarkierung(f
ring seal	Ringverschmelzung(f
ring winding, toroidal winding	Ringwicklung(f
ringed network	ringförmiges Netz(n
ripple tray	Wellboden(m
rise, slope	Steigung(f
rising characteristic	steigende Kennlinie(f
Ritter method	Verfahren(n nach Ritter
rocking grate	Schwingrost(m
rod mill	Stabmühle(f
rod reflector, - mirror	Stabreflektor(m
roll adjustment	Walzeneinstellung(f
roll coater	Walzenbeschichter(m
roll glazing	Walzenglasierung(f
roll neck	Walzenzapfen(m
roll preloading adjustment	Walzenvorspannung(f

roll, mill	Walzenmischer (m
roller train, - conveyor	Rollenbahn (f
rolling contact	Rollkontakt (m, Wälzkontakt (m
rolling resistance	Rollreibungskraft (f
root angle	Fusswinkel (m
root circle	Fusskreis (m
root diameter of a screw	Schneckenkerndurchmesser (m
root width of tooth	Zahndicke (f
rope friction	Seilreibung (f
rotary disk, rotary shelf	Drehteller (m
rotary feeder	Dreh-Dosierschleuse (f
rotary paddle	Drehschaufel (f
rotary phase changer	Drehphasenschieber (m
rotary plate feeder	Drehplattenspeiser (m
rotary shaker	Umlaufschüttelmaschine (f
rotating beacon	Drehbake (f
rotating joint	Drehkupplung (f
rotating knife	umlaufendes Messer (n
rotating machine	rotierende Maschine (f
rotation circulator	Rotationszirkulator (m
rotator	Rotator (m
rotor core	Rotorkern (m
rounded aperture	gerundete Öffnung (f
routine tests	Stückprüfung (f, Einzelprüfung (f
roving chopper, glass chopper	Roving-Schneidwerk (n
rubber adhesive, - solution	Gummiklebstoff (m, Klebkitt (m
rubbing fastness,	Scheuerfestigkeit (f
running down	Auslauf (m
safety circuit	Sicherheitsschaltung (f
safety valve, pop valve	Sicherheitsventil (n
salient pole	ausgeprägter Pol (m, Schenkelpol
sandblast nozzle	Sandstrahldüse (f
sandblasting	Sandstrahlen (n
saturation	Sättigung (f
saturation current	Sättigungsstrom (m
scale	Skala (f, Skalenteilung (f
scale of forces	Kräftemassstab (m
scaling factor, - ratio	Untersetzungsfaktor (m
scattering center, - centre	Streuzentrum (n
Schrage motor	Schrage-Motor (m
Scott connection	Scottsche Schaltung (f
scrap reprocessing	Abfallwiederverwendung (f
screen burn	Schirmeinbrennung (f
screen, sieving screen	Siebrost (m
screen-grid current	Schirmgitterstrom (m
screening of nucleus	Kernabschirmung (f
screening, shielding	Abschirmung (f
screw core pin	Gewindestift (m

screw extruder	Schneckenpresse(f
screw length	Schneckenlänge(f
screw mixer	Schneckenmischer(m
screw with decreasing pitch	Schnecke(f mit Steigungsabnahm
screw with equal pitch	Schnecke(m mit Konstantsteigur
screw, worm	Schnecke(f, Schraube(f
screwed conduit	Rohrverschraubung(f
screwed joint	Schraubverbindung(f
screwed socket, - bell	Schraubmuffe(f
seal a cable	ein Kabel ausgiessen
sealable equipment	veschliessbare Anordnung(f
sealing	Abdichtung(f
sealing compound	Dichtungsmasse(f
sealing-in, seal	Einschmelzen(n
sealing-off burner	Abschmelzbrenner(m
seam welding	Nahtschweissen(n
secondary feeder	sekundäre Speiseleitung(f
secondary radiation	Sekundärstrahlung(f
seconds-counter	Sekundenzähler(m
section modulus	Widerstandsmoment(n
sectional panel	unterteiltes Schaltfeld(n
sectionalized spherical cavity	abgeplatteter Kugelhohlraum(m
sediment	Ablagerung(f, Sediment(n
segment coupling, - connector	Segmentbogen-Kupplung(f
segmental rim rotor	Blechkettenläufer(m
segmental wheel	Segmentscheibe(f
selector switch	Umschalter(m
selenium cell	Selenzelle(f
self-cleaning filter	selbstreinigendes Filter(n
self-induction	Selbstinduktion(f
self-regulation	Selbstregulierung(f
self-ventilated	selbstbelüftet
semi thick covering	mitteldicke Umhüllung(f
semi-self-sustained discharge	halbselbständige Entladung(f
semiconductor	Halbleiter(m
sense of rotation	Drehsinn(m
sensitive time	empfindliche Zeit(f, wirksame
sensitiveness to percussion	Schlagempfindlichkeit(f
sensitivity	Empfindlichkeit(f
separating electrode	Trennelektrode(f
separator	Scheider(m, Separator(m
sequence of operation	Betätigungsfolge(f
series connection	Serienschaltung(f, Reihenschltg
series motor	Reihenschlussmotor(m
series winding	Reihenschlusswicklung(f
serpentine pipe	Spiralrohr(n, Rohrschlange(f
service cable	Verbraucherleitung(f
service capacity	Nutzleistung(f

service voltage	Gebrauchsspannung(f
setting	Einstellwert(m
setting angle	Einstellwinkel(m
shaft diameter	Wellendurchmesser(m
shaker	Schüttelmaschine(f
shear	Schub(m
shear stress	Schubspannung(f
shearing force	Scherkraft(f, Querkraft(f
sheath	Schicht(f, Wand(f
sheet extruder	Folien(press)maschine(f
sheet, foil	Folie(f
sheeting	Folienmaterial(n
sheeting machine, - mill	Folienwalzwerk(n
shell core, blow stick	Hohlkern(m
shield	Abschirmung(f, Schirm(m
shield grid	Abschirmgitter(n
shielding, shadowing	Abschirmung(f, Blenden(n
shifting gear	Schaltgetriebe(n
shock test	Stossprobe(f
short-circuit	Kurzschluss(m
short-circuit brake	Kurzschlussbremse(f
short-circuit loss	Kurzschlussverlust(m
short-circuit winding	Kurzschlusswicklung(f
short-time duty	kurzzeitiger Betrieb(m
shower proofing	wasserabstossend Impregnieren(n
shredder	Zerkleinerungsmaschine(f
shrink-coating	Aufschrumpfen(n eines Überzuges
shrinkage allowance	Schrumpfmass(n
shrinkage, contraction	Schwinden(n, Schrumpfen(n
shrunk-on ring	Schrumpfring(m
shunt coil	Nebenschlussspule(f
shunt motor	Nebenschlussmotor(m
shunt winding	Nebenschlusswicklung(f
side cap	Seitenanschlusskappe(f
side sheet	Seitenschirm(m
sieve plate	Siebplatte(f, Filterplatte(f
sieving machine	Siebmaschine(f
sight glass, sight hole	Schauglas(n, Schauloch(n
signal operation	Signalbetätigung(f
silicon carbide	Siliziumkarbid(n
silicon solar cell	Silizium-Sonnenzelle(f
silver-chloride cell	Silberchloridelement(n
silvering	Versilberung(f
simple electrode	Einfachelektrode(f
simple folding, single folding	einfache Faltung(f
simple leaf spring	gerade Biegungsfeder(f
single contact	Einfachkontakt(m
single feeder	Einzelspeiseleitung(f

single phase	einphasig, Einfasen-
single pole	einpolig
single-phase machine	Einphasenmaschine(f
single-phase rectifier	Einphasengleichrichter(m
single-wire	Einzeldraht-, eindratig
sinlge-break switch	Einzelunterbrecher(m
sintering bath	Sinterbad(n
siphon trap	Geruchverschluss(m
size reduction	Zerkleinerung(f
sizing	Grössensortierung(f
sleet hood	Frostkappe(f
sleeve welding	Muffenschweissen(n
slenderness	Schlankheitsgrad(m
slide follower	Schieberbacke(f
sliding bottom	Schiebeboden(m
sliding contact	Schleifkontakt(m
sliding contact	Gleitkontakt, Schleifkontakt(m
sliding friction	Gleitreibung(f
slinging wire	Einhängedraht(m
slot	Nut(f, Schlitz(m
slow accelerator	langsamer Beschleuniger(m
slush mo(u)lding	Schalenguss(m, Formguss(m
smoke filter	Rauchgasfilter(m, n
smoothing rolls	Glättwalzen(pl
snagging wheel	Putzscheibe(f
socket joint	Muffenverbindung(f
socket outlet	Steckdose(f
socket outlet and plug	Steckvorrichtung(f
softening plant	Enthärtungsanlage(f
solar battery	Sonnenbatterie(f
solar cell	lichtelektrische Sonnenzelle(f
soldering lamp	Lötlampe(f
solid body	fester Körper(m
solid conductor	massiver Leiter(m
solidifying agent	Verfestiger, Verfestigungsmittel
solvent	Lösungsmittel(n
sorting plant	Sortieranlage(f
spacer	Distanzstück(n
spacer block	Distanzblock(m
spacer, spacer plate	Abstandplatte(f
spacing clip, - clamp	Abstandschelle(f
spacing of coils	Windungsabstand(m
spark	Funke(m
spark trap	Funkenfänger(m
sparking potential, glow -	Zündspannung(f
specific heat	spezifische Wärmekapazität(f
specific volume	spezifisches Volumen(n
speed	Drehzahl(f, Umdrehungsfrequenz(f

speed controller	Geschwindigkeitsregler (m
spindle mill	Spindelmühle (f
spiral condenser, – radiator	Schlangenkühler (m
spiral spring	Spiralfeder (f
splicing ear	Verbindungsöse (f
splicing sleeve	Verbindungsmuffe (f
spontaneous ignition	Selbstentzündung (f
spoon agitator	Löffelrührer (m
spot welding	Punktschweissen (n
spray coating	Sprühbeschichten (n
spray dyeing	Zerstäubungsfärben (n
spray gun process	Spritzverfahren (n
spreading machine	Streichmaschine (f
spreading mixture, coating –	Streichmischung (f, Überzugs–
spring contact	Federkontakt (m
spring set	Federsatz (m
sprue ejector bar	Auswurfstab (m
spur gear	Stirnrad (n
square edge	Stirnfläche (f, Rechteckkante (f
squeeze roll	Quetschwalze (f
stability factor	Stabilitätsfaktor (m
stability to light	Lichtechtheit (f
stabilized glass	verfärbungsfreies Glas (n
stable position	stationäre Stellung (f
stack height	Stapelhöhe (f
stacked packing	geordnete Füllung (f
stamping press, – machine	Prägepresse (f
star-circuit	Sternschaltung (f
star-delta connection	Stern-Dreieck-Schaltung (f
starter	Starter (m, Anlasser (m
starter (electrode), igniter	el. Zündelektrode (f, Starter (m
starter current, striking –	Starterstrom (m
starting	Anlauf (m
starting anode	Zündanode (f, Anlassanode (f
starting current	Anlaufstrom (m, Anzugsstrom (m
starting current, striking –	Zündstrom (m
starting motor	Anwurfmotor (m
starting test	Anlaufversuch (m
starting voltage, striking –	Einsatzstrom (m
starting winding	Anlaufwicklung (f
starting-up	Anlassen (n, Starten (n
static characteristic	statische Kennlinie (f
static converter	Stromrichter (m
static friction	Haftreibung (f
static mixer, motionless –	statischer Mischer (m
stationary battery	ortsfeste Batterie (f
stationary lip	feststehende Lippe (f
stationary state	stationärer Zustand (m

stator	Ständer(m, Stator(m
steady flow	stationäre Strömung(f
steam autoclave	Dampfautoklav(m
steam channel, steam way	Dampfkanal(m
step aeration	Stufenbelüftung(f
step time	Schrittzeit(f
step-by-step excitation	stufenweise Anregung(f
stepped	abgestuft
stepped tray	Stufenboden(m
sticking voltage	Sperrspannung(f
stop	Anschlag(m, Puffer(m
stopping brake	Anhaltebremse(f
storage	Speicherung(f
storage element	Speicherelement(n
storage tank, accumulator –	Sammelbehälter(m, Speichertank(m
stored energy	gespeicherte Energie(f
stoving lacquer	Einbrennlack(m
straight blade	gerade Schaufel(f
straight vacuum forming	einfaches Vakuumformverfahren(n
straightening press	Richtpresse(f
straining clamp	Abspannklemme(f
stress	Spannung(f
stress ratio	Anstrengungs-Verhältnis(n
strip cutter	Streifenschneider(m
strip feed	Bandbeschickung(f
stripper plate	Abstreifplatte(f
stripping compound	Trennsubstanz(f
stuffing piston	Füllkolben(m
subassembly	Bauteil(m
subminiaturization	Subminiaturtechnik(f
suction conduit	Saugleitung(f
summation meter	Summenzähler(m
superheating	Überhitzung(f
supply terminal	Anschlusspunkt(m
supply voltage, feeding voltage	Speisespannung(f
support	Abstützung(f
support force	Auflagerkraft(f
support pillar	Stütze(f, Unterlegestück(n
support reaction, bearing –	Auflagerreaktion(f
supported flange joint	Klemmflansch(m
supporting plate	Trägerplatte(f, Halteplatte(f
supporting rolls	Stützwalzen(pl, Stützrollen(pl
supporting structure	Traggerüst(n
surface barrier	Oberflächensperrschicht(f
surface coating	Oberflächenüberzug(m
surface cooler	Oberflächenkühler(m
surface hardening	Oberflächenhärtung(f
surface layer	Oberflächenschicht(f

surface load	Oberflächenbelastung(f
surface of liquid	Flüssigkeitsspiegel(m
surface treating	Oberflächenbehandlung(f
suspension	Aufhängung(f
suspension insulator	Aufhängeisolator(m
swing pipe	Schwenkrohr(n
swinging scraper	pendelnder Wischer(m
switch	Schalter(m
switch base	Schaltersockel(m
switch group	Schaltgruppe(f
switch machine, point mechanism	Weichenmechanismus(m
switch starter	Anlassschalter(m
switchgear	Schaltgeräte(pl
switching	Schaltung(f
switching time	Schaltzeit(f
switching transistor	Schalttransistor(m
symbol	Schaltbild(n
synchronizing, synchronization	Synchronisieren(n
synchronous generator	Synchrongenerator(m
synchronous motor	Synchronmotor(m
synchronous scanning	Synchronabtastung(f
synchronous speed	Synchrondrehzahl(f
system of units	Einheitensystem(n
T-slot	T-Nut(f, Spann-Nut(f
tack coat	Klebeschicht(f
tack welding	Punktschweissen(n
take-off roller	Abnahmerolle(f, Abwickelrolle(f
tandem motor	Tandemmotor(m, Doppelmotor(m
tank	Behälter(m, Tank(m
tank lifter	Gefässheber(m, Tankheber(m
tank partition	Behältertrennwand(f
tap	Anzapfung(f
tap, cock	Hahn(m
tapered key	Querkeil-Verbindung(f
telecontrol	Fernsteuerung(f
temperature	Temperatur(f
temperature change	Temperatur-Änderung(f
temperature coefficient	Temperaturkoeffizient(f
temperature difference	Temperaturdifferenz(f
temperature-limited	tempertaturbegrenzt
tensile stress	Zugspannung(f
tension roll(er), pull roll	Spannrolle(f
termal equilibrium	thermisches Gleichgewicht(n
terminal	Klemme(f, Anschluss(m
terminal support	Endstütze(f
terminal velocity	Endgeschwindigkeit(f
terminal voltage	Klemmenspannung(f
test value	Prüfwert(m

testing joints	Prüfverbindungen(pl
tetravalent, quadrivalent	vierwertig
theoretical yield	theoretische Ausbeute(f
thermal activation	thermische Aktivierung(f
thermal barrier	Wärmesperre(f
thermal breakdown	thermischer Abbruch(m
thermal conduction	Wärmeleitzahl(f
thermal conductivity	Wärmeleitfähigkeit(f
thermal cutout	thermischer Unterbrecher(m
thermal insulation board	Wärmeschutzplatte(f
thermal resistance	thermischer Widerstand(m
thermal state	thermischer Zustand(m
thermionic current	Thermionenstrom(m
thermocouple	Thermofühler(m
thermoplastic	thermoplastisch
thermostat	Thermostat(m
thermostat (relay)	Thermostat(m
thickness control	Dickensteuerung(f
thickness ga(u)ge	Dickenmessgerät(n
thickness of covering	Hüllendicke(f
thickness of winding	Wicklungsdicke(f
thin covering	dünne Umhüllung(f
thorat	Kragen(m
thread guide	Fadenführung(f
thread, flight	Gewinde(n, Windung(f
three-phase	Dreiphasen-
three-phase motor	Drehstrommotor(m
three-roll calender	Dreiwalzenkalander(m
three-way cock	Dreiweghahn(m
threephase power	Drehstromleistung(f
threephase-transformer	Drehstrom-Transformator(m
through, undersize	Siebdurchfall(m
thrust roll	Andruckwalze(f
tilted cylinder mixer	Schrägtrommelmischer(m
time constant	Zeitkonstante(f
time limit	Zeitgrenze(f, Grenzzeit(f
time selector	Zeit-Diskriminator(m (Einkanal-
time-limit release	Zeitauslösung(f
timebase	Zeitbasis(f
tinning	Verzinnung(f
tinplating	Zinnschicht(f
tolerance	Tolleranz(f
tool box, equipment box	Werkzeugkiste(f
tooth calculation	Zahnberechnung(f
tooth spacing	Zahnlücke(f
tooth system	Verzahnung(f
tooth wheel rim	Zahnkranzstärke(f
toothed blade	gezahnter Flügel(m

top backing plate	obere Stanzplatte, Stanzauflage
top board, top plate	obere Platte(f
top cap	Kopfanschlusskappe(f
top discharge	Obenentleerung(f
top feed	Füllung(f von oben
top roll	Oberwalze(f
toroidal coil	Ringspule(f
torpedo head	Torpedokopf(m
torque	Drehmoment(n
torsion	Verdrehung(f, Torsion(f
torsion stress	Verdrehspannung(f
total number of teeth	Zähnezahlsumme(f
total resistance	Totalwiderstand(m
total resistance	Gesamtwiderstand(m
total time constant	Gesamtzeitkonstante(f
totally-enclosed	geschlossen
track braking	Schienenbremsung(f
traction machine	Antriebsmaschine(f
tractive effort, - force	Zugkraft(f
transfer characteristic	Übertragungskennlinie(f
transfer plate, loading plate	Füllplatte(f, Ladetablett(n
transformation	Umwandlung(f, Transformation(f
transformer	Transformator(m, Umspanner(m
transient	vorübergehend
transition	Übergang(m
transition effect	Übergangseffekt(m
transition loss	Übergangsverlust(m
transition point	Übergangspunkt(m
transmission coefficient	Übertragungsfaktor(m
transmission line	Übertragungsleitung(f
transmission loss	Übertragungsverlust(m
transmission ratio	Übersetzungsverhältnis(n
transmitted	übermittelt
transport factor, - ratio	Übergangsverhältnis(n
trash rack, coarse screen	Grobrechen(m
travelling grate	Wanderrost(m
triple motor	Dreifachmotor(m
triple pole	dreipolig
trolley head	Stromabnehmerkopf(m
trouble shooter, set analyzer	Fehlersucher(m, Prüfgerät(n
tube mill	Rohrmühle(f
tubular (space) grid	Rohrgitter(n
tumbling dryer, - drier	Taumeltrockner(m
turbine mixer	Turbinenmischer(m
turbo dryer, - drier	Turbotrockner(m
turbulent flow	turbulente Strömung(f
turning blades	Wendeschaufeln(pl
twin cable	zweiadriges Kabel(n

twin-screw extruder machine	Doppelschneckenextruder(m
two-arm kneader	zweiarmiger Kneter(m
two-component adhesive	Zweikomponenten-Klebstoff(m
two-phase current	Zweiphasenstrom(m
two-phase system	Zweiphasensystem(n
two-roll mill	Zweiwalzenmischer(m
two-stage compression	Zweistufencompression(f
two-way	Zweiweg-
two-way valve	Wechselventil(n
U-section, channel	U-Profil(n
ultimate position	Endstellung(f
ultimate stress, tensile stress	Zugfestigkeit(f
ultra-high-vacuum	Höchstvakuum(n
undercooling, supercooling	Unterkühlung(f
uniform connection	einheitliche Schaltung(f
uniformly distributed	gleichmässig verteilt
uninsulated	nichtisoliert
unit charge	Einheitsladung(f
universal motor	Universalmotor(m
unknown	gesucht, unbekannt
unloader, unloading device	Entladevorrichtung(f
unloading, discharge	Entladung(f), Entlastung(f
unstable	unbeständig, unstabil, labil
unwinding, uncoiling	Abwickeln(m, Abspulen(n
upper boom	Obergurt(m
upper ram	Oberstempel(m, Oberkolben(m
useful area	wirksamer Querschnitt(m
utilisation factor	Belastungsfaktor(m
utilization time	Nutzzeit(f
vacuum desiccator, - essicator	Vakuumexsikkator(m
vacuum drier	Vakuumtrockner(m
vacuum filter, suction filter	Vakuumfilter(m
vacuum pump	Vakuumpumpe(f
valley point	Talpunkt(m
valve	Ventil(n
valve seating	Ventilsitz(m
vapo(u)r jet pump	Dampfstrahlpumpe(f
variable coupling	veränderliche Kupplung(f
variable losses	veränderliche Verluste(pl
variable of state	Zustandsgrösse(f
varnishing machine	Lackiermaschine(f
vat, tank, vessel	Bottich(m, Tank(m
vector diagram	Zeigerbild(n, Vektordiagramm(n
vector product	vektorielles Produkt(n
velocity modulation	Geschwindigkeitssteuerung(f
vent	Entlüftungsöffnung(f
vent, ventilation	Lüftung(f, Entlüftung(f
ventilator, blower, fan	Ventilator(m, Lüfter(m

vertex plate	Scheitelplatte(f
vertical axis	vertikale Achse(f
vertical centring (control)	vertikale Einmittung(f
vertical conductor	Vertikalleiter, Senkrechtleiter
vertical deflection	Vertikalablemkung(f
vertical pipe, riser	Steigrohr(n, Vertikalrohr(n
vibrating mill	Vibrationsmühle, Schwingmühle(f
vibration damper	Schwingungsdämpfer(m
vibrator	Rüttler(m
viewing screen	Bildschirm(m
volatilization	Verflüchtigung(f
volt efficiency	Nutzspannung(f
voltage	elektrische Spannung(f
voltage build-up	Auferregung(f
voltage drop	Spannungsabfall(m
voltage limiter	Spannungsbegrenzer(m
voltage measuring	Spannungsmessung(f
voltage rating	Nennspannung(f
voltage regulator	Spannungsregler(m
voltage relay	Spannungsrelais(n
voltmeter	Voltmeter(n, Spannungsmesser(m
voltmeter	Spannungsmesser(m, Voltmeter(n
volume of outlet flow	Volumenstrom(m
vulcanized fiber, - fibre	Vulkanfiber(n
vulcanizing press	Vulkanisierpresse(f
vulcanizing, vulcanising	Vulkanisieren(n, Vulkanisation(f
wafer socket	Flachsockel(m
wall mounting	Wandmontage(f
wall socket	Wandsteckdose(f
warming (up) mill, preheating -	Vorwärmwalzwerk(n
washing tank, purifying -	Waschkammer(f, Waschtank(m
water channel, - line	Wasserkanal(m
water circulator	Wasserumlauf-Einrichtung(f
water fastness, fastness to -	Wasserbeständigkeit(f
water ga(u)ge, - level indicator	Wasserstandsanzeiger(m
water jacket	Kühlwassermantel(m
water jacket	Wassermantel(m
water reservoir, water tank	Wasserreservoir(n, Wassertank(m
water tube boiler	Wasserrohrkessel(m
water-repellent finishing	Wasserabstossendmachen(n
waterproof, watertight	wasserfest, wasserdicht
wave mechanics	Wellenmechanik(f
wave trap	Sperrkreis(m
waveform test	Aufnahme(f der Kurvenform(f
wavelength	Wellenlänge(f
wear	Abnutzung(f, Verschleiss(m
wear resistance	Verschleissfestigkeit(f
wear test	Abnutzungsprobe(f

web dryer	Bahnentrockner(m
weight per axle	Achslast(f
weighting agent, loading -	Beschwerungsmittel(n
weighting, loading	Beschweren(n, Ladung(f
weld area	Schweissfläche(f
weld structure	Nahtaufbau(m
weld, welding	Schweissstelle(f, Schweissung(f
welded sleeve	geschweisste Muffe(f
welding bead	Schweissraupe(f
welding joint	Schweissnaht(f
welding joint	Schweissverbindung(f
welding plant	Schweissanlage(f
welding time	Schweisszeit(f
welding-arc voltage	Schweissspannung(f
Wheatstone bridge	Wheatstonesche Brücke(f
whistle valve	Pfeifenventil(n
whole rubber	Vollgummi(m
wide-angle deflection	weitwinklige Ablenkung(f
width of chip	Spanbreite(f
width of coil	Spulenbreite(f
wind bracing	Windverstrebung(f
wind, winding	Wicklung(f
winder, winding device	Wickler(m
winding angle, helix angle	Wickelwinkel(m
winding drum	Wickeltrommel(f
winding operation	Wickeln(n
wiper blade	Abstreifer(m, Rakel(m
wire core	Drahtkern(m
wire gauze, wire gaze	Metallgaze(f
wiring	Verdrahtung(f
wiring diagram	Vertratungsschema(n
with of aperture	Öffnungsbreite(f
with of tooth	Zahnbreite(f
with sharp edges	scharfkantig
work per unit mass	massebezogene Arbeit(f
worm gearing	Schneckengetriebe(n
worm, coil	Rohrschlange(f
X-ray tube	Röntgenröhre(f
X-rays	Röntgenstrahlen(pl
Y-branch	Y-Verzweigung(f, Hosenrohr(n
yield	Ausbeute(f, Rendement(n
zero-energy level	Nullenergieniveau(n
zig-zag supporting wire	Zickzackdrahtseil(n
zig-zag-line coupler	Zickzackkopplung(f
zinc oxide	Zinkoxyd(n

Units

English	Units	German
absolute permittivity	F/cm, pF/m, As/(Vm)	elektrische Feldkonstante(f
acceleration	m/s²	Beschleunigung(f
amount of substance	mol	Stoffmenge(f
angle	rad, ″, ′, °	Winkel(m
ascending force, lift	N, kN	Auftrieb(m
bearing reaction	N, kN	Auflagerreaktion(f
bending moment	Nm, kNm	Biegemoment(n
bending stress	N/mm²	Biegespannung(f
capacitance	F(Farad), pF, nF	elektrische Kapazität(f
circulation	A, mA, kA	elektrische Durchflutung(f
compressive force	N, kN	Druckkraft(f
compressive strength	N/mm²	Druckfestigkeit(f
compressive stress	N/mm², MN/m²	Druckspannung(f
conductance	S(Siemens)	elektrischer Leitwert(m
conductivity	S/m, Sm/mm², S/cm	elektrische Leitfähigkeit(f
cube strength	N/mm²	Würfel(druck)festigkeit(f
current density	A/m², A/mm²	Stromdichte(f
current, intensity of current	A, mA, kA	Stromstärke(f
density	kg/m³	Dichte(f
density of heat flow	W/m²	Wärmestromdichte(f
dielectric displacement	C/m², As/m²	elektrische Flussdichte(f
dynamic viscosity	mPas, Ns/m²	dynamische Viskosität(f
earth pressure	N/mm², MN/m²	Erddruck(m
electric charge	C(Coulomb)	elektrische Ladung(f
electric field strength	V/m, kV/mm, kV/cm	elektrische Feldstärke(f
electrical power	W, kW, MW	elektrische Leistung(f
electrical work	J, Ws, Nm, kWh	elektrische Arbeit(f

English	Units	German
energy	J, Nm, kJ, MJ, Ws	Energie(f
excess pressure	bar, mbar	Überdruck(m
force	N, kN, MN	Kraft(f
frequency	Hz(Hertz)	Frequenz(f
gravitational force	N, kN, MN	Gewichtskraft(f
heat per unit mass	J/kg	massebezogene Wärme(f
heat, termal energy	J, Ws, kWh	Wärme(f, Wärmemenge(f
inductance	H(Henry), mH	Induktivität(f
latent heat	J, kJ	latente Wärme(f
length	mm, m, km	Länge(f
linear expansion	mm/m, m/m, %	Längenausdehnung(f
load	N, kN, MN	Last(f, Belastung(f
magnetic conductance	H, mH	magnetischer Leitwert(m
magnetic field strength	A/m, A/cm, A/mm	magnetische Feldstärke(f
magnetic flux	Wb(Weber)	magnetischer Fluss(m
magnetic flux density	T, mT, Vs/m², Wb/m²	magnetische Flussdichte(f
magnetic potential	A, mA, kA	elektrische Durchflutung(f
magnetic voltage	A	magnetische Spannung(f
modulus of elasticity	N/mm²	Elastizitätsmodul(m
molecular volume	m³/kmol, l/mol	molares Volumen(n
moment	Nm, kNm	Moment(n
moment of inertia	kgm², Ws³	Trägheitsmoment(n
outlet velocity	m/s	Ausflussgeschwindigkeit(f
period	s, min, h	Periode(f, Periodendauer(f
permeability	Wb/(Am), H/m	Permeabilität(f
permissible stress	N/mm²	zulässige Spannung(f
permissible torsion stress	N/mm²	zulässige Verdrehspannung(f
pressure, compression	Pa, bar, mbar	Druck(m
quantity of electricity	C(Coulomb), mC, As	Elektrizitätsmenge(f, Ladung(f
remanence	T, mT, VS/m², Wb/m²	Remanenz(f

English	Units	German
resistance	$\Omega, k\Omega, M\Omega$	elektrischer Widerstand (m
shear stress	$N/mm^2, N/m^2$	Schubspannung (f
shear(ing) force	N, mN, kN	Schubkraft (f
shear(ing) stress	$N/mm^2, kN/mm^2$	Scherspannung (f
shearing force	N, mN, kN	Scherkraft (f, Querkraft (f
specific heat	$J/(kgK), kJ/(kgK)$	spezifische Wärmekapazität (f
speed, velocity	$m/s, km/h$	Geschwindigkeit (f
stress	$N/mm^2, MN/m^2$	Spannung (f
support force	N, kN	Auflagerkraft (f
support reaction	N, kN	Auflagerreaktion (f
temperature	$K, °C$	Temperatur (f
temperature difference	$K, °C$	Temperaturdifferenz (f
tensile force	N, kN, MN	Zugkraft (f
tensile strength	N/mm^2	Zugfestigkeit (f
tensile stress	N/mm^2	Zugspannung (f
thermal conductivity	W/mK	Wärmeleitfähigkeit (f
torque	Nm, kNm	Drehmoment (n
voltage	$V(Volt)$	elektrische Spannung (f
work	$J, Nm, 1J=1Nm$	Arbeit (f
work per unit mass	J/kg	massebezogene Arbeit (f

A-Stellung(f	position A
Abblättern(n, Häuten(n	exfoliation, flaking
Abdeckfolie(f	covering film
Abdeckplatte(f, Deckplatte(f	coverplate, faceplate
Abdichtung(f	sealing
Abfallwiederverwendung(f	scrap reprocessing
Abfüllmaschine(f	filling machine
Abgase(pl	exhaust gases, waste gases
abgeplatteter Kugelhohlraum(m	sectionalized spherical cavity
abgeschrägte Kante(f	bevelled edge
abgestuft	stepped
Abgratbank(f	flash lathe
Abkantwinkel(m	folding angle, creasing –
Abklingzeit(f, Ausschwingdauer(f	dying-out time
Ablagerung(f, Sediment(n	sediment
Ablassrohr(n, Ausflussrohr(n	eduction pipe
Ablassventil(n	drain valve
ablativer Kunststoff(m	ablative plastics
Ablaufrinne(f	delivery chute
Ableitbleche(pl	deflecting blades
Ablenkjoch(n	deflection yoke
Abluftkamin(m	exhaust gas stack
Abnahme(f, Entladung(f	discharge, unloading
Abnahmeprüfungen(pl	accetance tests
Abnahmerolle(f, Abwickelrolle(f	take-off roller
Abnutzung(f, Verschleiss(m	wear
Abnutzungsprobe(f	wear test
Abnutzungstest(m	abrasion test
Abquetschfläche(f	land, land area
Abquetschrand(m, Abquetschfläche(f	flash land, – surface, – rid
Abquetschring(m	flash ring
Abreisskontakt(m	arcing contact
Abriebdauerversuch(m	attritation test
Abschirmgitter(n	shield grid
Abschirmschicht(f	barrier sheet
Abschirmung(f	screening, shielding
Abschirmung(f, Blenden(n	shielding, shadowing
Abschirmung(f, Schirm(m	shield
Abschlussschirm(m	end shield, end hat
Abschmelzbrenner(m	sealing-off berner
Abschmelzkunstharz(m	ablative resin
Abschmelzzeit(f	burning time
Abschrägung(f	bevel angle
Abschreckhärtung(f	quench hardening
absoluter Fehler(m	absolute error
Absorptionskoeffizient(m	absorption coefficient
Absorptionsschirm(m	absorbing screen
Absortionsmittel(n	absorber

Abspannkabel(n	anchoring cable
Abspannklemme(f	straining clamp
Abspannklemme(f	anchor clamp
Abspannring(m	bull ring
Abspantechnik(f	machining
Abstandplatte(f	spacer, spacer plate
Abstandschelle(f	spacing clip, - clamp
Abstossungskraft(f	force of repulsion
Abstrahlungswärme(f	heat of emission
Abstreifer(m, Rakel(m	wiper blade
Abstreifplatte(f	stripper plate
Abstützung(f	support
Abweichung(f	derivation
Abwickeln(m, Abspulen(n	unwinding, uncoiling
Abzugsventil(n, Auslassventil(n	eduction valve
Abzweigdose(f	conduit box
Abzweigung(f	branch
Ach(sen)abstand(m	axial spacing
Achse(f, Welle(f, Spindel(m	arbor, spindle
achsenparallel, paraxial	paraxial
Achslast(f	weight per axle
Achszähleinrichtung(f	axle-counter
Achtersockel(m, Oktalsockel(m	octal base
Äquipotentialkatode(f	equipotential cathode
Äquivalentladung(f	equivalent charge
Ätzen(n	etching
äusserer Zylinder(m	outer cylinder
Akkumulatorengefäss(n	accumulator box
Akkumulatorplattensatz(m	accumulator group
Aktionspotential(n	action potential
Aktivator(m, Aktivierungsmittel(n	activator, sensitizer
Aktivierung(f	activation, sensitization
Aktivierungs(über)spannung(f	activation overvoltage
Aktivierungsgeschwindigkeit(f	priming speed
Alarmschalter(m	alarm switch
Alkalimeter(n, Laugenmesser(m	alkali hydrometer, alkalimeter
Alterungsschutzmittel(n	age resistor, antioxidant
Aluminieren(n, Aluminisieren(n	alumetization, alumizing
aluminisierter Schirm(m	aluminized screen
Ampereleiter(pl	ampere-conductors
Ampèremeter(n	ammeter
Amperewindungen(pl	ampere-turns
Anbaumotor(m	built-on motor
Andruckwalze(f	thrust roll
Anfangstemperatur(f	initial temperature
Anfangswiderstad(m	initial resistance
Anfeuchtmaschine(f	dewing machine
angehobene Vorderwalze(f	raised front roll

Band M.0.3　　Seite 65

angenähert	approximate, approximative
angetriebene Walze(f	driven roll
Angriffspunkt(m	point of application
Anhaltebremse(f	stopping brake
Anheizzeit(f	preheating time, warm-up time
Anker(m	armature
Anker(zweig)paar(n	armature pair
Ankerfeder(f	armature reed, armature spring
Ankerkern(m	armature core
Ankernabe(f	armature hub
Ankerrückwirkung(f	armature reaction
Ankerstrom(m	armature current
Ankerwicklung(f	armature winding
Ankerwiderstand(m	armature resistance
Anlagerungskoeffizient(m	attachment coefficient
Anlassen(n, Starten(n	starting-up
Anlassschalter(m	switch starter
Anlauf mit direktem Einschalten	direct-on-line starting
Anlauf(m	starting
Anlauf(m mit Sparumspanner(m	auto-transformer starting
Anlauf-Hilfswicklung(f	auxiliary winding
Anlaufstrom(m, Anzugsstrom(m	starting current
Anlaufversuch(m	starting test
Anlaufwicklung(f	starting winding
Anlaufzeit(f	acceleration time
Annäherungssignal-System(n	approach control
Anode(f	anode, plate
Anodenbelastung(f	plate load, anode –
Anodenbügel(m	anode clamp
Anodeneffekt(m	anode effect
Anodeneingangsleistung(f	plate input power
Anodenhals(m	anode neck
Anodenkoppelleitung(f	anode strap
Anodenkühlrippe(f	anode fin, plate fin
Anodenschutzkappe(f	anode protecting cap
Anodenspannung(f	anode voltage, plate –
Anodenstrom(m	plate current, anode current
Anodenverankerung(f	anode anchoring
anomales magnetisches Moment(n	anomalous magnetic moment
Anpass(ungs)blende(f	matching diaphragm
Anpassung(f	balancing, matching
Anpresswalze(f	pressure roll
Anreicherung(f	enriching
Anreicherungszone(f	enriching section
Anschlag(m, Puffer(m	stop
Anschlussort(m	point of connection
Anschlusspunkt(m	supply terminal
Anschlussschema(n	connection diagram

Ansprechwert(m	pick-up value
Anstrengungs-Verhältnis(n	stress ratio
Anstrichfilm(m	paint film
Antiparallelschaltung(f	anti-parallel coupling
Antriebsaggregat(n	motor equipment
Antriebsleistung(f	drive rating, power demand
Antriebsmaschine(f	traction machine
Antriebsmoment(n	driving torque
Antriebsriemen(m, Treibriemen(m	drive belt
Anwärmdruck(m	pressure during heating time
Anwärmzeit(f	heating time
Anwurfmotor(m	starting motor
Anzahl(f der Arme	number of spokes
Anzapfung(f	tap
Anzeigefehler(m	error in indication
Anzeiger(m, Signaltafel(f	indicator
Anzugsmoment(n	breakaway torque
aperiodisch	aperiodic
aperiodische Zeitkonstante(f	aperiodic time constant
Arbeitsbereich(m	region of operation
Arbeitsbühne(f	operating platform, working -
Arbeitskontakt, Schliesskontakt	make contact
Arbeitsphase(f, Arbeitszyklus(m	duty cycle
Arbeitsphasenfaktor(m	duty factor
Arbeitspunkt(m	operating point
Arbeitsstellung, Ein-Stellung(f	on-position
Arbeitszeit(f, Leitperiode(f	on-period
Asphaltfutter(n	asphalt lining
Asphaltkitt(m	bituminous cement, - compound
Asphaltschicht(f	asphalt coating
astatisch	astatic
astatisches Organ(n	astatic element
Asynchron-Impedanz(f	asynchronous impedance
asynchroner Lauf(m	asynchronous operation
Asynchrongenerator(m	asynchronous generator
Asynchronmaschine(f	asynchronous machine
Asynchronmotor(m	induction motor
Asynchronreaktanz(f	asynchronous reactance
Asynchronwiderstand(m	asynchronous resistance
Aufbereitungsanlage(f	finishing plant
Auferregung(f	voltage build-up
Auffanggefäss(n	drip pan, catch pan
Aufhängeisolator(m	suspension insulator
Aufhängung(f	suspension
Auflagerkraft(f	support force
Auflagerreaktion(f	support reaction, bearing -
Auflockerungsmass(n	degree of lossening
Aufnahme(f der Kurvenform(f	waveform test

Aufschrumpfen(n eines Überzuges	shrink-coating
Aufspannplatte(f	adapter plate
Aufspannplatte(f	clamping plate, mounting –
Auftragwalze(f	casting roll
Aufzug(m, Fahrstuhl(m, Lift(m	elevator, lift
Aufzugmotor(m	lift motor
Aus-Stellung(f, Ruhestellung(f	off-position
Ausbeute(f, Rendement(n	yield
Ausbreitung(f, Fortpflanzung(f	propagation
Ausdehnung(f	expansion
Ausdehnungskoeffizient(m	coefficient of expansion
Ausdrückbolzen(m	ejector ram
Ausdrücker-Stange(f	ejection tie bar
Ausdrückstift(m	ejector pin, knock-out pin
Ausfallzeit(f	down time
Ausgang(m	output
Ausgangskapazität(f	output capacitance
Ausgangsleistung(f	output power, power output
Ausgangsmaterial(n	base material
ausgebohrte Walze(f	bored well, drilled roll
ausgeprägter Pol(m, Schenkelpol	salient pole
Ausgleichsdrossel, Saugdrossel(f	compensating choke
Ausgleichsladung(f	equalizing charge
Ausgleichsverbinder(m	equalizing connection
Aushärten(n, Härten(n	cementation
Auskleidung(f	lining, liner
Auslauf(m	running down
Auslaufversuch(m	retardation test
Ausleger(m	bracket
Auslöserrelais(n	release relay
Ausrüstung(f	equipment
Ausschaltkasten(m	cut-out box
Ausschaltstellung(f	disconnect position
Aussenbelag(m	outer coating
Aussendurchmesser(m	external diameter
Aussengewinde(n	external thread
Aussenisolator(m	outdoor insulator
Ausserbetriebsetzungszeit(f	disoperating time
Aussertrittfallen(n	pulling out of synchronism
Aussetzbetrieb(m	periodic duty
Ausstanzen(n, Fassonschnitt(m	blanking, outline cutting
Ausstossleistung(f	output, through-put
austauschbar	interchangeable
Austauscher(m	exchanger
auswechselbares Element(n	removable element
Auswerferkolben(m	ejector (connecting) bar, – rod
Auswurffeder(f	ejection spring, ejector –
Auswurfplatte, Ausdrückplatte(f	ejector (pin) plate

Auswurfstab(m	sprue ejector bar
Auswurfstift(m	ejection pin, knockout -
Auswurfvorrichtung(f	ejecting device, piece knockout
automatische Fokussierung(f	automatic focusing
automatischer Umschalter(m	automatic change-over switch
axialer Vektor(m	axial vector
Axialkraft(f	axial (bearing) force
azyklische Maschine(f	acyclic machine
Bahnentrockner(m	web dryer
Balanceregler(m	balance control
Bananenstecker(m	banana plug
Bandage(f	binding band
Bandbeschickung(f	strip feed
Bandförderer(m	band conveyer
Bandkabel(n, Flachkabel(n	ribbon cable
Bandmischer(m	ribbon blender, - mixer
Bandzuführer(m	band feed, belt -
Basisflansch(m	base lip
Basismetall(n	parent metal
Batterieladegerät(n	battery charger
Bauteil(m	subassembly
Bearbeitungsanlage(f	precessing plant
beewehrt, gepanzert	armo(u)red
Befestigungsschelle(f	clip, loop-type clamp
begrenzte Proportionalität(f	limited proportionality
Behälter(m, Tank(m	tank
Behältertrennwand(f	tank partition
Beharrungszustand, Gleichgewicht	equilibrium
beid(er)seitig	bilateral
beidseitige Beschichtung(f	double-face coating
beidseitiger Achsantrieb(m	bilateral transmission
bekannter Widerstand(m	known resistance
Belastungsart(f	loading
Belastungsdiagramm(n	rating chart
Belastungsfaktor(m	utilisation factor
Belastungsimpedanz(f	load impedance
Belastungsprobe(f	load test
Belastungsspitze(f	load peak
Beobachtungsfenster(n	observation window, peep-window
Beobachtungsrohr(n	observation pipe, - tube
Beschichten(n, Beschichtung(f	coating
Beschichten(n, Laminieren(n	laminating, doubling
Beschichtungsanlage(f	laminator, film laminator
Beschickung(f unten	bottom feed
Beschickung(f, Ladung(f	feed, load, mo(u)ld charge
Beschickungsöffnung(f	charging hole
Beschickungstrichter(m	feed funnel, - hopper
Beschickungszone(f	feed zone

Band M.O.3   Seite 69

Beschleunigen(n	accelerating
Beschleuniger(m, Härter(m	accelerator, hardener
Beschleunigung(f	acceleration
Beschleunigungsmoment(n	accelerating torque
Beschleunigungsrelais(n	accelerating relay
Beschleunigungszeit(f	acceleration time
Beschweren(n, Ladung(f	weighting, loading
Beschwerungsmittel(n	weighting agent, loading –
Bestrahlung(f	irradiation
Betätigungsfolge(f	sequence of operation
Betätigungsorgan(n	operating device
Betonpanzer(m	concrete shield
Betriebsart(f	duty-type
Betriebsdaten(pl	operating characteristics
Betriebssicherheit(f	reliability
Betriebsspannung(f	operating voltage, working –
Betriebsverhalten(n	operating conditions
Betriebszustand(m, Last(f	load
bewegliche Hälfte(f	movable part
bewegliche Spule(f	movable coil
beweglicher Leiter(m	movable conductor
bewegliches Organ(n	mouving element
Bezugsachse(f	reference axis
Bezugspunkt(m	reference point
biegekritische Drehzahlen(pl	critical whirling speeds
Biegen(n von Rohren	pipe bending
Biegespannung(f	bending stress
Biegung(f	bending
bifilare Wicklung(f	bifilar winding
Bildschirm(m	viewing screen
Bimetalldraht(m	bimetallic wire
Bimetallinstrument(n	bimetallic instrument
Bimetallsicherung(f	bimetal fuse
blanke Elektrode(f	bare electrode
Blas(e)druck(m	blow pressure
Blaskopf(m	blow head
Blasluft(f	blow air
Blasspule(f	blow-out coil
Blechkettenläufer(m	segmental rim rotor
Blechkontrolle(f	plate check
Blechlage(f	lamination layer
Blechpaket(n	laminated core
Bleifarbe(f	lead paint
Bleifeder(f	lead spring
Bleimuffe(f	lead sleeve
blinde Spule(f	dummy coil
Blindleistung(f	reactive power
Blindwiderstand(m	reactance

Blinkrelais(n	flasher relay
Blitzableiter(m	lightning conductor
Blockierschaltung(f	paralysis circuit
Blockschaltbild(n	block diagram
Bodengestell(n	bottom block
Bodenplatte(f, Grundplatte(f	bottom plate
Bogen(m, Krümmer(m	bend
Bohrer-Spitzenwinkel(m	drill tip angle
Bohrung(f	bore
bolckierte Auslösung(f	fixed trip
Bord(n, Bördelprofil(n	flange, elbow
Bottich(m, Tank(m	vat, tank, vessel
Brecher(m	crusher, breaker
Brechwalze(f	cracker roll
Brechwalze(f, Walzenbrecher(m	crushing roll
Bremsdynamo(m	brake dynamo
Bremsmagnet(m	braking magnet
Bremsmoment(n	braking torque
Brennschneiden(n	oxygen cutting, lance -
Brennstoff(m	fuel
Brenstoffwirtschaft(f	fuel economy
Brikettiermaschine(f	briquet machine
Bronzelack(m	bronze pigmented lacquer,-pai
Bronzieren(n	bronzing
Brückenausleger(m	bridge hanger
Brückenkontakt(m	bridge contact
Brustwalze(f	breast roll(air-knife coater)
Bügelgestell(n	bow frame
Bürste(f	brush
Bürstenbrücke(f	brush rocker
Bürstenfeder(f	brush spring
Bürstenhalter(m	brush holder
Bürstenkasten(m	brush box
bürstenlose Maschine(f	brushless machine
Celsius-Skala(f	centigrade scale
chemische Diffusion(f	chemical diffusion
Codier(ungs)system(n	code system
Cremona-Verfahren(n	Cremona method
Dämpfer(m	damper
Dämpfungsgrad(m	damping ratio
Dampfautoklav(m	steam autoclave
Dampfkanal(m	steam channel, steam way
Dampfstrahlpumpe(f	vapo(u)r jet pump
Dauerfehler(m	permanent fault
Dauerfestigkeitsprüfung(f	endurance test, fatigue -
Dauerleistung(f	continuous output
Dauerprobe(f	long duration test
Deckenplatte(f	ceiling plate

Dehnungsfuge(f	expansion joint
Dehnungskoeffizient(m	coefficient of elongation
Dehnungsmesser(m	extensometer
Densimeter(n, Dichtemesser(m	densimeter, densometer
Depolarisation(f	depolarization
Diagonalstab(m	diagonal member
Diagramm(n	diagram
diamantarti	adamantine
Dichtungsmasse(f	sealing compound
Dichtungsring(m	gasket ring, joint - , packing -
Dickenmessgerät(n	thickness ga(u)ge
Dickensteuerung(f	thickness control
Dielektrizitätskonstante(f	dielectric constant
Dielektrizitätszahl(f	relative permittivity
Differentialkalorimeter(n	differential calorimeter
differenzierendes Verhalten(n	derivation action
Differenzstrom(m	differential current
Diffusionskoeffizient(m	diffusion coefficient
Dilatometer(n, Dehnungsmesser(m	dilatometer
direkt geheizter Ofen(m	direct fired furnace
direkte Kupplung(f	direct coupling
direkter Antrieb(m	direct drive
Dispersionsharze(pl	dispersion resins
Distanzblock(m	spacer block
Distanzstück(n	spacer
Dochtkohle(f, Kernkohle(f	cored carbon
Doppel-Achsialbelüftung(f	double ventilation
Doppelkegelmischer(m	double cone mixer, - - blender
Doppelkolbenpresse(f	double force press, - ram -
Doppelschicht(f	double layer
Doppelschlussmotor(m	compound wound motor
Doppelschneckenextruder(m	twin-screw extruder machine
Doppelspeisung(f	double-feeding
doppelwandiges Rohr(n	double walled tube
Dorn(m	mandrel, mandril
Dornhalter(m	mandrel carrier
Dosiereinrichtung(f	doser, dosing device
Dosiergefäss(n	metering tank
Dosiermaschine(f	batcher
Dosierrakel(f, Dosiermesser(n	doctor blade, doctor knife
Dosierschieber(m	feed slide
Dosierstab(m, Dosierrakel(m	metering rod, meter bar
Drahtkern(m	wire core
Drahtquerschnitt(m	cross section of wire
Drahtziehdose(f	pull box
Drallrichtung(f	direction of lay
Dreh-Dosierschleuse(f	rotary feeder
Drehbake(f	rotating beacon

Drehfeldimpedanz (f	cyclic impedance
Drehkupplung (f	rotating joint
Drehmoment (n	torque
Drehphasenschieber (m	rotary phase changer
Drehplattenspeiser (m	rotary plate feeder
Drehschaufel (f	rotary paddle
Drehsinn (m	sense of rotation
Drehstrom-Transformator (m	threephase-transformer
Drehstromleistung (f	threephase power
Drehstrommotor (m	three-phase motor
Drehteller (m	rotary disk, rotary shelf
Drehzahl (f, Umdrehungsfrequenz (f	speed
Dreieckschaltung (f	delta-circuit
Dreifachmotor (m	triple motor
Dreifingerregel (f	hand rule
Dreiphasen-	three-phase
dreipolig	triple pole
Dreiwalzenkalander (m	three-roll calender
Dreiweghahn (m	three-way cock
Drosselkolben (m	choke piston
Drosselkupplung (f	choke coupling, choke joint
Drosselspule (f	choke coil
Druckaufbau (m	pressure build-up
Druckdüse (f	pressure nozzle
Druckflasche (f	pressure bottle
Druckkessel (m	pressure boiler
Druckknopf (m	pushbutton
Druckluft (f, Pressluft (f	pressure air, compressed air
Druckrelais (n, pneumatisches R.	pressure relay
Druckspannung (f	compressive stress
Druckventil (n, Ablassventil (n	discharge valve
Druckwandler (m	pressure converter
Drückplatte (f, Ausdrückplatte (f	ejection plate, ejector -
dünne Umhüllung (f	thin covering
Düse (f, Strahlrohr (f	jet, nozzle
Düsen(spalt)verstellung (f	die gap adjustment
Düsenkanal (m	die approach, die channel
Düsenmundstück (n	nozzle
Düsenplatte (f, Düsenhalter (m	die body, die base
Durchdringung (f	punch-through, penetration
Durchflusskalorimeter (n	continuous-flow calorimeter
Durchflussmischer (m	flow mixer, pipeline mixer
Durchlassrichtung (f	forward direction
Durchlassstellung (f	on-state
Durchlaufofen (m	continuous furnace
Durchschlagspannung (f	disruptive voltage
dynamische Empfindlichkeit (f	dynamic sensitivity
dynamischer Widerstand (m	dynamic resistance

Dynamo(n	dynamo
Dynamometer-Test(m	dynamometer test
E-Bogen(m	E bend
E-Verzweiger(m	E plane Tee junction
E-Winkel(m	E corner
Ebonit(m, Hartgummi(m	ebonite, hard rubber, vulcanite
Eckstoss(m, Winkelstoss(m	corner joint
Edison-Effekt(m	Edison effect
Effektivwert(m	effective value
Egalisieren(n	equalizing
Eichspule(f	reference coil
Eichung(f	calibration
Eigenbeweglichkeit(f	intrinsic mobility
Eilganggeschwindigkeit(f	rapid traverse speed
ein Kabel ausgiessen	seal a cable
Einbetten(n	embedding
Einbrennlack(m	stoving lacquer
Eindringtiefe(f	penetration depth
einfache Faltung(f	simple folding, single folding
Einfachelektrode(f	simple electrode
einfaches Vakuumformverfahren(n	straight vacuum forming
Einfachkontakt(m	single contact
Einfärbetrommel(f, Farbtrommel(f	coloring barrel, colouring dru
Eingangskapazität(f	input capacitance
Eingangsspannung(f	input voltage
Eingangstransformator(m	input transformer
eingefügte Wicklung(f	inserted winding
eingeschlossenes Gleitmittel(n)	internal lubricant
eingetauchte Walze(f	immersed roll
Eingriffsstrecke(f	area of contact, length - -
Eingriffswinkel(m	pressure angle
Einhängedraht(m	slinging wire
Einhängegestell(n	plating rack
Einheitensystem(n	system of units
einheitliche Schaltung(f	uniform connection
Einheitsladung(f	unit charge
Einkapseln(n	encapsulation
Einkapselung(f, Kapselung(f	encapsulating
Einlass(m, Zugang(m	inlet, gate
Einlassrohr(n	admission pipe
Einphasengleichrichter(m	single-phase rectifier
Einphasenmaschine(f	single-phase machine
einphasig, Einfasen-	single phase
einpolig	single pole
Einsatzfilter(m	hanging filter, insertion -
Einsatzspannung(f	cut-off voltage
Einsatzstrom(m	starting voltage, striking -
Einschmelzen(n	sealing-in, seal

Band M.0.3 Seite 74

Einschraubenmontage(f	one-screw mounting
Einspritzverfahren(n	injection process
Einsteckblock(m	plug-in unit
einstellbarer Widerstand(m	adjustable resistor
Einstellwert(m	setting
Einstellwinkel(m	setting angle
Eintauchthermostat(m	immersion thermostat
Einzeldraht-, eindratig	single-wire
Einzelkreiskontakt(m	independent contact
Einzellast(f	concentrated load
Einzelpol(m	pole unit
Einzelspeiseleitung(f	single feeder
Einzelsteuerung(f	individual drive
Einzelunterbrecher(m	sinlge-break switch
Eisenlänge(f	iron length
Eisenmasse(f	mass of iron
Eisenverlust(m	iron losses
elastische Nachwirkung(f	elastic aftereffect
elastisches Fliessen(n	plastic flow
Elastizitätsgrenze(f	elastic limit
Elastizitätsmodul(m	modulus of elasticity
Elastomer(n	elastomer
elastomerer Kunststoff(m	elastomeric plastic
Elastometer(n	elastometer
elektrische Arbeit(f	electrical work
elektrische Durchflutung(f	circulation, magnetic potential
elektrische Feldkonstante(f	absolute permittivity
elektrische Feldstärke(f	electric field strength
elektrische Flussdichte(f	dielectric displacement
elektrische Kapazität(f	capacitance
elektrische Kupplung(f	electric clutch
elektrische Ladung(f	electric charge
elektrische Leistung(f	electrical work
elektrische Leitfähigkeit(f	conductivity
elektrische Leitfähigkeit(f	electrical conductivity
elektrische Leitung(f	electric line
elektrische Spannung(f	voltage
elektrischer Leitwert(m	conductance
elektrischer Stromkreis(m	electric circuit
elektrischer Widerstand(m	resistance
elektrischer Wirkungsgrad(m	electrical efficiency
elektrisches Feld(n	electric field
Elektrizität(f	electricity
Elektrizitätsleitung(f	electric conduction
Elektrizitätsmenge(f, Ladung(f	quantity of electricity
Elektro-Sauerstoffschneiden(n	oxy-arc cutting
Elektroden-Durchmesser(m	diameter of the electrode
Elektrodenhalter(m	electrode support

Elektrodynamik(f	electrodynamics
elektrodynamisch	electrodynamic
elektrodynamisches Relais(n	electrodynamic relay
Elektromagnet(m	electromagnet
elektromagnetische Ablenkung(f	electromagnetic deflection
elektromagnetische Linse(f	electromagnetic lens
Elektronegativität(f	elektronegativity
elektronegtives Element(n	electronegative element
Elektronenmikroskop(n	electron microscope
Elektronenschalter(m	electronic commutator
elektronisch	electronic
elektronische Abtastung(f	electronic scanning
elektronische Auswuchtung(f	dynetric balancing
elektronische Lunge(f	electronic lung
elektronische Steuerung(f	electronic control
elektronische Uhr(f	electronic clock
elektronische Verarbeitung(f	elecronic processing
elektronische Wägung(f	electronic weighing
elektronischer Graukeil(m	electronic grey wedge
elektronischer Höhenmesser(m	electronic altimeter
elektronischer Locher(m	electronic punch-card machine
elektronischer Luftfilter(m	electronic air cleaner
elektronischer Multiplikator(m	electronic multiplier
elektronischer Rauheitsmesser(m	electronic profilometer
elektronischer Rechner(m	electronique calculator
elektronischer Regler(m	electronic controller
elektronischer Taster(m	electronic key
elektronischer Zähler(m	electronic counter
elektronischer Zeitschalter(m	electronic timer
elektronisches Bauelement(n	electronic component
elektronisches Echolot(n	electronic fathometer
elektronisches Mikrometer(n	electronic micrometer
elektronisches Nähen(n	electronic sewing
elektronisches Tachometer(n	electronic tachometer
elektronisches Voltmeter(n	electronic voltmeter
elektronisches Wattmeter(n	electronic wattmeter
Elektrostatik(f	electrostatics
elektrostatischer Druck(m	electrostatic pressure
elektrostatisches Beschichten(n	electrostatic coating
Emailüberzug(m	enamel coating
Emittervorspannung(f	emitter bias
Empfängermagnet(m	receiver magnet
Empfangsoszillator(m	local oscillator
empfindliche Zeit(f, wirksame -	sensitive time
Empfindlichkeit(f	sensitivity
Emulsionsauftragmaschine(f	emulsifying machine, coating -
Endgeschwindigkeit(f	terminal velocity

Endlos-Bandmischer(m	continuous belt mixer
Endstellung(f	ultimate position
Endstütze(f	terminal support
Endversiegeln(n	end sealing
Energie-Austausch(m	exchange of energy
Energiebilanz(f	energy balance
Energieverlust(m	dissipation of energy
Entfettungsmittel(n	degreaser, cleaner
entflammbar, feuergefährlich	inflammable
Entgasung(f	degassing
Enthärtungsanlage(f	softening plant
Entionisierungsgitter(n	de-ionization grid
Entladevorrichtung(f	unloader, unloading device
Entladung(f), Entlastung(f	unloading, discharge
Entleerung(f von unten	bottom discharge
Entlüfter(m	de-aerator
Entlüftungsgebläse(n	exhausting fan, air exhauster
Entlüftungsöffnung(f	vent
Entlüftungsrohr(n	exhaust tube, pumping tube
Entlüftungszyklus(m	breathing cycle, degassing -
entmagnetisieren	demagnetize
epizyklischer Schneckenmischer	epicyclic screw mixer
Erdkabel(n	earthing cable, grounding -
Erdplatte(f	ground plate, earth plate
erdsymmetrisches System(n	balanced-line system
Erdungsstange(f	grounding rod, earthing pole
Erhitzungsband(n	cuff heater band, heater band
Erholungszeit(f	recovery time
Erregermaschine(f	exciter
Erregerstrom(m	exciting current
Erregung(f, Anregung(f	excitation
Ersatzteile(pl	renewal parts
Etagen-Plattenpresse(f	multi-platen press, day-light -
Evakuiermaschine(f	evacuating machine
Evolventen-Verzahnung(f	involute-tooth system
Extruderdüse(f	extrusion die
Extruderkopf(m	extruder head, extrusion -
Extrudieren(n	extrusion
Extrusionsbeschichten(n	extrusion laminating
Extrusionsbeschichten(n	extrusion coating
Extrusionslaminieren(n	extrusion-lamination
Extrusionsschweissen(n	extrusion welding
Exzenterpresse(f	eccentric press
Fachwerkträger(m	lattice girder
Fadenführung(f	filament guide
Fadenführung(f	thread guide
Fadenführungsschlitten(m	filament delivery carriage
fahrbarer Transformator(m	mobile transformer

fallende Kennlinie (f	falling characteristique
Faltenfilter (m	fluted filter, folded filter
Farbe (f, Anstrichfarbe (f	paint
Farbenscheibe (f	color disk, colour disk
Farblack (m	color lake, colour lake
Farbspritzpistole (f	paint-spraying gun
Federkontakt (m	spring contact
Federsatz (m	spring set
feeding voltage	feeding voltage
Fehlersucher (m, Prüfgerät (n	trouble shooter, set analyzer
Feinen (n mit Schleifmittel	abrasive finishing
Feinmühle (f	fine grinding mill
Feldkonstante (f (magnetische)	absolute permeability
Feldspule (f	magnet(izing) coil
Fernsteuerung (f	telecontrol
feste Formplatte (f	fixed plate
feste Rolle (f	fixed sheave
feste Spule (f	fixed coil
fester Körper (m	solid body
fester Leiter (m	fixed conductor
Festrolle (f, Festwalze (f	fixed roll
feststehende Lippe (f	stationary lip
Fett (n	fat
fettfeste Farbe (f	greaseproof paint
Fettspritze (f	grease gun
Feuchtfänger (m	moisture trap
Feuchtigkeitsregler (m	humidity controller
Feuchtluftgebläse (n	damp air blower
feuerabweisende Farbe (f	fire protecting paint
feuerfest, feuersicher	fireproof
feuerfeste Auskleidung (f	refractory coating
feuerfestes Futter (n	refractory lining
Feuerschutzanstrich (m	fireproof paint
Film (m, Feinfolie (f	film
Filterdeckschicht (f	filtering surface layer
Filtermantel (m	filter mantle
Filtermittel (n	filtering medium
Filterrohr (n	filter tube
Filtrieren (n, Filterung (f	filtering
Filtrierfilz (m	filter felt
Filz (m	felt
Filzführung (f	felt guide
Fischschwanzkneter (m	double naben kneader
Flachfolie (f	flat sheet
Flachsockel (m	wafer socket
Flammenhärtung (f	flame hardening
Flammenschutz (m, Feuerschirm (m	flame guard
Flammenschweissen (n	flame welding

Flanschverbindung(f	flange joint
Flaschenzug(m	pulley block
flexibel, biegsam	flexible
flexible Kupplung(f	flexible coupling
Fliessfähigkeit(f	flowability, fluidity
Flügeltorpedo(n	finned torpedo
flüssiger Körper(m	liquid body
Flüssigkeitsspiegel(m	surface of liquid
Flüssigkeitsstandanzeiger(m	liquid level indicator
Fluoreszenzschirm(m	fluorescent screen
Förderband(n	conveying belt
Förderschnecke(f	helical conveyor, screw -, worm -
Förderwalze(f	pinch roll
Folgeeinrichtungen(pl	auxiliary equipment
Folie(f	sheet, foil
Folien(press)maschine(f	sheet extruder
Folienmaterial(n	sheeting
Folienwalzwerk(n	sheeting machine, - mill
Formel(f, Rezept(n	formula, formulation
Formentrennmittel(n	mo(u)ld release agent
Formfaktor(m	coefficient of shape
Formierungsstrom(m	baking current
Formpresse(f	mo(u)lding press
Formrahmen(m	mo(u)ld chase
Fräsbreite(f	milling width
freier Lauf(m	free-running
Freifall-Verdampfer(m	free-falling evaporator
Freifallmischer(m	free-falling mixer
Frequenz(f	frequency
frequenzabhängig	frequency-dependent
Frequenzbereich(m	frequency range
Frequenzgleiten(n	frequency change
frequenzunabhängig	frequency-independent
Friktionskalander(m	friction calender
Frostbeständigkeit(f	freeze resistance
Frostkappe(f	sleet hood
Führerstandsignal(n	cab signal, car signal
Führungsarm(m	guide bracket
Führungsbuchse(f	guide bushing
Führungsring(m	guard ring
Führungsstift(m	guide pin, dowel -, leader -
Führungsstift(m, Suchstift(m	guide pin, aligning plug
Füllkolben(m	stuffing piston
Füllmetall(n	filler metal
Füllplatte(f	filler plate, loading shoe
Füllplatte(f	loading tray, charging tray
Füllplatte(f, Ladetablett(n	transfer plate, loading plate
Füllstoff(m	filler

Füllstoff(m, Streckmittel(n	extender
Fülltrichter(m, Zuführöffnung(f	loading funnel
Füllung(f von oben	top feed
Füllventil(n	feed valve, filling valve
Füllzylinder(m	feed cylinder
Fünfwalzenmühle(f	five roller mill
Fundament(n, Gründung(f	foundation, footing
Funke(m	spark
Funkenfänger(m	spark trap
Fuss(m, Fundament(n	base
Fusshöhe(f	dedendum
Fusskreis(m	root circle
Fussschalter(m	foot switch, floor switch
Fusswinkel(m	root angle
galvanisches Element(n	galvanic cell
galvanomagnetischer Effekt(m	galvanomagnetric effect
Gammastrahlen(pl	gamma rays
Gaseinschluss(m	gas pocket
Gasentladung(f	gas discharge
gasförmiger Brennstoff(m	gaseous fuel
Gasschicht(f	gas layer
Gebläse(n	blower
gebohrte Walze(f	drilled roll
Gebrauchsspannung(f	service voltage
gedrängter Aufbau(m	cramped construction
gedruckte Schaltung(f	printed circuit
geerdeter Kreis(m, Erdkreis(m	earthed circuit
Gefässheber(m, Tankheber(m	tank lifter
Gegendruckplatte(f	back-pressure plate
Gegendruckwalze(f	backing roll, counter-pressure -
Gegenelektrode(f	counter electrode
Gegengewicht(n	counterweight
Gegenrichtung(f	inverse direction, reverse -
Gegenvakuum(n	anti-vacuum
Gehäuse(n	housing
Gehäuse(n, Hülse(f	case, jacket
geheizte Sonde(f	hot probe
Geiger-Zähler(m	Geiger counter
gekrümmte Fläche(f	curved surface
Gel-Coat(m, Gel-Feinschicht(f	gel coat
Gelenkkopf(m	hinged nose piece
gemeinsame Katode(f	common cathode
Gemeinschaftskollektor(m	common collector
Gemisch(n, Mischung(f	mixture
gemischte Bremsung(f	composite braking
Genauigkeit(f	accuracy
Genauigkeitsgrad(m	accuracy grade, degree of accuracy
geneigter Flügel(m	pitched blade, inclined -

Generator(m	generator
Generator(m	generator
genormte Spannung(f	conventional voltage
geordnete Füllung(f	stacked packing
gerade Biegungsfeder(f	simple leaf spring
gerade Schaufel(f	straight blade
Geradeaus-Düse(f	in-line die, straight through -
geriffelte Fläche(f	ribbed surface
Geruchverschluss(m	siphon trap
gerundete Öffnung(f	rounded aperture
Gesamtwiderstand(m	total resistance
Gesamtwirkungsgrad(m	overall efficiency
Gesamtzeitkonstante(f	total time constant
geschlossen	totally-enclosed
geschlossene Leitung(f, Pipeline	pipeline, closed conduit
geschlossener Filter(m)	closed filter
geschützt	protected
geschweisste Muffe(f	welded sleeve
Geschwindigkeitsregler(m	speed controller
Geschwindigkeitssteuerung(f	velocity modulation
gespeicherte Energie(f	stored energy
Gestängeaufhängung(f	bar suspension, yoke -
gesucht, unbekannt	unknown
getauchte Elektrode(f	dipped electrode
Getriebe(n	gear, gearing
Gewichtsdosierer(m	dosing feeder, weight feeder
Gewichtsdosierung(f	feed dosing
Gewichtskraft(f	gravitational force
Gewinde(n, Windung(f	thread, flight
Gewindestift(m	screw core pin
gewundene Feder(f	coiled spring
gezahnter Flügel(m	toothed blade
Gill-Morell-Oszillator(m	Gill-Morell oscillator
Gipfelpunkt(m, Höckerpunkt(m	peak point
Gipfelspannung(f	peak point voltage
Gipfelstrom(m, Höckerstrom(m	peak point current
Gittergegenstrom(m	reverse grid current
Gitterreckdorn(m	grid stretcher
Gitterrückstrom(m	backlash
Gitterspannung(f	grid voltage
Gittertransformator(m	grid transformer
Gitterzündspannung(f	critical grid voltage
Glättkalander(m, Glättwerk(n	glazing calender
Glättwalzen(pl	smoothing rolls
Glanzlackfarbe(f	gloss paint
Glanzmesseinrichtung(f	glossmeter
Glas-Metall-Verschmelzung(f	glass-to-metal seal
Glasfaser(f	glass fibre, - fiber, fiberglas

Glasfaserschichtstoff(m	glass fibre laminate, - fiber -
Glaspapier(n	glasspaper
Glasplatte(f	glass plate
Glaswolle(f	glass wool, spun glass
gleichgerichteter Strom(m	rectified current
Gleichgewichtsbedingung(f	condition of equilibrium
Gleichgewichtskammer(f	equilibrium chamber
Gleichgewichtskraft(f	equilibrium force
Gleichgewichtsmethode(f	equilibrium methode
Gleichlauf(m	even speed
gleichmässig verteilt	uniformly distributed
Gleichrichter(m	rectifier
Gleichrichteranode(f	rectifier anode
Gleichrichtwert(m	rectified value
Gleichstrom(m	direct current
Gleichstrommaschine(f	direct-current machine
Gleichstrommotor(m	direct current motor
Gleichstromrelais(n	direct current relay
Gleitgrenze(f	limiting friction
Gleitkontakt, Schleifkontakt(m	sliding contact
Gleitlack(m	lubricating lacquer
Gleitmittel(n, Schmiermittel(n	lubricant
Gleitreibung(f	sliding friction
Glimmerplatte(f	mica plate
Glimmerunterlagsscheibe(f	mica washer
Glühlampe(f	filament lamp
Glutfestigkeitsprüfung(f	glow-bar test
Goldbeschichtung(f	gold coating
Granulator(m, Abfallmühle(f	granulating mill, granulator
graphische Lösung(f	graphical solution
Graphitelektrode(fd	graphite electrode
Grenzdichte(f	limiting density
Grenzfläche(f, Zwischenfläche(f	interface
Grenzfrequenz(f	critical frequency
Grenzwerte(pl	limiting values
Grobfilter(m	coarse filter, roughing filter
Grobrechen(m	trash rack, coarse screen
Grössensortierung(f	sizing
Grundeinheiten(pl	fundamental units
Grundgleichung(	basic equation
Grundlast(f	base load
Grundmaterial(n	matrix, base material
Grundmodus(m	principal mode
Grundplatte(f	bed plate
Grundplatte(f, Fundament(n	base plate
Grundstellung(f	normal position
Grundzeit(f	basic time
Grundzustand(m	ground state, normal energy level

Gruppenschaltung(f	multiple connection
Güte(f	quality, figure of merit
Gummi(n, m	gum
Gummiklebstoff(m, Klebkitt(m	rubber adhesive, - solution
Gussstahlrost(m	cast steel grate
Gyrator(m	gyrator
H-Bogen(m, H-Winkel(m	H bend, H corner
H-Flachlinse(f	H plane lens
Haarrisse(pl	hairlines
Härteprüfer(m, Durometer(n	durometer, hardness tester
Härter(m, Härtungsmittel(n	hardener
Härtungstemperatur(f	curing temperature
Haftfestigkeitsprüfung(f	bond testing
Haftmittel(n	coupling agent
Haftreibung(f	static friction
Hahn(m	tap, cock
Hakenbetätigung(f	hook operation
halb geschlossen	half-closed
Halbleiter(m	semiconductor
halbselbständige Entladung(f	semi-self-sustained discharge
Halseinsatz(m, Halsring(m	neck insert, neck ring
Haltestift(m, Fixierdorn(m	insert pin, carrier pin
Hammermühle(f	hammer mill
Handpunktschweissen(n	poke welding
hart, spröde	rigid
Hauptachse(f	main axis
Hauptkontakt(m	main contact
Hauptschalter(m	master switch
Hauptschutz(m	main protection
Hauptuhr(f	master clock
Hebebühne(f	raising platform
Hebelregler(m	dimmer lever
Hebelschalter(m	lever switch
Heisspressverfahren(n	hot press mo(u)lding
Heizbatterie(f	heater battery
Heizelement(n	heater, heating element
Heizkabel(n	heating cable
Heizkanal(m	heating bore, - passage
Heizkreis(m	heater circuit
Heizmantel(m	heating jacket
Heizplatte(f, Wärmeplatte(f	heater plate
hermetischer Verschluss(m	hermetic seal, hermetic closur
Heteropolarmaschine, Wechselpolm.	heteropolar machine
Hilfskontakt(m	auxiliary contact
Hilfsmotor(m	auxiliary motor
Hilfsschalter(m	auxiliary switch
Hilfswiderstand(m	auxiliary resistor
Hitzebeständigkeit(f	heat resistance

Hochdruckplastifizierung (f	compression melting
Hochdruckpressung (f	high-pressure mo(u)lding
Hochdruckrohr (n	compressed air pipe
Hochfrequenzgenerator (m	high frequency generator
Hochspannung (f	high voltage
Hochspannungsbeschleuniger (m	high-voltage accelerator
Hochvakuum (n	high vacuum
Hochvakuumhahn (m	high-vacuum stopcock
Höchstbelastung (f	peak load
Höchstleistung (f	maximum capacity
Höchstspannung (f	extra high tension, E.H.T.
Höchstvakuum (n	ultra-high-vacuum
Hohlkern (m	shell core, blow stick
Homopolarmaschine (f, Gleichpolm.	homopolar machine
Horizontalablenkung (f	horizontal deflection
Horizontalaustastung (f	horizontal blanking
horizontale Achse (f	horizontal axis
Hotmelt-Beschichter (m	hot-melt coater
Hüllendicke (f	thickness of covering
hydraulische Maschine (f	hydraulic machine
hydraulische Presse (f	hydraulic presse, hydropress
hydraulischer Auswerfer (m	pushback
hydraulischer Durchmesser (m	hydraulic diameter
hydraulischer Radius (m	hydraulic radius
Hydrodynamik (f	hydrodynamics
Hydrostatik (f	hydrostatics
Hydrotometer (n	hydrotometer
Hysteresismotor (m	hysteresis motor
Immersionslinse (f	immersion lens
Implosion (f	implosion
Imprägnierkessel (m	impregnation pan
Impulserregung (f	impulse excitation
Impulssatz (m	momentum equation
Impulsübertrager (m	pulse transformer
Impulszähler (m	impulse meter
in Bewegung (f	in motion
in Ruhe (f, ruhend	at rest
indirekte Betätigung (f	indirect operation
indirekte Trockenzentrifuge (f	indirect rotary drier
Induktionseffekt (m	induction effect
Induktionsgesetzt (n	induction law
Induktionsmaschine (f	induction machine
Induktionsmotor (m	induction motor
induktiver Beschleuniger (m	induction accelerator
induktiver Stromkreis (m	inductive circuit
Induktivität (f	inductance
Induktormaschine (f	inductor machine
induzierte Spannung (f	induced voltage

Infrarotabtaster(m	infrared scanner
Infrarotstrahlung(f	infrared radiation
Injektordüse(f	inductor, jet agitator
Innengewinde(n)	internal thread, female -
Innengitter(n	inner grid
Innenmischer(m)	kneader
Innenraumgerät(n	indoor apparatus
Innenwiderstand(m	internal resistance
innere Ecke(f), Innenwinkel(m)	internal angle
innere Leistung(f	internal power
innerer Zylinder(m	inner cylinder
Instrumentenlampe(f	instrument lamp
integrierte Schaltung(f	integrated circuit
intertmetallische Verbindung(f	intermetallic compound
Ionenfluss(m	ion flow
Ionenhalbleiter(m	ionic semiconductor
Ionenladung(f	ionic charge
Ionenmotor(m	ion engine
Ionenschicht(f)	ion sheath
Ionisationsenergie(f	ionizing energy
irreversible Elektrode(f	irreversible electrode
isoelektronisch	isoelectronic
Isolationsstrom(m	insulation current
Isolator(m	insulator
Isolierrost(m	insulating grid, grid
Isolierschicht(f	insulating layer
Isolierstoss(m	insulated joint
isoliert	insulated
Joule-Effekt(m	Joule effect
Kabelbündel(n	bundle of cables
Kabelrohreingang(m	duct entrance
Kabeltrommel(f	cable drum, cable reel
Kabelverbindungsstelle(f	cable joint, splice
Kalander(m	calender
Kalibrierung(f	calibration, gauging
Kalibrierwalzen(pl	gage rolls, gauging rolls
Kalorimeter(n	calorimeter
Kalorisieren(n	calorizing
kalte Fixierung(f	cold setting
kalthärtender Leim(m	cold setting adhesive, - - glu
Kantenschneidwalze(f	edge trim roll
Kantenwinkel(m	pitch angle
Kapazität(f	capacitance, capacity
Kardanantrieb(m	cardan drive
Kardiotachometer(n	cardiotachometer
Kaseinleim(m	casein glue
Kaskadenrührwerk(n	cascade agitator
Katalysator(m	catalyst

Kathodenreaktion(f	cathodic reaction
Katode(f	cathode
Katodenanschluss(m	cathode terminal
Katodenfall(m	cathode fall, potential fall
Katodenhals(m	cathode neck
Katodennagel(m	cathode tack
Katodenspannung(f	cathode voltage
Katodenstrom(m	cathode current
Katodenvorspannung(f	cathode bias
katodische Reinigung(f	cathodic cleaning
Kautschuk(m, Rohgummi(m	caoutchouc, india rubber
Kegelform(f	mo(u)ld with conical splits
Kegelklassierer(m, Konuskl.(m	cone classifier
Kegelkreiselmischer(m	cone impeller mixer
Kegelrad(n	bevel gear
Kehlnaht(f	fillet weld
Kehrrolle(f	return pulley
Kelvin-Skala(f	Kelvin scale
Kennlinie(f	characteristic curve
Kennzahl(f, Kennziffer	key number
Keramikabschmelzung(f	ceramic seal
Kernabschirmung(f	screening of nucleus
Kernbildung(f	nucleation
Kerndraht(m	core wire
kinematische Viskosität(f	kinematic viscosity
kinetisches Moment(n	kinetic momentum
Kipp-Presse(f	inclinable press, tilting press
Kitt(m	putty, stopper
Klampe(f, Klemmisolator(m	cleat
Klarlack(m	clear lacquer
Klassierer(m, Klassifizierer(m	classifier
klassisches System(n	classical system
Klebefläche(f	adhesive surface, adherend
Klebekaschieren(n	adhesive bonding
Klebekitt(m	gap-filling adhesive
Klebelack(m	adhesive varnish
Klebelösung(f	adhesive solution
Klebeschicht(f	tack coat
Klebeverbindung(f	adhesive joint
Klebmuffe(f	cemented socket joint
Klebstoff(m	adhesive, glue
Klebstoff(m, Leim(m	cement, glue
Klemme(f	clamp
Klemme(f, Anschluss(m	terminal
Klemmenspannung(f	terminal voltage
Klemmflansch(m	supported flange joint
Klemmplatte(f	adjusting clip
Klemmring(m, Schliessring(m	locking ring

Klemmwalzen(pl, Haltewalzen(pl	nip rolls, nipper rolls
Knicken(n, Knickung(f	buckling
Knickspannung(f	buckling stress
Kniehebel(m	bell crank
koaxialer Zylinder(m	coaxial cylinder
Koaxialkabel(n	concentric cable, coaxial cabl
Körnigkeit(f, Körnung(f	graininess
Koerzitiv-Feldstärke(f	coercive force
Kohäsion(f	cohesion
Kohäsionskraft(f	cohesive force
Kohlebogen(m	carbon arc
kohlenstoffartig, -haltig	carbonaceous
Kohlenstoffverbindungen(pl	carbon compounds
Kolben(m	plunger
Kolbendruckmesser(m	piston manometer
Kolbenstrangpresse(f	ram extruder
Kollektor-Wirkungsgrad(m	collector efficiency
Kollision(f, Stoss(m	collision
Kommutator(m, Stromwender(m	commutator
Kommutatortragvorrichtung(f	commutator spider
Kompensationskreis(m	bucking circuit
kompensierte Abtastung(f	expandet sweep
Komponente(f	component
Komponenten(pl	components
Kompound(n, Compound(n	compound
Kompressionsverhältnis(n	compression ratio
Kompressionswärme(f	heat of compression
Kompressormantel(m	compressor jacket
Komprimieren(n, Verdichten(n	compacting, compression
Kondensator(m	capacitor
Kondensatorbatterie(f	bank of capacitors
Kondensatorkapazität(f	capacitor-capacitance
Kondensatorleistung(f	cpacitor power
Kondensatorplatte(f	capacitor plate
konstante Expansion(f	fixed expansion
konstante Verluste(pl	constant losses
konstante Verzögerung(f	definite time
Kontakt(m	contact
Kontakt-Elektrode(f	contact electrode
Kontaktelement(n	contact member
Kontaktfeder(f	contact spring, make spring
Kontaktfläche(f	land area
Kontaktklammer(f	contact clip
Kontaktkleber(m	contact adhesive, impact -
kontinuierliche Färbmaschine(f	continuous dyeing machine
kontinuierliche Umlaufpumpe(f	recirculating pump
Kontinuitätsgleichung(f	continuity equation
Kontrast(m	contrast

Kontrolllehre (f, Prüflehre (f	reference gage, master gauge
konzentrierte Wicklung (f	concentrated winding
Koordinaten (pl	coordinates (pl
Kopfanschlusskappe (f	top cap
Kopfhöhe (f	addendum
Kopfkreis (m	outside circle
Kopfwinkel (m	crest angle
Koppelkondensator (m	blocking capacitor
Kopplungskoeffizient (m	coupling coefficient
Kopplungswiderstand (m	coupling resistance
Korkgummiplatte (f	corkrubber sheet
Korngrössenbestimmungsapparat (m	particle size apparatus
Korona-Entladung (f	corona discharge
Koronaerscheinung (f	corona effect
Korrosion (f	corrosion
Korrosionsschutz (m	protection against corrosion
Korrosionsschutzfarbe (f	anticorrosive paint
Korrosionsschutzmittel (n	corrosion inhibitor
Kräftemassstab (m	scale of forces
Kräfteplan (m	diagram of forces
Krählwerk (n	raking mechanism, rabbling -
Kraft (f	force
Kraft (f, Leistung (f	power
Krafteck (n	force polygon
Kraftspeiseleitung (f	power feeder
Kraftweg (m	path of load
Kraftzerlegung (f	resolution of a force
Kragen (m	thorat
Kreis (m, Schaltung (f	circuit
kreisförmig	circular
kreisförmiges Rohr (n	circular pipe
Kreisfrequenz (f	angular frequency
Kreislauf (m, Umlauf (m	circuit, circulation
Kreiswindungen (pl	circular windings (pl
Kreuzspule (f	cross coil
Kreuzstück (n	cross
kreuzweise Schichten (pl	cross-layers
kritische Abmessung (f	critical dimension
kritische Geschwindigkeit (f	critical speed
Kühlanlage (f	refrigeration plant
Kühlluft (f	cooling air
Kühlmantel (m	cooling jacket
Kühlmittel (n	coolant, cooling agent
Kühlmittel (n	refrigerant, coolant
Kühlplatte (f	cooling plate
Kühlpresse (f	cooling press
Kühlrinne (f	cooling trough
Kühlrippe (f	cooling fin

Kühlschlange(f, -serpentine(f	condensing coil, cooling -
Kühlschlange, Kühlspirale(f	cooling coil
Kühlschlangensystem(n	evaporator coil
Kühlstrecke(f	annealing range
Kühlung(f, Abkühlung(f	cooling
Kühlwalze(f	cooling roll
Kühlwalze(f, Kühlzylinder(m	chill roll, cooling cylinder
Kühlwassermantel(m	water jacket
Kugelschieber(m, Kugelhahn(m	ball cock
Kunst(harz)stoff(m	plastic (material)
Kunstharz(n	artificial resin, synthetic -
Kunstharzrohr(n	plastic pipe, - tube
Kunststoffe(pl, Plaste(pl	plastics(pl
Kunststoffrohrleitung(f	plastic piping
Kunststoffschlosser(m	plastics welder
Kupfer(n	copper
Kupferdraht(m	copper wire
Kupferoxyd(n	cuprous oxide
Kurzschluss(m	short-circuit
Kurzschlussbremse(f	short-circuit brake
Kurzschlussverlust(m	short-circuit loss
Kurzschlusswicklung(f	short-circuit winding
kurzzeitiger Betrieb(m	short-time duty
Lack(m, Farbstofflack(m	lacquer, lake, lac
Lackieren(n	lacquering
Lackiermaschine(f	varnishing machine
Ladevorrichtung(f	loading device
Ladezeit(f	charging time
Ladungsausgleich(m	charge neutralization
Ladungsvervielfachung(f	charge multiplication
Länge(f	length
Längenausdehnung(f	linear expansion
Längskopf(m	axial head, straight head
Lagerreibung(f	bearing friction
laminare Strömung(f	laminar flow
langsamer Beschleuniger(m	slow accelerator
Laser(m	laser
lastabhängig	load-dependent
Lastweg(m	path of force
latente Wärme(f	latent heat
Lederpackung(f	leather gasket, - packing
Lederscheibe(f	leather wheel
Leerlauf(m	idle run
Legierdiode(f	alloy diode
Leimen(n unter Druck	press bonding
Leimfolie(f	film glue
Leimschicht(f, Klebefläche(f	glue layer
Leimsiedekessel(m	glue cooker

Leistungsfaktor(m	power factor
Leistungsteiler(m	power divider
Leistungsverstärkung(f	power amplification
Leiter(m	conductor
Leiterstromstärke(f	line current
Leiterwiderstand(m	resistance of conductor
Leiterzahl(f	number of conductors
Leitwalze(f	master roll, control –
Leitwalze(f, Führungsrolle(f	guide roll
Leuchtschirm(m	fluorescent screen
lichte Weite(f	free opening, daylight –
lichtecht	light resistant, lightfast
Lichtechtheit(f	stability to light
Lichtechtheitsprobe(f	fading test
lichtelektrische Sonnenzelle(f	solar cell
lichtelektrische Zelle(f	photoelectric cell
lichtelektrischer Zähler(m	photoelectric counter
lichtempfindlich	photosensitive, light sensitive
Linearbeschleuniger(m	linear accelerator
lineare Zeitbasis(f	linear timebase
Linse(f	lens
Lochstift-Halteplatte(f	core-pin retainer plate
Löffelrührer(m	spoon agitator
lösbare Verbindung(f	detachable joint
Löschung(f	extinction
Lösungsmittel(n	solvent
Lötlampe(f	soldering lamp
lose Rolle(f	free sheave
Lüftung(f, Entlüftung(f	vent, ventilation
Luftabdichtung(f	air seal
luftdichter Verschluss(m	hermetic seal
Lufteinlass(m	air inlet
Luftfilter(m	air filter
Luftfilter(m, Luftreiniger(m	air cleaner, – filter
luftgestützte Konstruktion(f	pneumatic structure
lufthydraulische Presse(f	air-hydraulic press
Luftkissen(n	air-inflated cushion
Luftleitung(f	air conduit
Luftrakel-Streichmaschine(f	floating knife coater
Luftspaltlänge(f	length of the air gap
Luftstrahlmühle(f	air-jet mill
Luftventil(n	air valve
Luftzirkulation(f	recycling air, recirculating –
magnetische Ablenkung(f	magnetic deflection
magnetische Abschirmung(f	magnetic screen, – shield
magnetische Feldkonstante(f	absolute permeability
magnetische Feldstärke(f	magnetic field strength
magnetische Flussdichte(f	magnetic flux density

magnetische Fokussierung(f	magnetic focusing
magnetische Richtungsregeln(pl	magnetic rules
magnetische Spannung(f	magnetic voltage
magnetischer Fluss(m	magnetic flux
magnetischer Kreis(m	magnetic circuit
magnetischer Leitwert(m	magnetic conductance
magnetischer Streufluss(m	leakage flux
magnetischer Widerstand(m	reluctance
Magnetismus(m	magnetism
Magnetnadel(f	magnetic needle
Magnetpol(m	magnetic pole
Manometer(n	ga(u)ge, manometer
Mantel(m	blanket
Mantel(m, Gehäuse(n	jacket
Maschennetz(n	meshed network
Maschine(f mit konischem Läufer	conical rotor machine
Maschinenelement(n	machine part
massebezogene Arbeit(f	work per unit mass
massebezogene Wärme(f	heat per unit mass
Masseleitung(f, Erdkabel(n	earth lead, work -, ground -
massiver Leiter(m	solid conductor
Mastikator-Schaufel(f	masticator blade, kneader -
Materialprüfung(f	material testing
Materie(f, Stoff(m	matter
Mattieren(n	frosting
Mattierungsmittel(n	gloss-reducing agent, flatting
mechanische Eigenschaften(pl	mechanical properties
mechanische Flotation(f	mechanical flotation
mechanische Leistung(f	mechanical power
mechanische Prüfung(f	mechanical test
mechanische Verluste(pl	mechanical loss(es)
mechanischer Wirkungsgrad(m	mechanical efficiency
mehrere Kräfte(pl	a number of forces(pl
Mehrfachantrieb, Mehrachsantrieb	multiple transmission
Mehrfachelektrode(f	polyelectrode, multiple elect
Mehrfachwicklung(f	multi-circuit winding
mehrgängige Schraube(f	multiple thread, multi-flighte
Mehrlagen-Schweissung(f	multi-layer welding
Mehrphasenmaschine(f	polyphase machine
mehrphasig	polyphase
mehrschichtige Katode(f	multilayered cathode
Messbereich(m	range of measurement
Messer(m, Meter(n, Zähler(m	meter
Messerkontakt(m	blade contact
Messersperre(f	blade latch
Messinstrument(n	measuring instrument
Messwertgeber(m	measuring comparator
Messzylinder(m	measuring cylinder, graduated

Metadyngenerator (m	metadyne generator
Metallgaze (f	wire gauze, wire gaze
Metallgleichrichter (m	metal rectifier
metallische Bindung (f	metallic bond
Metallisieren (n	metallization, metal plating
Metallkeramik (f	metal-ceramic, cermet
Metallspritzverfahren (n	metal spraying
Metallüberzug (m	metallic coating
Mikro-Elektronik (f	microelectronics
Mikrolegierung (f	microalloy
Mikrowaage (f	microbalance
Mikrowellenfilter (n	microwave filter
Mischarm (m	mixing blade
Mischer (m	blender, mixer
Mischkneter (m	kneader-mixer
Mischtrommel (f	mixing drum
Mischzylinder (m	mixing cylinder
mit dem Gehäuse verbinden	connect to frame
mitlaufende Schneidevorrichtung	flying shears
mitteldicke Umhüllung (f	semi thick covering
Mittelleiter (m	middle wire
Mittelschicht (f	centre layer, center –
mittelstarker Beschleuniger (m	moderate accelerator
mittlere Beschleunigung (f	average acceleration
mittlere freie Zeit (f	mean free time
mittlere Geschwindigkeit (f	medium speed
mittlere Katodenbelastung (f	mean cathode loading
mittlere Spannung (f	average voltage
Modellsand (m	facing sand
modifiziertes Harz (n	modified resin
molares Volumen (n	molecular volume
Moment (n	moment
Momentengleichung (f	equation of moments
Momentenkonstante (f	moment constant
Momentensatz (m	moment theorem
Montagekleber (m	assembly adhesive, structural –
Montagestellung (f	mounting position
Muffenschweissen (n	sleeve welding
Muffenverbindung (f	socket joint
n gleiche Widerstände (pl	n equal resistances
Naben-Durchmesser (m	hub diameter
Nabenlänge (f	hub length
Nachbearbeitungsmittel (n	finishing agent
Nachbehandlung (f	postcuring
Nachbehandlung (f	aftertreatment
Nachbeschleunigung (f	post-acceleration
Nachdehnung (f	afterexpansion
Nachdicken (n	afterbodying, afterthickening

nachgiebige Stütze (f	flexible support
Nachkühlung (n	aftercooling
Nachreinigung (f	final cleaning
Nachschwinden (n	aftercontraction
Nadelausschlag (m	needle-deflection
Nadelschmiergerät (n	needle lubricator
Nadelzähler (m	needle counter
Nahtaufbau (m	weld structure
Nahtschweissen (n	seam welding
natürliche Kennlinie (f	natural characteristic
Nebenschlussmotor (m	shunt motor
Nebenschlussspule (f	shunt coil
Nebenschlusswicklung (f	shunt winding
negative Ladung (f	negative charge
negativer Leiter (m	negative conductor
Nenn-	rated
Nennbetrieb (m	rating
Nennfrequenz (f	rated frequency
Nennspannung (f	voltage rating
Nennstrom (m	rated current
Nennwert (m, Nenngrösse (f	rated quantity
Nennwirkungsgrad (m	declared efficiency
Neonlampe (f, Neonröhre (f	neon lamp
Netztransformator (m	power transformer
neutrale Achse (f, - Faser (f	neutral axis
neutrale Zone (f	neutral zone
nicht ineinandergreifend	non-intermeshing
nicht kreisförmig	non circular
nichtangeschlossene Elektrode (f	open-circuited electrode
nichtisoliert	uninsulated
nichtkritische Dimension (f	non-critical dimension
nichtlineare Skala (f	non-linear scale
Nickelschicht (f	nickel layer
Niederdruckverdampfer (m	low-pressure vaporizer
niedrige Geschwindigkeit (f	low speed
niedrige Spannung (f	low voltage
niedriges Vakuum (n	low vacuum
Nitrozellulose (f	nitrocellulose
Niveau (m, Pegel (m	level
Nocken (m, Nocke (f	boss
Nockenfahrschalter (m	cam controller
Normalband (n	normal band
Normalwiderstand (m	resistance standard
Normalzustand (m	normal state, ground state
Notausschalter (m	emergency stop switch
Nullenergieniveau (n	zero-energy level
Nullleiter (m	neutral conductor
Nut (f	groove

Nut(f, Schlitz(m	slot
Nutzbremsung(f	regenerative braking
Nutzleistung(f	service capacity
Nutzspannung(f	volt efficiency
Nutzzeit(f	utilization time
Obenentleerung(f	top discharge
obere Platte(f	top board, top plate
obere Stanzplatte, Stanzauflage	top backing plate
Oberflächenbehandlung(f	surface treating
Oberflächenbelastung(f	surface load
Oberflächenhärtung(f	surface hardening
Oberflächenkühler(m	surface cooler
Oberflächenschicht(f	surface layer
Oberflächensperrschicht(f	surface barrier
Oberflächenüberzug(m	surface coating
Obergurt(m	upper boom
Oberstempel(m, Oberkolben(m	upper ram
Oberwalze(f	top roll
Öffnung(f	orifice
Öffnungsbreite(f	with of aperture
Öffnungsfläche(f	opening surface
Oeffnungswinkel(m	angle of Vee
Ölabscheider(m	oil separator
Ölbad(n	oil bath
ölbeständig	oil resistant
Ölfilter(m	oil filter
Ölgehalt(m	oil length
Ölkanal(m, Ölrinne(f	oil channel
Ölkühler(m	oil cooler
Ölmantel(m	oil jacket
Ölpresse(f	pot press, oil press
Ölpumpe(f	oil pump
Ölzufuhrgefäss(n	oil-feeding reservoir
örtliche Einwirkung(f	local action
offener Filter(m	open filter
offener Kreis(m	open circuit
Ohmscher Kontakt(m	ohmic contact
Ohmsches Gesetz(m	Ohm's law
optisches Pyrometer(n	optical pyrometer
ortsfeste Batterie(f	stationary battery
oxydierende Umhüllung(f	oxide covering
Paar(n, Kräftepaar(n	couple
Paddelrührer(m, Paddelmischer(m	paddle mixer, - agitator
Pannensignal(n	breakdown signal
Parallel-Schwingkreis(m	parallel resonant circuit
parallele Kräfte(pl	parallel forces
paralleler Leiter(m	parallel conductor
Parallelschalten(n	paralleling

Parallelschaltung(f	parallel connection
parametrischer Verstärker(m	parametric amplifier
Passring(m	adapter ring
Passstück(n	adapter, adaptor, adopter
pendelnder Wischer(m	swinging scraper
Penetrometer(n	penetrometer, quotimeter
Periode(f, Periodendauer(f	period
periodischer Strom(m	periodic current
Permeabilität(f	permeability
Permeabilitätszahl(f	relative permeability
Pfeifenventil(n	whistle valve
pH-Messer(m	pH-meter
pH-Registrierer(m	pH-recorder
Phasendifferenz-Abschnitt(m	differential phase section
Phasenkonstante(f	phase constant
Phasenleiter(m	phase conductor
Phasenschieber(m	phase changer
Phasenverschiebung(f	phase shift
Phasenwicklung(f	phase winding
Phasenwinkel(m	phase anlge
photoelektrischer Zeitschalter(m	photoelectric timer
Photoleiter(m	photoconductor
Planetengetriebe(n	epicyclic gearing
Planetenrührwerk(n	planetary mixer
Plastifizier(ungs)zone(f	plastification zone
Plastifizierbehälter(m	plasticizer tank
Plastometer(n	plastimeter, plastometer
Platte(f	plate
Platte(f), Tafel(f)	panel, sheet
Plattenanode(f	plate anode
Plattenblock(m	plate block
Plattenfläche(f	plate area
Plattenhalter(m	plate support
Plattenkühler(m	plate cooler, surface cooler
Plattenstütze(f	plate support
pneumatische Schleuse(f	air lock
pneumatischer Schalter(m	pneumatic switch
pneumatischer Trockner(m	pneumatic dryer
Poissonsche Gleichung(f	Poisson's equation
polare Öffnung(f	polar port
polarer Kontakt(m	polar contact
Polarisationsstrom(m	polarization current
Polarität(f	polarity
Polarrelais(n	polarized relay
Polfläche(f	pole face
Polieren(f), Schwabbeln(n)	buffing
Polieren(n	polishing, brightening, ashing
Polierkalander(m	polishing calender

Poliermaschine(f	polishing machine
Polierscheibe(f	grinding wheel, polishing wheel
Poliertrommel(f	polishing barrel, - drum
Polpaar(n	pole pair
Polpaarzahl(f	number of pairs of poles
Polprüfer(m	polarity indicator
Polrad(n	magnet wheel
Polteilung(f	pole pitch
Polumschalter(m, Umpoler(m	pole reverser
Polwicklung(f	polar wind(ing)
Polymerisierung(f	polymerizing
positive Ladung(f	positive charge
positiver Leiter(m	positive conductor
Potentialgradient(m	potential gradient
Prägekalander(m	embossing calender
Prägeplatte(f	embossing plate
Prägepresse(f	stamping press, - machine
Prägevorrichtung(f	embosser, embossing machine
Präzisionswaage(f	precision balance
Prallbrecher(m	impact breaker, - crusher
Prallmühle(f	impact mill
Press-Stumpfschweissen(n	pressure butt welding
Pressdruck(m	mo(u)lding pressure
Presse(f	press
Presse(f mit hohem Hub	long-stroke press
Pressform(f	pressing mould, block mold
Pressformbeschickung(f	mold load, mould charge
Pressglassockel(m	pressed-glass base
Pressglasverschmelzung(f	button seal
Presskissen(n	pressure pad, forming -
Presslufttrocknen(n	pneumatic drying
Pressplatte(f, Druckplatte(f	press plate
primär	primary
primäre Strahlung(f	primary radiation
Produktionsstrasse(f	line, production line
Propellerrührwerk(n, Schrauben-(n	propeller agitator, - stirrer
Proportionalbereich(m	proportional region
Proportionalitätsgrenze(f	proportional limit
Prozessrechner(m	process computer
Prüfstromkreis(m	proving circuit
Prüfverbindungen(pl	testing joints
Prüfwert(m	test value
Pulszahl(f	pulse number
Pumpfrequenz(f	pumping frequency
Punktkatode(f	point cathode
Punktkontakt(m	point contact
Punktschweissen(n	tack welding
Punktschweissen(n	spot welding

Putzen(n, Reinigen(n	cleaning, dressing
Putzscheibe(f	snagging wheel
Putzwalze(f	polishing roll(er), wheel roll
Quantenzahl(f	quantum number
Quecksilberkontakt(m	mercury contact
Quecksilbersäule(f	mercury column
Querkeil-Verbindung(f	tapered key
Quetschwalze(f	squeeze roll
Radarschirm(m	radar screen
Radialablenkung(f	radial deflection
Radialkraft	radial (bearing) force
Radiator(m, Strahler(m	radiator
Raffinierwalze(f	refiner mill
Rahmenkonstruktion(f, Fachwerk(n	framework structure
Rahmenmontage(f	frame mounting
Rahmenpresse(f	frame press, strain plate press
Rasterwalze(f, gravierte Walze	gravure roll, print -
Rauchgasfilter(m, n	smoke filter
Raumdehnung(f, räumliche Dehnung	cubic expansion
Reaktionskraft(f	reaction force
Rechenmischer(m	rake mixer
rechnerisch	mathematical
rechteckiger Heizkörper(m	frame heater
rechteckiger Querschitt(m	rectangular cross section
Rechteckkatode(f	rectangular cathode
Reduktionsmuffe(f	reducing joint
Reduzierstück(n	reducing fitting, reducer
Regelungssystem(n	control system
Regulierhahn(m	regulating tap
Regulierschraube(f	adjusting screw
Reibungsarbeit, Reibungsverlust	friction losses
Reibungsbeiwert(m	friction coefficient
Reibungskoeffizient(m	adhesion coefficient
Reibungskoeffizient(m	coefficient of friction
Reibungskontakt(m	friction contact
Reibungskraft(f	friction force
Reibungsmoment(n	moment of friction
Reibungszahl(f	coefficient of friction
Reihenschlussmotor(m	series motor
Reihenschlusswicklung(f	series winding
Rekombinationskoeffizient(m)	recombination coefficient
Rektifizierteil(m	rectifying section
Relais(n, Schütz(n	relay
relative Rauhigkeit(f	relative roughness
relativer Fehler(m	relative error
Reluktanzmotor(m	reluctance motor
Remanenz(f	remanence
Remanenz-Induktion(f	remanent-flux density

Repulsionsmotor(m	repulsion motor
Resonanzbedingung(f	resonance condition
Resonanzfrequenz(f	resonant frequency
Resonanzmodus(m	resonant mode
Restfehler(m	residual error
resultierende Kraft(f	resultant force
Rhenium-Wolframlegierung(f	rhenium-tungsten alloy
Richtpresse(f	straightening press
Richtungsrelais(n	directional relay
Riemengeschwindigkeit(f	belt velocity
Riementrieb(m	belt drive
Riffelwalze(f	grooved cylinder, - roll
rinförmiger Querschnitt(m	annular cross section
ringförmiges Netz(n	ringed network
Ringheizkörper(m	ring heater
Ringkreis(m	ring circuit
Ringmarkierung(f	ring marking
Ringspule(f	toroidal coil
Ringverschmelzung(f	ring seal
Ringwicklung(f	ring winding, toroidal winding
Ringzähler(m	ring counter
Rippenplatte(f	ribbed panel
Rippenrohr(n	finned tube
Röhrenkühler(m	pipe cooler
Röntgenröhre(f	X-ray tube
Röntgenstrahlen(pl	X-rays
Rohmetall(n	crude metal
Rohr(n, Röhre(f	pipe, tube
Rohrbogen(m	pipe bend
Rohrdurchmesser(m	diameter of pipe
Rohrgitter(n	tubular (space) grid
Rohrhalter(m	pipe support
Rohrkabel(n	pipe-type cable
Rohrmühle(f	tube mill
Rohrnippel(m	pipe nipple
Rohrpresse(f	pipe extruder
Rohrschelle(f	pipe clip, pipe clamp
Rohrschlange(f	worm, coil
Rohrströmung(f	pipe flow
Rohrverbindung(f	pipe joint, - connection
Rohrverschraubung(f	screwed conduit
Rollenbahn(f	roller train, - conveyor
Rollenwechsel(m	reel change
Rollkontakt(m, Wälzkontakt(m	rolling contact
Rollreibungskraft(f	rolling resistance
Rolltreppe(f	escalator
Rostschutzmittel(n	antirust agent
Rotationszirkulator(m	rotation circulator

Rotator(m	rotator
rotierende Maschine(f	rotating machine
Rotorkern(m	rotor core
Roving-Schneidwerk(n	roving chopper, glass chopper
Rückgangswert(m	resetting value
Rückgewinnung(f	recovery, recuperation
Rücklaufbehälter(m	drum reflux
Rücklicht(n	rear light, tail light
Rückstellzeit(f	reset time
Rückstoss(m	recoil
Rückwärtssperrstellung(f	inverse blocking state
Rückzündung(f	back fire, arc-back
Rückzugkolben(m	pull-back ram
Rührtank(m, Agitator(m	agitator
Rührwerk(n mit Radialströmung	radial flow agitator
Rüttler(m	vibrator
Ruhekontakt(m	back contact
Ruhepotential(n	resting potential
Ruhewert(m	quiescent value
runder Tank(m, Kreisbehälter(m	circular tank
Rundplattenanode(f	disk anode
Sättigung(f	saturation
Sättigungsstrom(m	saturation current
Säule(f	column
säurebeständig, säurefest	acidproof
säurefeste Anstrichfarbe(f	acid-resisting paint
Sammelbehälter(m, Speichertank(m	storage tank, accumulator –
Sammelschiene(f	bus bar
Sammelsteuerung(f	collective control
Sandstrahldüse(f	sandblast nozzle
Sandstrahlen(n	sandblasting
Satinierkalander(m	glazing rolls, calender stack
Saugleitung(f	suction conduit
saurer feuerfester Stoff(m	acid refractory
Schalenguss(m, Formguss(m	slush mo(u)lding
Schaltbild(n	symbol
Schalter(m	switch
Schaltersockel(m	switch base
Schaltgeräte(pl	switchgear
Schaltgetriebe(n	shifting gear
Schaltgruppe(f	switch group
Schaltmechanismus(m	circuit breaker
Schaltraum(m	control room
Schalttransistor(m	switching transistor
Schaltung(f	switching
Schaltzeit(f	switching time
scharfkantig	with sharp edges
Scharnierklemme(f	hinge clamp

Band M.0.3 Seite 99

Schauglas(n, Schauloch(n	sight glass, sight hole
Schauloch(n	peep-hole, spy glass
Schaumkunststoff(m	aerated plastic, foamed –
Schaumleim(m	foam glue
Schaumstoffe(pl	foamed plastics, expanded –
Scheibeneinschmelzung(f	disk seal
Scheibenkreiselrührer(m	disc impeller, disk –
Scheibenmischer(m	disk mixer
Scheibenrad(n	disk wheel
Scheider(m	liner
Scheider(m, Separator(m	separator
Scheidetrichter(m	extraction funnel, separating –
Scheinleistung(g	apparent power
Scheinleitwert(m	conductivity, admittance
Scheinwiderstand(m	impedance
Scheitelplatte(f	vertex plate
Scheitelwert(m, Höchstwert(m	peak value
Scherkraft(f, Querkraft(f	shearing force
Scheuerfestigkeit(f	rubbing fastness,
Schicht(f, Lage(f	ply, layer
Schicht(f, Wand(f	sheath
Schichtentrennung(f	delamination
Schichtgitter(n	layer lattice
Schichtplatte(f, Schichttafel(f	laminated sheet, – board
Schiebeboden(m	sliding bottom
Schieberbacke(f	slide follower
schiefe Ebene(f	inclined plane
Schienenbremsung(f	track braking
Schienenkontakt(m	rail contact
Schirmeinbrennung(f	screen burn
Schirmgitterstrom(m	screen-grid current
Schlagempfindlichkeit(f	sensitiveness to percussion
Schlagzähigkeit(f	impact strength
Schlangenkühler(m	spiral condenser, – radiator
Schlankheitsgrad(m	slenderness
Schleifapparat(m	abrader, abrading device
Schleifen(n	grinding
Schleiferei(f	grindery
Schleifkontakt(m	sliding contact
Schleifmaschine(f	grinding machine
Schleifscheibe(f	abrasive wheel
Schliessbewegung(f	closing travel
Schliessdruck(m	clamping pressure, locking –
Schliesseinheit(f	closing unit
Schliesskolben(m	clamping plunger
Schliesskraft(f	clamping force, locking –
Schliessseite(f	force side, movable side
Schliesszeit(f	closing time

Schliesszylinder(m	closing cylinder
schmelzende Umhüllung(f	fusible covering
Schmelzgeschwindigkeit(f	melting rate
Schmelzpunkt(m	melting point
Schmelzpunkt(m	fusion point
Schmelzschweissen(n	fusion welding
Schmelzstrom(m	fusing current
Schmelzwärme(f	heat of fusion
Schmelzzone(f	fusion zone
Schmiermittel(n, Fett(n	grease
Schmierrille(f, Ölring(m	oil ring, scraper ring
Schmirgel(m	emery
Schmirgelmühle(f	emery grinder
Schmirgelwalze(f	emery roll
Schnecke(f mit Steigungsabnahme	screw with decreasing pitch
Schnecke(f, Schraube(f	screw, worm
Schnecke(m mit Konstantsteigung	screw with equal pitch
Schneckengetriebe(n	worm gearing
Schneckenkerndurchmesser(m	root diameter of a screw
Schneckenlänge(f	screw length
Schneckenmischer(m	screw mixer
Schneckenpresse(f	screw extruder
Schneidmaschine(f	cutting machine
Schneidvorrichtung(f	cutting device, chopper, cutter
Schnellauslösung(f	rapid release, quick release
Schnellauslösung(f	instantaneous release
Schnellausschalter(m	quick-break switch
Schnellrührer(m	high-speed agitator
Schnittantrieb(m	cutting drive
Schnittgeschwindigkeit(f	cutting speed
Schnittpunkt(m	point of intersection
Schnittzeit(f	cutting time
Schräganode(f	oblique anode
Schrägkopf(m, Winkelkopf(m	oblique head
Schrägstellung(f, Schrägaufbau(m	oblique structure
Schrägtrommelmischer(m	tilted cylinder mixer
Schrage-Motor(m	Schrage motor
Schrauben-Beanspruchung(f	load on screw
Schraubmuffe(f	screwed socket, - bell
Schraubverbindung(f	screwed joint
Schrittzeit(f	step time
Schrumpfen(n, Schwinden(n	contraction, shrinkage
Schrumpfmass(n	shrinkage allowance
Schrumpfring(m	shrunk-on ring
Schub(m	shear
Schubspannung(f	shear stress
Schüttelmaschine(f	shaker
Schüttelrinne(f	jigging conveyor, shaking shoot

Schüttelsiebmaschine (f	pulsator jig
Schütteltisch (m	reciprocating table
Schutzgehäuse (n	protection cap
Schutzhandschuhe (pl	protective gloves
Schutzring (m	arcing ring
Schutzrohr (n	conduit
Schutzsystem (n	protective system
Schutzüberzug (m	protective coating
schwankende Spannung (f	fluctuation voltage
schwebender Ring (m	floating ring
Schwebeplatte (f, Schwebetisch (m	floating plate
Schweissanlage (f	welding plant
Schweissblase (f, Schweisskrater (m	arc crater
Schweissfläche (f	weld area
Schweisslöten (n	braze welding
Schweissnaht (f	welding joint
Schweissraupe (f	welding bead
Schweissspannung (f	welding-arc voltage
Schweissstelle (f, Schweissung (f	weld, welding
Schweissverbindung (f	welding joint
Schweisszeit (f	welding time
Schwenkrohr (n	swing pipe
Schwerkraftverschluss (m	gravity closing
Schwerpunkt (m	centre of gravity
Schwimmer (m	float
Schwinden (n, Schrumpfen (n	shrinkage, contraction
Schwingförderband (n	oscillating conveyor
Schwingkreis (m	resonant circuit
Schwingrost (m	rocking grate
Schwingungsdämpfer (m	vibration damper
Schwingungsdauer (f	resonant period
Scottsche Schaltung (f	Scott connection
Segmentbogen-Kupplung (f	segment coupling, - connector
Segmentscheibe (f	segmental wheel
Seileck (n	link polygon
Seilreibung (f	rope friction
Seitenanschlusskappe (f	side cap
Seitenleitung (f	lateral conductor
Seitenöffnung (f	lateral aperture
Seitenschirm (m	side sheet
sekundäre Speiseleitung (f	secondary feeder
Sekundärstrahlung (f	secondary radiation
Sekundenzähler (m	seconds-counter
Selbstanlasser (m	automatic starter
Selbstauslüsung (f	automatic release
selbstbelüftet	self-ventilated
Selbstentzündung (f	spontaneous ignition
Selbstinduktion (f	self-induction

Selbstregulierung (f	self-regulation
selbstreinigendes Filter (n	self-cleaning filter
selbsttätige Einschaltung (f	automatic switching on
selbsttätige Fernbedienung (f	automatic control
selbsttätiger Teiler (m	automatic scaler
Selenzelle (f	selenium cell
Serienschaltung (f, Reihenschltg.	series connection
Sicherheitsfaktor (m	factor of safety, safety factor
Sicherheitsschaltung (f	safety circuit
Sicherheitsventil (n	safety valve, pop valve
Sicherung, Schmelzsicherung (f	fuse
Siebblech (n	perforated plate, slotted –
Siebboden (m	perforated bottom
Siebdurchfall (m	through, undersize
Siebmaschine (f	sieving machine
Siebplatte (f, Filterplatte (f	sieve plate
Siebrost (m	screen, sieving screen
Signalbetätigung (f	signal operation
Silberchloridelement (n	silver-chloride cell
Silizium-Sonnenzelle (f	silicon solar cell
Siliziumkarbid (n	silicon carbide
Sinterbad (n	sintering bath
Skala (f, Skalenteilung (f	scale
Sonnenbatterie (f	solar battery
Sortieranlage (f	sorting plant
Sortierzylinder (m	cylindrical grader
Spaltweite (f, Walzenspalt (m	mill opening, bite
Spanbreite (f	width of chip
Spandicke (f	chip thickness
Spannring (m	clamping ring
Spannrolle (f	tension roll(er), pull roll
Spannung (f	stress
Spannungsabfall (m	voltage drop
Spannungsbegrenzer (m	voltage limiter
Spannungsmesser (m, Voltmeter (n	voltmeter
Spannungsmessung (f	voltage measuring
Spannungsregler (m	voltage regulator
Spannungsrelais (n	voltage relay
Spannungsteiler (m	potential divider
Spannungsverhältnis (n	ratio of voltages
Spannweite (f	length of a span, span length
Sparumspanner (m	auto-transformer
Speicher (m, Akku (m	accumulator, store
Speicherbecken (n	holding basin, storing basin
Speicherelement (n	storage element
Speicherkopf (m	accumulator head
Speichertank (m	retention tank
Speicherung (f	storage

Speiserolle (f, Zufuhrrolle (f	feed roller
Speisespannung (f	supply voltage, feeding voltage
Sperrkondensator (m	commutating capacitor
Sperrkreis (m	wave trap
Sperrschicht (f	barrier layer
Sperrspannung (f	sticking voltage
Sperrstellung (f	off-state
Sperrzeit (f	blocking period
spezifische Wärmekapazität (f	specific heat
spezifischer Widerstand (m	resistivity
spezifisches Volumen (n	specific volume
Spindelmühle (f	spindle mill
Spirale (f, Rohrspirale (f	coil, worm, spiral tube
Spiralfeder (f	spiral spring
Spiralrohr (n	helically wound pipe
Spiralrohr (n, Rohrschlange (f	serpentine pipe
Spitzenwert (m	crest factor, peak value
Spritzdorn (m	extrusion mandril
Spritzdorn (m	extruder core, extrusion core
Spritzverfahren (n	spray gun process
Spritzzylinder, Füllzylinder (m	injection cylinder, feed -
Sprühbeschichten (n	spray coating
Sprühkopf (m	actuator, spray gun
Spule (f	bobbin, coil
Spule (f	cop
Spulenbreite (f	width of coil
Spulenhalter (m	coil holder
Spulenwicklung (f	bobbin winding
Stabilitätsfaktor (m	stability factor
Stabmühle (f	rod mill
Stabreflektor (m	rod reflector, - mirror
Stabrost (m, Stangenrost (m	bar screen
Ständer (m, Stator (m	stator
Stanzen (n	punching
Stanzgrat (m	punching ridges
Stanzmaschine (f	blanking machine
Stanzmesser (n mit Auswerfer	ejecting blanking cutter
Stapelhöhe (f	stack height
Starter (m, Anlasser (m	starter
Starterstrom (m	starter current, striking -
stationäre Stellung (f	stable position
stationäre Strömung (f	steady flow
stationärer Zustand (m	stationary state
statische Kennlinie (f	static characteristic
statischer Mischer (m	static mixer, motionless -
Staubfilter (m	dust filter
Staubsammelrohr (n	dust collecting tube
Steckdose (f	socket outlet

Stecker (m	plug
Stecksockelrelais (n	plug-in relay
Steckvorrichtung (f	socket outlet and plug
steigende Kennlinie (f	rising characteristic
Steigrohr (n	ascending tube
Steigrohr (n, Vertikalrohr (n	vertical pipe, riser
Steigung (f	rise, slope
Steigungswinkel (m (Gewinde-)	angle of lead
Stellknopf (m	button
Stern-Dreieck-Schaltung (f	star-delta connection
Sternschaltung (f	star-circuit
Steuerabschnitt (m	controlling section
Steuergitter (n	control grid
Steuerkabel (n	control cable
Steuerkreis (m	control circuit
Steuerleitung (f	control line
Steuerleitung (f	cab cable, car cable
Steuerpult (n	control desk
Steuerspannung (f	gate voltage
Steuerventil (n	delivery valve, head valve
Stirnfläche (f, Rechteckkante (f	square edge
Stirnrad (n	spur gear
Stirnstoss (m	edge joint
Stoffmenge (f	amount of substance
Stopfbüchse (f	compression gland
Stossfuge (f, Stossnaht (f	butt joint
Stossprobe (f	shock test
Stossstrom (m	impulse current
Strahlbelastung (f	beam loading
Strahlenquelle (f	radiation source
Strahler (m	radiator
Strahlungs(ober)fläche (f	radiating surface
Strahlungsdichte (f	radiation density
Strahlungsintensität (f	radiation intensity
Strahlungsverlust (m	radiation loss
Strangpresse (f, Spritzmaschine (f	extruder, extruding machine
Strangpressen (n	extrusion mo(u)lding
Strangpresskolben (m	extrusion plunger
Strangspannung (f	phase voltage
Streichmaschine (f	spreading machine
Streichmasse (f, Überzugmasse (f	coating compound, - resin
Streichmischung (f, Überzugs-	spreading mixture, coating -
Streifenschneider (m	strip cutter
Streutransformator (m	leakage transformer
Streuungswinkel (m	angle of divergence
Streuzentrum (n	scattering center, - centre
Strömungsmesser (m	flowmeter
Strömungsregelung (f	flow control

Stromabnehmerkopf(m	trolley head
Stromdichte(f	current density
Stromempfindlichkeit(f	current sensitivity
Strommesser(m, Amperemeter(n	ammeter
Stromrichter(m	static converter
Stromschiene(f	contact rail, conductor rail
Stromstärke(f	current, intensity of current
Stromverhältnis(n	ratio of current
Stromverstärkung(f	current amplification
Stromzuführung(f	current supply
Stückprüfung(f, Einzelprüfung(f	routine tests
Stütze(f, Unterlegestück(n	support pillar
Stützwalzen(pl, Stützrollen(pl	supporting rolls
Stufenbelüftung(f	step aeration
Stufenboden(m	stepped tray
Stufensprung(m	progressive ratio
stufenweise Anregung(f	step-by-step excitation
Stundenbetrieb(m	one-hour duty
Sublimationswärme(f	heat of sublimation
Subminiaturtechnik(f	subminiaturization
Summenzähler(m	summation meter
Summer(m	buzzer
Synchronabtastung(f	synchronous scanning
Synchrondrehzahl(f	synchronous speed
Synchrongenerator(m	synchronous generator
Synchronisieren(n	synchronizing, synchronization
Synchronmotor(m	synchronous motor
synthetischer Gummi(m	artificial rubber
T-Nut(f, Spann-Nut(f	T-slot
Tablettenpresse(f	pelleting machine, tablets press
Tageslichteinheit(f	daylight unit
Talpunkt(m	valley point
Tandemmotor(m, Doppelmotor(m	tandem motor
Tangens(m des Verlustwinkels	loss tangent
Tauchbad(n	dipping bath, immersion bath
Tauchbeschichten(n, Tränken(n	dip coating, impregnating
Tauchgefäss(n	dipping tank
Tauchlack(m	dipping lacquer
Tauchlackierung(f	dip coating, immersion -
Tauchröhrchen(n	dip tube
Tauchschmierung(f	bath lubrication
Tauchwalze(f	dip roll
Tauchzylinder(m	dipping barrel
Taumelmischer(m	eccentric tumbler
Taumeltrockner(m	tumbling dryer, - drier
Teerfarbstoffe(pl	coal tar dyes
Teilkreis(m	pitch circle
Teilung(f	pitch

tellerförmiger Halter(m	cup-shaped base
Temperatur(f	temperature
Temperatur-Änderung(f	temperature change
Temperaturdifferenz(f	temperature difference
Temperaturkoeffizient(f	temperature coefficient
Temperaturprogrammierung(f	programmed heating
Temperaturregelung(f	attemperation
Temperaturregulator(m	attemperator
tempertaturbegrenzt	temperature-limited
Testbild(n	pattern
theoretische Ausbeute(f	theoretical yield
Thermionenstrom(m	thermionic current
thermische Aktivierung(f	thermal activation
thermischer Abbruch(m	thermal breakdown
thermischer Unterbrecher(m	thermal cutout
thermischer Widerstand(m	thermal resistance
thermischer Zustand(m	thermal state
thermisches Gleichgewicht(n	termal equilibrium
Thermofühler(m	thermocouple
thermoplastisch	thermoplastic
Thermostat(m	thermostat (relay)
Thermostat(m	thermostat
Tiefätzprobe(f	deep-etch testing
Tolleranz(f	tolerance
Topfkern(m	pot core
Torpedokopf(m	torpedo head
Totalwiderstand(m	total resistance
tote Zone(f	dead zone
Totzeit(f	dead time, insensitive time
Tourenzähler(m	revolution counter
Träger(m	beam
Träger(m auf 2 Stützen	girder on two supports
Trägerplatte(f	carrier plate
Trägerplatte(f, Halteplatte(f	supporting plate
Trägheitsmoment(n	moment of inertia, second mome
Traggerüst(n	supporting structure
Transformator(m, Umspanner(m	transformer
transportable Batterie(f	portable battery
Traverse(f, Querriegel(m	cross brace
Treibgas(n	gas propellant
Trennblech(n	baffle
Trennelektrode(f	separating electrode
Trennlasche(f	isolating link
Trennmittel(n	parting agent
Trennrelais(n	cut-off relay
Trennsubstanz(f	stripping compound
Triebeinheit(f, Motoreinheit(f	motive power unit
Triebfahrzeug(n	motor vehicle

Trockenboden (m	hot floor
Trockenfüllstoff (m	dry filler
Trockenkammer (f	drying chamber
Trockner (m	dryer
Trockner (m mit Abteilen	compartment dryer
Trockner (m, Exsikkator (m	essiccator, dessiccator
Trocknungsmittel (n	desiccant, drying agent
Trommelgalvanisierung (f	barrel electro-plating
Trommelmischer (m	drum mixer, barrel -, tumbler
Trommeltrockner (m	drum dryer
Trommelwicklung (f	drum winding
Türschalter (m	gate switch, door switch
Turbinenmischer (m	turbine mixer
Turbotrockner (m	turbo dryer, - drier
turbulente Strömung (f	turbulent flow
U-Profil (n	U-section, channel
Überdeckungsgrad (m	arc of contact
Überdruck (m	excess pressure
Übergang (m	transition
Übergangseffekt (m	transition effect
Übergangspunkt (m	transition point
Übergangsstecker (m	plug adaptor
Übergangsverhältnis (n	transport factor, - ratio
Übergangsverlust (m	transition loss
Übergangszeit (f	change-over time
überheizte Stelle (f	hot spot
Überhitzung (f	superheating
Überkompression (f	overcompression
überlappende Knetschaufeln (pl	overlapping blades
Überlappstoss (m mit Kehlnaht	overlap fillet weld
Überlappung (f	overlap
Überlappungswinkel (m	overlap angle
Überlappungszeit (f	overlap period
Überlast (f, Überlastung (f	overload
Überlauf (m	excess overflow, spew, spue
Überlaufauslass (m	overflow trap
Überlaufkammer (f	flash chamber, overflow space
Überlaufkonus (m	overflow cone
Überlaufleitung (f	overflow conduit
Überlaufrohr (n	jack-leg, overflow pipe
Überlauftrichter (m	outlet hopper, discharge -
übermittelt	transmitted
Überschichtungs-Schaumstoff (m)	foam laminate
Überschuss (m	excess, excess material
Überschussleitung (f	excess conduction
Übersetzungsverhältnis (n	transmission ratio
Überspannung (f	overvoltage
Überstromfaktor (m	overcurrent factor

Übertragungsfaktor(m	transmission coefficient
Übertragungskennlinie(f	transfer characteristic
Übertragungsleitung(f	transmission line
Übertragungsverlust(m	transmission loss
Überwachungskreis(m	checking circuit
Überwurfmutter(f	cap nut, screwed cap
Überzugs-Aktivierung(f	coatingt activation
Überzugslack(m	coating varnish
Umfangskomponenten(pl	circumferential components(pl
Umfangwickeln(n	circumferential winding
Umformer(m	converter
Umgebungsbeleuchtung(f	ambient light
umgekehrte Polung(f	reversed polarity
umkehrbarer Stromrichter(m	reversible converter
Umkehrwalze(f	reverse cylinder
umlaufender Rücklauf(m	circulating reflux
umlaufendes Messer(n	rotating knife
Umlaufkühlung(f	circulation cooling
Umlaufschüttelmaschine(f	rotary shaker
Umriss(m, Kontur(f	outline
Umschalter(m	selector switch
Umstellzeit(f	change-over time
Umwandlung(f, Transformation(f	transformation
Umwandlungsgrad(m, -verhältnis(n	conversion ratio
Umwandlungsverlust(m	conversion loss
un(ver)brennbar	incombustible
unabhängige Zündung(f	independent firing
unbeständig, unstabil, labil	unstable
undurchdringlich	imperveous
ungeordnete Anordnung(f	irregular pattern
Universalmotor(m	universal motor
unlösbare Verbindung(f	permanent joint
unterbliebenes Arbeiten(n	missing operation
Unterbrechungsfeder(f	break spring
Unterbrechungszeit(f	interrupting time
unteres Querhaupt(n	lower cross head, - traverse
Untergurt(m	lower boom
Unterkolbenpresse(f	bottom force press, - ram -
Unterkühlung(f	undercooling, supercooling
Unterschneidung(f	interference
Untersetzungsfaktor(m	scaling factor, - ratio
Untersetzungsgetriebe(n	reduction gear
unterteiltes Schaltfeld(n	sectional panel
Unterwalze(f	bottom roll
unverkleidete Konstruktion(f	non-lined construction
Vakuumexsikkator(m	vacuum desiccator, - essicato
Vakuumfilter(m	vacuum filter, suction filter
Vakuumpumpe(f	vacuum pump

Vakuumtrockner(m	vacuum drier
vektorielles Produkt(n	vector product
Ventil(n	valve
Ventilator(m, Lüfter(m	ventilator, blower, fan
Ventilsitz(m	valve seating
veränderliche Kupplung(f	variable coupling
veränderliche Verluste(pl	variable losses
Verbiegung(f	bending
Verbindung(f	compound
Verbindung(f, Verbindungsstück(n	joint
Verbindungsdose(f	junction box
Verbindungsmuffe(f	splicing sleeve
Verbindungsöse(f	splicing ear
Verbraucherleitung(f	service cable
Verbrennung(f)	burning, combustion
Verbund-Schaumstoff(m	composite foam
Verbundplatte(f	composite panel
Verbundstoffe(pl	composites
Verdampfer(m	evaporator, vaporizer
Verdampferanlage(f	evaporating plant
Verdampfungskühlung(f	evaporative cooling
Verdampfungswärme(f	heat of vapourisation
Verdichtungsverhältnis(n	compression ratio
Verdichtungszone(f	compression zone
Verdrahtung(f	wiring
Verdrehspannung(f	torsion stress
Verdrehung(f, Torsion(f	torsion
Verdrehwinkel(m	angle of twist
verfärbungsfreies Glas(n	stabilized glass
Verfahren(n nach Ritter	Ritter method
Verfestiger, Verfestigungsmittel	solidifying agent
Verflüchtigung(f	volatilization
Verflüssigung(f	fluidification
Verformungstest(m	distorsion testing
Vergleichsspannung(f	equivalent stress
Vergussharz(n, Gussharz(n	casting resin
Vergussmasse(f, Vergiessmasse(f	casting compound
Verhältnis(n Länge/Durchmesser	L/D ratio, length/diametre rati
Verhältnis(n Reichweite-Energie	range-energy relation
Verleimung(f	glue joint
Verluste(pl	losses
Verlustfaktor(m	loss factor, damping factor
Verlustwinkel(m	loss angle
Vernetzung(f	crosslinking, interlacing
Verriegelungskontakt(m	locking contact
Verriegelungsvorrichtung(f	interlocking device
Verschiebungsfluss(m	displacement flux
Verschleissfestigkeit(f	wear resistance

verschleisshindernde Zugabe(f	antiwear additive
Verschlussmaschine(f	capsuling machine, sealing -
Verschmutzung(m, Verkrustung(f	fouling
Versilberung(f	silvering
Verstärker(m	amplifier
verstärkter Kunststoff(m	reinforced plastics
Verstärkungsfaktor(m	amplification factor
verstellbare Kapazitäten(pl	adjustable capacitances
Verstrecken(n	drawing
Verteiler(m, Abzweigung(f	manifold
Verteilerscheibe(f	disk feeder
Verteilerschrank(m	kiosk
Verteilerwalzen(pl	distributor rolls, - rolls
verteilte Konstante(f	distributed constant
verteilte Last(f	distribuited load
Verteilungsfunktion(f	distribution function
Verteilungspunkt(m	distribution point
Verteilungsrohr(n	distributor duct
Vertikalablemkung(f	vertical deflection
vertikale Achse(f	vertical axis
vertikale Einmittung(f	vertical centring (control)
Vertikalleiter, Senkrechtleiter	vertical conductor
Vertratungsschema(n	wiring diagram
Vervielfachungsfaktor(m	multiplication factor
Verzahnung(f	tooth system
Verzinnung(f	tinning
Verzögerer(m	retarder
Verzögerung(f	deceleration
Verzögerungsband(n	delaying belt
Verzögerungskabel(n	delay cable, delay line
Verzögerungskraft(f	retarding force
Verzögerungszeit(f	delay time
veschliessbare Anordnung(f	sealable equipment
Vibrationsmühle, Schwingmühle(f	vibrating mill
Vierwalzenkalander(m	four-roll calender
vierwertig	tetravalent, quadrivalent
Vollgummi(m	whole rubber
Voltmeter(n, Spannungsmesser(m	voltmeter
Volumenstrom(m	volume of outlet flow
Vor-Dimensionierung(f	preliminary dimensioning
Vorbeschichtung(f	precoating
Vorbohrung(f	pre-drilled hole
Vorbrecher(m, Grobbrecher(m	primary crusher
Vorhub(m	initial deflection
Vorkühler(m	forecooler
Vorschub(m	feed
Vorschubkraft(f	feed force
vorübergehend	transient

vorverdichtet	precompressed
Vorwärmer (m	preheater
Vorwärmung (f	preheating
Vorwärmwalze (f	feed mill
Vorwärmwalzwerk (n	warming (up) mill, preheating -
Vorwärtsspannung (f	forward voltage
Votrockner (m	predrier
Vulkanfiber (n	vulcanized fiber, - fibre
Vulkanisieren (n, Vulkanisation (f	vulcanizing, vulcanising
Vulkanisierpresse (f	vulcanizing press
Wärme (f, Wärmeenergie (f	heat, termal energy
Wärme-Ausbiegung (f	bending due to heat
Wärme-Speichervermögen (n	heat storage capacity
Wärmeaufnahme (f	heat absorption
Wärmeaustausch (m	heat exchange, - exchanging
Wärmeleitfähigkeit (f	thermal conductivity
Wärmeleitzahl (f	thermal conduction
Wärmeschutz (m	heat shield
Wärmeschutzplatte (f	thermal insulation board
Wärmespeicher (m	heat accumulator
Wärmespeicherung (f	heat accumulation
Wärmesperre (f	thermal barrier
Wärmestrahlung (f	heat radiation
Wärmestrom (m	heat flow, heat current
Wärmestromdichte (f	density of heat flow
Walzenbeschichter (m	roll coater
Walzeneinstellung (f	roll adjustment
Walzenglasierung (f	roll glazing
Walzenkalander (m	bowl calender, roll -
Walzenkörper (m	body of the roll, roller body
Walzenmischer (m	roll, mill
Walzenrakelmaschine (f	knife-over-roll coater
Walzenvorspannung (f	roll preloading adjustment
Walzenwölbung (f	arching of a cylinder
Walzenzapfen (m	roll neck
Wanderrost (m	travelling grate
Wandmontage (f	wall mounting
Wandsteckdose (f	wall socket
Wanne (f)	pan, flat tank
Warmschweissen (n	heat sealing
Waschkammer (f, Waschtank (m	washing tank, purifying -
wasserabstossend Imprägnieren (n	shower proofing
Wasserabstossendmachen (n	water-repellent finishing
Wasserbeständigkeit (f	water fastness, fastness to -
wasserfest, wasserdicht	waterproof, watertight
Wasserkanal (m	water channel, - line
Wassermantel (m	water jacket
Wasserreservoir (n, Wassertank (m	water reservoir, water tank

Wasserrohrkessel (m	water tube boiler
Wasserstandsanzeiger (m	water ga(u)ge, - level indicat
Wasserumlauf-Einrichtung (f	water circulator
Wechselfeld (n	alternating field
Wechselfluss (m	alternating flux
Wechselsteuerung (f	alternating control, dual -
Wechselstrom (m	AC, alternating current
Wechselstrom (m	alternating current
Wechselstrombrücke (f	alternating-current bridge
Wechselstromkreis (m	alternating-current circuit
Wechselstrommotor (m	alternating current motor
Wechselventil (n	two-way valve
Wechselwirkungszeit (f	interaction time
Weichenmechanismus (m	switch machine, point mechanism
Weichenmotor (m	point motor, switch motor
weitwinklige Ablenkung (f	wide-angle deflection
Wellboden (m	ripple tray
Wellendurchmesser (m	shaft diameter
Wellenlänge (f	wavelength
Wellenmechanik (f	wave mechanics
Wellplatte (f	corrugated sheet, - panel
Wendepol (m	commutating pole
Wendeschaufeln (pl	turning blades
Wendestange (f	angle bar, turning bar
Werkzeugkiste (f	tool box, equipment box
Werkzeugmaschine (f	machine tool
Wheatstonesche Brücke (f	Wheatstone bridge
Wickeln (n	winding operation
Wickeltrommel (f	winding drum
Wickelwinkel (m	winding angle, helix angle
Wickler (m	winder, winding device
Wicklung (f	wind, winding
Wicklung (f	coiling, winding
Wicklungsdicke (f	thickness of winding
Wicklungsquerschnitt (m	coil cross section
Widerstand (m	resistance
Widerstandsbeiwert (m	coefficient of resistance
Widerstandselement (n	resistor element
Widerstandsheizung (f	resistance heating
Widerstandsmoment (n	section modulus
Widerstandsschweissen (n	resistance welding
Wiedereinschaltzeit (f	reclosing time
wiederholte Erstarrung (f	repeated solidification
Wiederverwendung (f	recycling
Wiederzündspannung (f	reignition voltage, restriking
Windungsabstand (m	spacing of coils
Windungslänge (f	length of winding
Windungszahl (f	numbre of turns

Windverstrebung(f	wind bracing
Winkel(m, Kniestück(n	elbow, knee
Winkelpresse(f	angle press
Winkelstütze(f	angle support
Wirbelströme(pl	Eddy currents
Wirkleistung(f	active power
wirkliches Eisenvolumen(n	real iron volume
wirksame Oberfläche(f	active area
wirksame Schneckenlänge(f	effective length of a screw
wirksamer Querschnitt(m	useful area
Wirkstrom(m	active current, actual –
Wirkungsgrad(m	efficiency
Wirkungsgrad(m	efficiency
Wirkungslinie(f	line of application
Würfelmischer(m	cube mixer
Würfelschneider(m	dicer, cube dicer, cutter
Y-Verzweigung(f, Hosenrohr(n	Y-branch
Zähler(m	counter
Zählergehäuse(n	meter case
Zählerprüfung(f	inspection of a meter
Zählertotzeit(f	counter dead time
Zählerverzögerung(f	counter tome-lag
Zählgeschwindigkeit(f	counting rate
Zähnezahlsumme(f	total number of teeth
Zahl(f der Lagen	number of layers
Zahnberechnung(f	tooth calculation
Zahnbreite(f	with of tooth
Zahndicke(f	root width of tooth
Zahnhöhe(f	depth of teeth
Zahnkranzstärke(f	tooth wheel rim
Zahnlücke(f	tooth spacing
Zahnrad(n	gear wheel
Zeichenleser(m	character reader
Zeiger(m	pointer
Zeigerbild(n, Vektordiagramm(n	vector diagram
Zeigerinstrument(n	pointer instrument
Zeit-Diskriminator(m (Einkanal-)	time selector
Zeitauslösung(f	time-limit release
Zeitbasis(f	timebase
Zeitgrenze(f, Grenzzeit(f	time limit
Zeitkonstante(f	time constant
Zeitperiode(f	periodic time
Zeitzähler(m	hour meter
Zentrierungsregler(m	centering control
Zentrifugalkompressor(m	centrifugal compressor
Zentrifugalventilator(m	centrifugal fan
Zerkleinerung(f	size reduction
Zerkleinerungsmaschine(f	shredder

Zerstäuber(m	atomizer
Zerstäubungsfärben(n	spray dyeing
Zickzackdrahtseil(n	zig-zag supporting wire
Zickzackkopplung(f	zig-zag-line coupler
Ziehknopf(m, Zuggriff(m	pulling knob
Ziffernmaske(f	figure mask, cipher mask
Zinkoxyd(n	zinc oxide
Zinnschicht(f	tinplating
Zündanode(f, Anlassanode(f	starting anode
Zündelektrode(f, Starter(m	starter (electrode), igniter el
Zündintervall(n	ignitor firing time
Zündkerze(f	ignition plug, sparking plug
Zündmagnet(m	ignition magneto
Zündspannung(f	sparking potential, glow –
Zündstift(m	ignitor rod
Zündstrom(m	starting current, striking –
Zufuhröffnung(f	inlet opening
Zufuhrtrommel(f	pay-off drum
Zugfestigkeit(f	ultimate stress, tensile stress
Zugkraft(f	tractive effort, – force
Zugspannung(f	tensile stress
zulässige Spannung(f	permissible stress
zulässige Verdrehspannung(f	permissible torsion stress
Zumesszone(f	metering zone
zusätzliche Induktion(f	incremental induction
zusammengesetzte Kennlinie(f	composite characteristic
zusammengesetzte Spannungen(pl	composite stresses
Zusammenschalten(n	electrical interconnecting
Zustandsgleichung(f	equation of state
Zustandsgrösse(f	variable of state
Zustandsveränderung(f	change of state
Zustellung(f	infeed
Zwangsumlauf(m	forced circulation, – flow
zweiadriges Kabel(n	twin cable
zweiarmiger Kneter(m	two-arm kneader
Zweikomponenten-Klebstoff(m	two-component adhesive
Zweiphasenstrom(m	two-phase current
Zweiphasensystem(n	two-phase system
zweipolig	bipolar
zweipolige Maschine(f	bipolar machine
Zweirichtungskoppler(m	bidirectional coupler
Zweistufencompression(f	two-stage compression
Zweiwalzenmischer(m	two-roll mill
Zweiweg-	two-way
Zwischenschicht(f	intermediate couting, – layer
zyklische Belastung(f	cyclical load
Zylinderzähler(m	cylindrical counter

Einheiten

Einheiten

Deutsch	Einheit	English
Arbeit (f	J, Nm, 1J=1Nm	work
Auflagerkraft (f	N, kN	support force
Auflagerreaktion (f	N, kN	support reaction, bearing reaction.
Auftrieb (m	N, kN	ascending force, lift
Ausflussgeschwindigkeit (f	m/s	outlet velocity
Beschleunigung (f	m/s²	acceleration
Biegemoment (n	Nm, kNm	bending moment
Biegespannung (f	N/mm²	bending stress
Dichte (f	kg/m³	density
Drehmoment (n	Nm, kNm	torque
Druck (m	Pa, bar, mbar	pressure, compression
Druckfestigkeit (f	N/mm²	compressive strength
Druckkraft (f	N, kN	compressive force
Druckspannung (f	N/mm2, MN/m²	compressive stress
dynamische Viskosität (f	mPas, Ns/m²	dynamic viscosity
Elastizitätsmodul (m	N/m²	modulus of elasticity
elektrische Arbeit (f	J, Ws, Nm	electrical work
elektrische Durchflutung (f	A, mA, kA	circulation, magnetic potential
elektrische Feldkonstante (f	F/cm, pF/m, As/(Vm)	absolute permittivity
elektrische Feldstärke (f	V/m, kV/mm, kV/cm	electric field strength
elektrische Flussdichte (f	C/m², As/m²	dielectric displacement
elektrische Kapazität (f	F (Farad), pF, nF	capacitance
elektrische Ladung (f	C (Coulomb)	electric charge
elektrische Leistung (f	W, kW, MW	electrical work
elektrische Leitfähigkeit (f	S/m, Sm/mm², S/cm	conductivity
elektrische Spannung (f	V (Volt)	voltage

elektrischer Leitwert (m	S(Siemens)	conductance
elektrischer Widerstand (m	Ω, kΩ, MΩ	resistance
Elektrizitätsmenge (f	C(Coulomb), mC, As	quantity of electricity
Energie (f	J, Nm, kJ, MJ, Ws	energy
Erddruck (m	N/mm²	earth pressure
Frequenz (f	Hz(Hertz)	frequency
Geschwindigkeit (f	m/s, km/h	speed, velocity
Gewichtskraft (f	N, kN, MN	gravitational force
Induktivität (f	H(Henry), mH	inductance
Kraft (f	N, kN, MN	force
Ladung (f	C(Coulomb), mC, As	quantity of electricity
Länge (f	mm, m, km	length
Längenausdehnung (f	mm/m, m/m, %	linear expansion
Last (f, Belastung (f	N, kN, MN	load
latente Wärme (f	J, kJ	latent heat
magnetische Feldstärke (f	A/m, A/cm, A/mm	magnetic field strength
magnetische Flussdichte (f	T, mT, Vs/m², Wb/m²	magnetic flux density
magnetische Spannung (f	A	magnetic voltage
magnetischer Fluss (m	Wb(Weber)	magnetic flux
magnetischer Leitwert (m	H, mH	magnetic conductance
massebezogene Arbeit (f	J/kg	work per unit mass
massebezogene Wärme (f	J/kg	heat per unit mass
molares Volumen (n	m³/kmol, l/mol	molecular volume
Moment (n	Nm, kNm	moment
Periode (f, Periodendauer (f	s, min, h	period
Permeabilität (f	Wb/(Am), H/m	permeability
Remanenz (f	T, mT, VS/m², Wb/m²	remanence
Scherkraft (f, Querkraft (f	N, mN, kN	shearing force
Scherspannung (f	N/mm², kN/mm²	shear(ing) stress
Schubkraft (f	N, mN, kN	shear(ing) force

Schubspannung (f	$N/mm^2, N/m^2$	shear stress
Spannung (f	$N/mm^2, MN/m^2$	stress
spezifische Wärmekapazität (f	$J/(kgK), kJ/(kgK)$	specific heat
Stoffmenge (f	mol	amount of substance
Stromdichte (f	$A/m^2, A/mm^2$	current density
Stromstärke (f	A, mA, kA	current, intensity of current
Temperatur (f	K, °C	temperature
Temperaturdifferenz (f	K, °C	temperature difference
Trägheitsmoment (n	kgm^2, Ws^3	moment of inertia, second moment
Überdruck (m	bar, mbar	excess pressure
Wärme (f, Wärmemenge (f	J, Ws, kWh	heat, termal energy
Wärmeleitfähigkeit (f	W/mK	thermal conductivity
Wärmestromdichte (f	W/m^2	density of heat flow
Winkel (m	rad, ″, ′, °	angle
Würfel(druck)festigkeit (f	N/mm^2	cube strength
Zugfestigkeit (f	N/mm^2	tensile strength
Zugkraft (f	N, kN, MN	tensile force
Zugspannung (f	N/mm^2	tensile stress
zulässige Spannung (f	N/mm^2	permissible stress
zulässige Verdrehspannung (f	N/mm^2	permissible torsion stress

Unser Verlag gibt **Zweisprachige Fachwörterbücher** heraus. Diese entstanden aus dem Bestreben, die schwierigsten und wichtigsten Fachausdrücke des jeweiligen Fachgebietes in handlichen Taschenbüchern zusammenzufassen. In jedem Band sind beide Sprachen in je einem Abschnitt in übersichtlicher Weise alphabetisch aussortiert und übersetzt. Die Kleinausgaben enthalten etwa 2500–3500 Ausdrücke, und die Grossausgaben wurden zusätzlich noch durch verwandte oder spezifische Gebiete erweitert. Ein grosser Teil des Inhaltes sind Spezialausdrücke, welche man in den meisten Wörterbüchern nicht findet. Die Bücher dienen so dem Wissenschafter, Ingenieur, Studenten und dem Übersetzer von Fachtexten als zweckmässige Ergänzung zu Wörterbüchern der Umgangssprache, in welchen die leichteren Fachausdrücke meistens bereits enthalten sind. Erhältlich sind über 100 verschiedene Bände, d.h. 2–sprachige Kombinationen gemäss folgendem Bandnummern–Schlüssel:

A	= Automobilindustrie *(In Vorbereitung)*	
B	= Bautechnik (Architektur und Ingenieurbauten)	0 = Deutsch
CD	= Computer und Datenverarbeitung	1 = Italienisch
CHE	= Chemische Industrie– und Laborausrüstung	2 = Französisch
CHP	= Chemische Prozesse und Produkte	3 = Englisch
E	= Elektronik und Wellenleiter	4 = Spanisch
ECD	= Elektronik, Wellenleiter, Computer und Datenverarbeitung	5 = Niederländisch
ET	= Elektrotechnik	
G	= Druckindustrie *(In Vorbereitung)*	
H	= Handel und Finanzen	
K	= Kunststofftechnik	
M	= Maschinenbau	
MA	= Maschinen– und Automobilbau	
T	= Textilindustrie *(In Vorbereitung)*	

z.B.Band–Nr. M.0.3 = Maschinenbau,Englisch–Deutsch/Deutsch–Englisch.
Es sind zur Zeit folgende Bände lieferbar:

KLEINAUSGABEN, mit etwa 120 Seiten Inhalt:
B.0.1;B.0.2;B.0.3;B.0.4;B.0.5;B.2.3;B.2.4;B.3.4;CD.0.1;CD.0.2;CD.0.3;CD.0.4;CD.0.5;
CD.1.3;CD.2.3;CD.2.4;CD.3.4;CD.3.5;CHE.0.1;CHE.0.2;CHE.0.3;CHE.0.4;CHE.0.5;
CHE.2.3;CHE.2.4;CHE.3.4;CHE.3.5;CHP.0.1;CHP.0.2;CHP.0.3;CHP.0.4;CHP.0.5;
CHP.1.3;CHP.2.3;CHP.2.4;CHP.3.4;CH.3.5;E.0.1;E.0.2;E.0.3;E.0.4;E.0.5;E.1.3;E.1.5;
E.2.3;E.2.4;E.2.5;E.3.4;E.3.5;E.4.5;ET.0.1;ET.0.2;ET.0.3;ET.0.4;ET.0.5;ET.1.3;ET.1.5;
ET.2.3;ET.2.4;ET.2.5;ET.3.4;ET.3.5;K.0.1;K.0.2;K.0.3;K.0.4;K.0.5;K.1.3;K.2.3;K.2.4;
K.3.4;K.3.5;M.0.1;M.0.2;M.0.3;M.0.4;M.0.5;M.2.3;M.2.4;M.3.4;H.0.1;H.0.2;H.0.3;
H.0.4. Weitere Ausgaben sind in Vorbereitung.

GROSSAUSGABEN, mit 240 bis 310 Seiten Inhalt:
B.0.1;B.0.2;B.0.3;B.0.4;CHE.0.1;CHE.0.2;CHE.0.3;CHE.0.4;ECD.0.1;FCD.0.2;
ECD.0.3;ECD.0.4; ET.0.1;ET.0.2;ET.0.3;ET.0.4;MA.0.1;MA.0.2;MA.0.3;MA.0.4.
Weitere Ausgaben sind in Vorbereitung.

SCHNELLMANN VERLAG, CH–9443 Widnau (Schweiz)

Electric motors, generators, transformers

A

ability to bridge	Überbrückungsfähigkeit(f
acyclic machine	azyklische Maschine(f
adjustable resistor	einstellbarer Widerstand(m
adjustable transformer	Einstelltransformator(m

adjustable-speed motor, variable-speed motor Motor(m mit
    Drehzalregelung
adjustable-variable-speed motor Motor(m mit einstellbarer
    Drehzahlregelung

air-blast transformer	Transformator(m mit Luftstromkühlung
air-cooled transformer	luftgekühlter Transformator(m, Lufttransformator, Trockentransformator
air-gap transformer	Luftspalttransformator(m
alternating current generator	Wechselstrom-Generator(m
alternating current motor	Wechselstrommotor(m
alternating-current bridge	Wechselstrombrücke(f
alternating-current circuit	Wechselstromkreis(m

alternating-current commutator motor
    Wechselstrokommutatormotor(m
alternating-current series motor
    Hauptschlusswechselstrommotor(m

ammeter	Strommesser(m, Amperemeter(r
angular frequency	Kreisfrequenz(f

anti-compound motor, decompounded motor
    Gegencompoundmotor(m, Gegenverbundmotor(m,
    Nichtverbundmotor(m
arc-welding transformer
    Lichtbogen-Schweisstransformator(m

armature current	Ankerstrom(m
armature resistance	Ankerwiderstand(m
armature winding	Kurzschlusswicklung(f

armature-reaction excited machine durch Ankerrückwirkung(
    erregte Maschine(f

asynchronous generator	Asynchrongenerator(m
asynchronous machine	Asynchronmaschine(f

asynchronous motor Asynchronmotor(m
attraction motor, contact type motor, impulse motor
    Kontaktmotor(m, Unterbrechermotor(m
audio-frequency transformer Niederfrequenztransformator(m
auto-compounded current transformer Stromwandler(m mit
    stromproportionaler Zusatzmagnetisierung
automatic change-over switch automatischer Umschalter(m
auxiliary elevator motor, auxiliary lift motor
    Aufzugshilfsmotor(m
auxiliary resistor Hilfswiderstand(m
axle-driven generator Achsdynamo(m
axle-hung motor, nose suspension motor nasenaufgehängter
    Motor(m, Tatzlagermotor(m

B

balanced-unbalanced transformer, balun Symmetriertopf(m,
    Symmetriertransformator(m
balancer transformer Ausgleichtransformator(m
bar-current-transformer Stangenstromwandler(m
bar-type transformer Schienenstromwandler(m,
    Stabwandler(m
base load Grundlast(f
bauch transformer Bauch-Transformator(m
bell transformer Klingeltransformator(m
bipolar machine zweipolige Maschine(f
blocking capacitor Koppelkondensator(m
booster transformer, step-down transformer
    Zusatztransformator(m für Gegenschaltung
booster transformer, step-up transformer
    Zusatztransformator(m für Zuschaltung
boucherot squirrel-cage motor, double squirrel-cage motor
    Doppelkäfigmotor(m
bracket Lagerschild(n
brake dynamo Bremsdynamo(m
braking magnet Bremsmagnet(m
bridge transformer, differential transformer
    Brückenübertrager(m, Differentialtransformator(m
brushless machine bürstenlose Maschine(f
built-in electric motor Einbau-Elektromotor(m
bushing transformer Durchsteckwandler(m
bushing-type current transformer, inlet-current-transformer
    Durchführungsstromwandler(m

A

cab retarder motor, car retarder motor
    Geschwindigkeitsbegrenzungsmotor(m

cable current transformer, slip over current transformer	
	Kabelstromwandler(m
cable drum, extension reel	Kabeltrommel(f
cable joint, splice	Kabelverbindungsstelle(f
cage synchronous motor	Synchronmotor(m mit Dämpferkäfig
cam controller	Nockenfahrschalter(m
capacitor	Kondensator(m
capacitor motor	Kondensatormotor(m
capacitor-start motor	Motor(m mit Anlaufkondensator
carbon electrode	Kohleelektrode(f
change-speed motor, varying-speed motor Motor(m mit Drehzahländerung, Motor(m mit veränderlicher Drehzahl	
charging rectifier	Ladegleichrichter(m
choke coil	Drosselspule(f
circular windings(pl	Kreiswindungen(pl
coil cross section	Wicklungsquerschnitt(m
coiled electrode	aufgespulte Elektrode(f
coiling, winding	Wicklung(f
column-type transformer, core-type transformer	
	Säulentransformator(m, Kerntransformator(m
commutator	Kommutator(m, Stromwender(m
compensated induction motor	kompensierter Induktionsmotor(m
compensated instrument transformer kompensierter Messwandler(m	
compensated motor	kompensierter Motor(m
compensating choke	Ausgleichsdrossel, Saugdrossel(f
compound wound motor	Doppelschlussmotor(m
compound-wound current transformer Stromwandler(m mit Zusatzmagnetisierung	
conductivity	Leitfähigkeit(f
conical rotor machine	Maschine(f mit konischem Läufer
connected load	Anschlusswert(m
constant-current transformer	Konstantstrom-Transformator(m
constant-speed motor	Motor(m mit konstanter Drehzahl
continuous output	Dauerleistung(f
control room	Schaltraum(m
control-circuit transformer	Steuerapparat(m
controlled-speed axle generator Achsgenerator(m mit Geschwindigkeitsregelung	
converter for welding	Umformer(m zum Schweissen
coreless transformer	kernloser Transformator(m
crest factor, peak value	Spitzenwert(m

cross coil	Kreuzspule(f
cross section of wire	Drahtquerschnitt(m
cross-field generator, Rosenberg generator	
Querfeldgenerator(m	
current tranformer	Stromtransformator(m,
Stromwandler(m	
current, intensity of current	Stromstärke(f
cut-out box	Ausschaltkasten(m
cynchronous motor	Synchronmotor(m

D

D.C. welding generator
    Gleichstrom-Schweissgenerator(m
delta-circuit   Dreieckschaltung(f
Déri motor   Déri-Motor(m
diffenrential shunt motor   Reihenschlussmotor(m mit
    Gegennebenschlusserregung
differential current   Differenzstrom(m
direct current   Gleichstrom(m
direct current generator   Gleichstrom-Generator(m
direct current motor, D.C. motor Gleichstrommotor(m
direct current voltage transformer
    Gleichstrom-Spannungswandler(m
direct drive motor   Achsmotor(m
direct starting circuit   direkte Einschaltung(f
direct-current machine   Gleichstrommaschine(f
disconnect position   Ausschaltstellung(f
disruptive voltage   Durchschlagspannung(f
double motor   Doppelmotor(m
double wound synchronous generator
    Zweiwicklungs-Synchrongenerator(m
double-commutator motor   Doppelkollektormotor(m,
    Doppelkommutatormotor(m
double-current generator   Doppelstromgenerator(m
double-feed polyphase shunt commutator motor
    ständergespeister Mehrphasen-Nebenschlussmotor(m,
    statorgespeister - -
double-feeding   Doppelspeisung(f
draining transformer   Saugtransformator(m
drive belt
    Antriebsriemen(m, Treibriemen(m
drum motor   Trommelmotor(m
duct entrance   Kabelrohreingang(m
dynamic characteristic   dynamischde Kennlinie(f
dynamo   Dynamo(n

E

earth clamp, ground clamp	Werkstückklemme(f
earth lead, work lead	Erdkabel(n, Massekabel(n
earthing cable, grounding -	Erdkabel(n
earthing transformer, grounding transformer	geerdeter Transformator(m
effective value	Effektivwert(m
electric circuit	Stromkreis(m
electric clutch	elektrische Kupplung(f
electric field	elektrisches Feld(n
electric heating	elektrische Heizung, Elektro-H.(f
electric motor	Elektromotor(m
electric traction generator	Bahngenerator(m, elektrischer Zuggeneratur(m
electrical characteristics	elektrische Charakteristiken(pl
electrical contact	elektrischer Kontakt(m
electrical interconnecting	Zusammenschalten(n
electrical work	elektrische Arbeit(f
electrically screened transformer	Transformator(m mit elektrischer Abschirmung
electricity generating set	Generator-Anlage(f
elevator motor, hoisting motor, lift motor	Aufzugmotor(m
emergency set	Notstromaggregat(n
emergency stop switch	Notausschalter(m
enclosed-type motor, protected motor	geschlossener Motor(m
engine-driven generator	vom Flugzeumotor angetriebener Generator(m
exciter	Erregermaschine(f
extension line, - cable, - cord	Verlängerungsschnur(f
external diameter	Aussendurchmesser(m
external-pool flywheel generator	Aussenpol-Schwungradgenerator(m
external-rotor motor	Aussenläufermotor(m

F

fan	Lüfter(m, Ventilator(m
fan housing	Lüfterhaube(f
Ferraris motor	Ferraris-Motor(m
field-displacement motor	Feldverdrängungsmotor(m
fixed coil	feste Spule(f
fixed conductor	fester Leiter(m
fixed electric motor	Standmotor(m
flange motor	Flanschmotor(m
flat belt drive	Flachriemenantrieb

flywheel generator	Schwungradgenerator (m
forced-ventilated motor	Motor (m mit Fremdbelüftung, fremdbelüfteter Motor (m
fractional horsepower motor	Kleinmotor (m unterhalb einer Pferdestärke
frame supended motor, suspended motor	Gestellmotor (m, aufgehängter Motor (m
frequency	Frequenz (f
frequency transformer	Frequenztransformator (m
frequency-dependent	frequenzabhängig
frequency-independent	frequenzunabhängig

G

Gear motor	Getriebemotor (m
gearless motor	getriebeloser Motor (m
generator	Generator (m
group, set	Gruppe (f, Satz (m

H

hand rule	Dreifingerregel (f
high frequency	Hochfrequenz (f
high voltage	Hochspannung (f
high-tension transformer, high-voltage transformer	Hochspannungs-Transformator (m
homopolar machine	Homopolarmaschine (f, Gleichpolm.
housing with cooling ribs	Gehäuse (n mit Kühlrippen
hysteresis motor	Hysteresismotor (m

I

ideal transformer	idealer Transformator (m
ignition transformer	Zündtransformator (m
impedance transformer	Impedanzwandler (m
impulse current	Stossstrom (m
impulse generator, surge generator	Impulsgenerator (m, Stossgenerator (m
independent contact	Einzelkreiskontakt (m
indoor transformer	Innenraumtransformator (m
induced voltage	induzierte Spannung (f
inductance	Induktivität (f
induction generator	Induktionsgenerator (m, Asynchrongenerator (m
induction machine	Induktionsmaschine (f
induction motor	Induktionsmotor (m
inductor generator	Induktorgenerator (m
inductor machine	Induktormaschine (f

initial resistance	Anfangswiderstad(m
inner cylinder	innerer Zylinder(m
input transformer	Eingangstransformator(m
instrument lamp	Instrumentenlampe(f
instrument transformer	Messwandler(m
insulator type transformer	Isoliertransformator(m, Topfwandler(m
internal power	innere Leistung(f
interphase transformer	Ausgleichstransformator(m, Saugtransformator(m
isolating transformer	Trenntransformator(m, Isoliertransformator(m

K

kiosk	Verteilerschrank(m
known resistance	bekannter Widerstand(m

L

Latour motor	Latour-Motor(m
law-tension transformer, low-voltage transformer	Niederspannungs-Transformator(m
layer winding	Lagenwicklung(f
leakage transformer	Streutransformator(m
length of winding	Windungslänge(f
level-crossing-gate motor	Schrankenantrieb(m
line current	Leiterstromstärke(f
line transformer	Leitungsübertrager(m
linear induction motor	Wanderfeldmotor(m
load peak	Belastungsspitze(f
loss angle	Verlustwinkel(m
low voltage	niedrige Spannung(f
low-tension regulating transformer	Regeltransformator(m für Niederspannungssteuerung

M

magnetic needle	Magnetnadel(f
magnetic pole	Magnetpol(m
magnetically screened transformer	Transformator(m mit magnetischer Abschirmung(f
magnetism	Magnetismus(m
main contact	Hauptkontakt(m
main exciter	Haupterregermaschine(f
main generator	Hauptgenerator(m
main transformer, scott transformer, teaser transformer	Scottscher Transformator(m

mains transformer	Netztransformator(m
make contact	Arbeitskontakt, Schliesskontakt
master switch	Hauptschalter(m
matching transformer	Anpassungstransformator(m, Anpassungsübertrager(m
mechanical power	mechanische Leistung(f
metadyne generator	Metadyngenerator(m
metal rectifier welding set	Plattenschweissgleichrichter(m
metal wrapped	metallbandumwickelt
mobile motor	fahrbarer Motor(m
mobile transformer	fahrbarer Transformator(m
monocarcase	Eingehäuse-
motor equipment	Antriebsaggregat(n
motor with combined ventilation	Motor(m mit gemischter Belüftung, Motor mit Eigen- und Fremdbelüftung(f
motor with reciprocating movement	Schwingmotor(m
motor with series characteristic	Motor(m mit Reihenschlussverhalten(n
motor with shunt characteristic	Motor(m mit Nebenschlussverhalten(n
mounted generating set	Anbaugenerator(m
multiple connection	Gruppenschaltung(f
multiple current generator	Mehrstromgenerator(m
multiple-speed motor, multispeed motor	Motor(m mit mehreren Drehzahlstufen
mutator motor	Mutatormotor(m
mutator transformer	Mutatortransformator(m

N

neutral conductor	Nullleiter(m
neutral-point transformer	Nullpunkttransformator(m
normal position	Grundstellung(f
number of conductors	Leiterzahl(f
numbre of turns	Windungszahl(f

O

off-time	Pausendauer(f, Leerlaufzeit(f
oil-cooled transformer	ölgekühlter Transformator(m, Öltransformator(m
oil-immersed forced air-cooled transformer	Öltransformator(m mit Druckluftkühlung
oil-immersed forced oil-cooled transformer	Öltransformator(m mit Ölumlaufkühlung

oil-immersed natural cooling transformer, oil-immersed
   self-cooler transformer   Öltransformator(m mit
   Selbstlüftung
oil-immersed water-cooled transformer Transformator(m mit
   Ölumlauf mit äusserer Wasserkühlung
one-way   Einweg-, in 1 Richtung
open circuit voltage   Leerlaufspannung(f
open-air transformer   Freilufttransformator(m
outdoor transformer   Aussentransformator(m,
   Freilufttransformator(m
output transformer   Ausgangstransformator(m
overload switch   Motorschutz-Schalter(m

P

parallel connection   Parallelschaltung(f
peak load   Höchstbelastung(f
peak value   Scheitelwert(m, Höchstwert(m
period   Periode(f, Periodendauer(f
permanent magnet generator   Dauermagnetgenerator(m
phase shift   Phasenverschiebung(f
phase voltage   Strangspannung(f
phase-number transformer
   Phasenzahl-Differenzstromwandler(m
pilot exciter   Hilfserregermaschine(f
plate area   Plattenfläche(f
plug   Stecker(m
plug-in transformer   Stecktransformator(m,
   Steckertransformator(m
point machine with hand crank, point mechanism with hand
   crank   Weichenantrieb(m mit Kurbel
point machine with long lever, point mechanisme with long
   lever   Weichenantrieb(m mit
   Umstellhebel(m
point machine, point mechanism, point motor, switch motor
   Weichenantrieb(m, Weichenmotor(m
polarity   Polung(f
pole reverser   Polumschalter(m, Umpoler(m
pole-type transformer   Masttransformator(m
polyphase commutator motor   Mehrphasen-Kommutatormotor(m
polyphase compound commutator motor
   Mehrphasen-Nebenschlussmotor(m mit Begrenzung der
   Leerlaufdrehzahl
polyphase machine   Mehrphasenmaschine(f
polyphase series commutator motor
   Mehrphasen-Reihenschlussmotor(m
polyphase synchronous generator
   Mehrphasen-Synchronmaschine(f

polyphase transformer	Mehrphasen-Transformator(m
portable battery	transportable Batterie(f
portable generating set	tragbarer Generator,- Erzeuger(m
potential transformer, voltage transformer	
Spannungstransformator(m. Spannungswandler(m	
power feeder	Kraftspeiseleitung(f
power socket	Steckdose(f
power transformer	Leistungstransformator(m
pre-amplifier transformer, driver-transformer	
Vorverstärkertransformator(m	
pressure relay	Druckrelais(n, pneumatisches R.
prime mover	Kraftmaschine(f, Primärmaschine(f
prong-type instrument transformer,	
tongs-current-transformer	Zangenstromwandler(m
protective transformer	Schutztransformator(m, Schutzwandler(m
push-pull transformer	Gegentakttransformator(m
pushbutton	Druckknopf(m

Q

quartz cooled transformer   Quartztransformator(m, quartzgekühlter Transformator(m

R

radio-frequency transformer, R.F. transformer
    Hochfrequenztransformator(m

rail-current-transformer	Schienenstromwandler(m
range	Bereich(m
range of regulation	Einstellbereich(m
rated short circuit current	höchster Kurzschlussstrom(m
reactance transformer	Reaktanztransformator(m
reaction alternating-current	generator mit Wechselstrom erregter Synchron-Generator(m
reaction motor	Reaktionsmotor(m
reactor-start motor	Motor(m mit Anlassdrossel
rectified value	Gleichrichtwert(m
rectifier anode	Gleichrichteranode(f
rectifier transformer	Gleichrichtertransformator(m
rectifier welding set	Schweissgleichrichter(m
regulating transformer	Regeltransformator(m
reluctance	magnetischer Widerstand(m
reluctance generator	Reaktionsgenerator(m
reluctance motor	Reluktanzmotor(m

repulsion motor	Repulsionsmotor(m
repulsion motor with double set of brushes Repulsionsmotor(m mit Doppelbürstensatz	
resistance	Widerstand(m
resistance of conductor	Leiterwiderstand(m
resistance-start motor	Motor(m mit Anlasswiderstand
resistivity	spezifischer Widerstand(m
resonance capacitor transformer kapazitiver Spannungswandler(m	
resonance transformer, tuned transformer Resonanztransformator(m	
reversed polarity, straight - negative Polung(f	
reversible voltage transformer umschaltbarer Spannungstransformator(m	
ring winding, toroidal winding Ringwicklung(f	
ring-type transformer	Ringtransformator(m, Toroidtransformator(m
rotary	rotierend
rotary current generator, triphaser Drehstrom-Erzeuger(m	
rotating machine	rotierende Maschine(f
rotating-field transformer	Drehfeldtransformator(m
rotor(m	Läufer(m, Anker(m

S

safety transformer	Schutztransformator(m
Schrage motor	Schrage-Motor(m
self adjusting	selbstregelnd
self-compensated motor with primary rotor läuferpespeister kompensierter Induktionsmotor(m, rotorgespeister - -	
self-excited alternating-current generator with revolving armature selbsterregender Wechselstromgenerator(m mit umlaufender Kommutatorwicklung	
self-exciting motor	Selbsterregermotor(m
self-regulating arc-welding transformer selbstregelnder Lichtbogenschweissumspanner(m	
self-regulating D.C. welding generator selbstregelnder Gleichstrom-Schweissgenerator(m	
self-starting synchronous motor selbstanlassender Synchronmotor(m	
self-ventilated motor	Motor(m mit Eigenbelüftung, selbstbelüftender Motor(m
sense of rotation	Drehsinn(m
separatly ventilated motor	Motor(m mit Fremdbelüftung
series connection	Serienschaltung(f
series motor	Reihenschlussmotor(m

setting	Einstellwert(m
shaded-pole motor	Motor(m mit Kurzschlusswicklung
shell-type transformator	Manteltransformator(m
shifting transformer	Schubtransformator(m
short circuit current	Kurzschlussstrom(m
short-circuit brake	Kurzschlussbremse(f
short-circuit loss	Kurzschlussverlust(m
shunt dynamo	Nebenschlussgenerator(m
shunt motor	Nebenschlussmotor(m
shunt winding	Nebenschlusswicklung(f
shunt-characteristic polyphase commutator motor with double set of brushes	läufergespeister Mehrphasen-Nebenschluss-Kommutatormotor(m, rotorgespeicherter - - -
shunt-wound motor	Shunt-Motor(m
sigle-phase commutator motor with self-excitation	kompensierter Repulsionsmotor(m
signal machine with disengager, signal mechanism with disengager	Signalantrieb(m mit Kupplung
signal machine, signal mechanisme	Signalantrieb(m
single contact	Einfachkontakt(m
single-phase	Einphasen-, einphasig
single-phase alternat. current m.	Einphasen-Wechselstrommotor(m
single-phase commutator motor	Einphasenkommutatormotor(m,
single-phase commutator motor with series compensating winding	Einphasen-Reihenschlussmotor(m mit Kompensationswicklung
single-phase machine	Einphasenmaschine(f
single-phase series commutator motor with short-circuited compensating winding	Einphasen-Reihenschlussmotor(m mit kurzgeschlossener Kompensationswicklung
single-phase synchronous genrator	Einphasensynchrongenerator(m
single-phase transformer	Einphasentransformator(m
single-winding multispeed motor	Mehrgeschwindigkeitenmotor(m
sliding contact	Gleitkontakt, Schleifkontakt(m
sliding contact	Schleifkontakt(m
slinging wire	Einhängedraht(m
slip-ring motor, wound-rotor induction motor	Schleifringmotor(m
solid pole synchronous motor	Massivpol-Synchronmotor(m

special purpose motor	Sonderzweckmotor(m
speed	Drehzahl(f, Umdrehungsfrequenz(f
split-core transformer	Anlegewandler(m, Zangenwandler(m
squirrel-cage induction motor, squirrel-cage motor	Käfigankermotor(m, Käfigmotor(m
stabilising inductance	Stabilisierungsdrossel(f
star-circuit	Sternschaltung(f
star-delta connection	Stern-Dreieck-Schaltung(f
star-delta starting circuit	Stern-Dreieck-Einschaltung(f
starting motor	Anwurfmotor(m
stator	Stator(m, Ständer(m
stator windings	Ständerwicklung(f
step-by-step motor	Schrittschaltmotor(m
stored energy	gespeicherte Energie(f
straight polarity, reversed -	positive Polung(f
striking voltage	Zündspannung(f
submersible transformer, subway type transformer	wasserdichter Transformator(m
subsynchronous reluctance motor	Subsynchronreaktionsmotor(m
switch	Schalter(m
switch group	Schaltgruppe(f
switch machine, point mechanism	Weichenmechanismus(m
symbol	Schaltbild(n
synchronous generator	Synchrongenerator(m
synchronous induction motor	synchronisierter Induktionsmotor(m
synchronous motor with asynchronous starting	asynchron anlaufender Synchronmotor(m
synchronous speed	Synchrondrehzahl(f

T

tandem motor	Tandemmotor(m, Doppelmotor(m
tapping transformer	Anzapftransformator(m
terminal box	Klemm(en)kasten(m
terminal voltage	Klemmenspannung(f
Tesla transformer	Tesla-Transformator(m
testing transformer	Prüftransformator(m
thawing transformer	Auftautransformator(m
thickness of covering	Umhüllungsdicke(f
thickness of winding	Wicklungsdicke(f
three-phase	Dreiphasen-, dreiphasig
three-phase current	Drehstrom(m
three-phase motor	Drehstrommotor(m
threephase power	Drehstromleistung(f
threephase-transformer	Drehstrom-Transformator(m

time factor, duty cycle	relative Einschaltdauer(f
toroidal coil	Ringspule(f
torque	Drehmoment(n
total resistance	Gesamtwiderstand(m
total resistance	Totalwiderstand(m
totally enclosed motor	geschlossener Motor(m, ungelüfteter Motor(m
track braking	Schienenbremsung(f
traction machine	Antriebsmaschine(f
traction motor	Fahrmotor(m, Triebmotor(m, Schleppmotor(m, Zugmotor(m
transformation	Umwandlung(f, Transformation(f
transformation of elentric energy	Umwandlung(f elektrischer Energie, Transformierung(f − − −
transformer	Transformator(m, Umspanner(m
transformer for regulating in phase	Längsregeltransformator(m
transformer for regulating in quadrature	Querregeltransformator(m
transformer group	Transformatorgruppe(f
transformer with adjustable leakage	Transformator(m mit regelbarer Streuung
transformer with artificial cooling	Transformator(m mit Fremdbelüftung, − − künstlicher Belüftung
transformer with evaporative cooling	Transformator(m mit Verdampfungskühlung
transformer with forced air cooling	Transformator(m mit Luftumlaufkühlung
transformer with forced oil circulation	Transformator(m mit Ölumlaufkühlung
transformer with natural cooling	Transformator(m mit Selbstlüftung
triple motor	Dreifachmotor(m
triple pole	dreipolig
trolley head	Stromabnehmerkopf(m
turbine-type alternating current generator	Turbogenerator(m
twin arc welding set	Zweiphasen-Schweissgerät(n
twin cable	zweiaderiges Kabel(n
two-phase	Zweiphasen-, zweiphasig

U

unipolar generator	Unipolargenerator(m
unit charge	Einheitsladung(f
universal motor	Universalmotor, Lichtstrommotor(m
utilisation factor	relative Belastung(f

V

V-belt drive	Keilriemenantrieb(m
value of welding current	Schweissstromstärke(f
variable losses	veränderliche Verluste(pl
variable transformer	Transformator(m mit regelbarer Übersetzung
variable-speed axle generator	Achsengenerator(m mit veränderlicher Drehzahl
variable-voltage welding source	Schweissgenerator(m mit veränderlicher Spannung
vault type transformer	Gewölbetransformator(m
ventilated commutator riser motor, ventilated riser motor	Motor(m mit durchgelüfteten Fahnen
ventilated motor	belüfteter Motor(m
ventilated totally-enclosed motor	Motor(m mit Mantelkühlung
voltage	Spannung(f
voltage limiter	Spannungsbegrenzer(m
voltage measuring	Spannungsmessung(f
voltage regulator	Spannungsregler(m
voltage relay	Spannungsrelais(n
voltmeter	Spannungsmesser(m, Voltmeter(n

W

wave trap	Sperrkreis(m
weather proof switch	Feuchtraumschalter(m
welding alternator	Wechselstrom-Schweissgenerator(m
welding cable	Schweisskabel(n, -leitung(f
welding current	Schweissstrom(m
welding transformator	Schweisstransformator(m
width of coil	Spulenbreite(f
wind-driven generator	Windgenrator(m
wind-type current transformer	Durchsteckwandler(m ohne Primärleiter
wire core	Drahtkern(m
wire-guide	Drahtführung(f
work head transformer	Anpasstransformator(m
working point	Antriebspunkt(m, Arbeitspunkt(m
working time	Belastungsdauer(f
working values	Antriebswerte(pl
working voltage	Arbeitsspannung(f

**Elektromotoren,
Generatoren,
Transformatoren**

A

Achsdynamo(m	axle-driven generator
Achsengenerator(m mit veränderlicher Drehzahl	variable-speed axle generator
Achsgenerator(m mit Geschwindigkeitsregelung	controlled-speed axle generator
Achsmotor(m	direct drive motor
Anbaugenerator(m	mounted generating set
Anfangswiderstad(m	initial resistance
Ankerstrom(m	armature current
Ankerwiderstand(m	armature resistance
Anlegewandler(m, Zangenwandler(m	split-core transformer
Anpasstransformator(m	work head transformer
Anpassungstransformator(m, Anpassungsübertrager(m	matching transformer
Anschlusswert(m	connected load
Antriebsaggregat(n	motor equipment
Antriebsmaschine(f	traction machine
Antriebspunkt(m, Arbeitspunkt(m	working point
Antriebsriemen(m, Treibriemen(m	drive belt
Antriebswerte(pl	working values
Anwurfmotor(m	starting motor
Anzapftransformator(m	tapping transformer
Arbeitskontakt, Schliesskontakt	make contact
Arbeitsspannung(f	working voltage
asynchron anlaufender Synchronmotor(m	synchronous motor with asynchronous starting
Asynchrongenerator(m	asynchronous generator
Asynchronmaschine(f	asynchronous machine
Asynchronmotor(m	asynchronous motor
aufgespulte Elektrode(f	coiled electrode
Auftautransformator(m	thawing transformer
Aufzugmotor(m	elevator motor, hoisting motor, lift motor
Aufzugshilfsmotor(m	auxiliary elevator motor, auxiliary lift motor
Ausgangstransformator(m	output transformer

Ausgleichsdrossel, Saugdrossel(f	compensating choke
Ausgleichstransformator(m, Saugtransformator(m	interphase transformer
Ausgleichtransformator(m	balancer transformer
Ausschaltkasten(m	cut-out box
Ausschaltstellung(f	disconnect position
Aussendurchmesser(m	external diameter
Aussenläufermotor(m	external-rotor motor
Aussenpol-Schwungradgenerator(m	external-pool flywheel generator
Aussentransformator(m, Freilufttransformator(m	outdoor transformer
automatischer Umschalter(m	automatic change-over switch
azyklische Maschine(f	acyclic machine

B

Bahngenerator(m, elektrischer Zuggeneratur(m	electric traction generator
Bauch-Transformator(m	bauch transformer
bekannter Widerstand(m	known resistance
Belastungsdauer(f	working time
Belastungsspitze(f	load peak
belüfteter Motor(m	ventilated motor
Bereich(m	range
Bremsdynamo(m	brake dynamo
Bremsmagnet(m	braking magnet
Brückenübertrager(m, Differentialtransformator(m	bridge transformer, differential transformer
bürstenlose Maschine(f	brushless machine

D

Dauerleistung(f	continuous output
Dauermagnetgenerator(m	permanent magnet generator
Déri-Motor(m	Déri motor
Differenzstrom(m	differential current
direkte Einschaltung(f	direct starting circuit
Doppelkäfigmotor(m	boucherot squirrel-cage motor, double squirrel-cage motor
Doppelkollektormotor(m, Doppelkommutatormotor(m	double-commutator motor
Doppelmotor(m	double motor
Doppelschlussmotor(m	compound wound motor
Doppelspeisung(f	double-feeding
Doppelstromgenerator(m	double-current generator
Drahtführung(f	wire-guide
Drahtkern(m	wire core
Drahtquerschnitt(m	cross section of wire

Drehfeldtransformator(m	rotating-field transformer
Drehmoment(n	torque
Drehsinn(m	sense of rotation
Drehstrom(m	three-phase current
Drehstrom-Erzeuger(m generator, triphaser	rotary current
Drehstrom-Transformator(m	threephase-transformer
Drehstromleistung(f	threephase power
Drehstrommotor(m	three-phase motor
Drehzahl(f, Umdrehungsfrequenz(f	speed
Dreieckschaltung(f	delta-circuit
Dreifachmotor(m	triple motor
Dreifingerregel(f	hand rule
Dreiphasen-, dreiphasig	three-phase
dreipolig	triple pole
Drosselspule(f	choke coil
Druckknopf(m	pushbutton
Druckrelais(n, pneumatisches R.	pressure relay
durch Ankerrückwirkung(f erregte Maschine(f	armature-reaction excited machine
Durchführungsstromwandler(m	bushing-type current transformer, inlet-current-transformer
Durchschlagspannung(f	disruptive voltage
Durchsteckwandler(m	bushing transformer
Durchsteckwandler(m ohne Primärleiter	wind-type current transformer
dynamischde Kennlinie(f	dynamic characteristic
Dynamo(n	dynamo

E

Effektivwert(m	effective value
Einbau-Elektromotor(m	built-in electric motor
Einfachkontakt(m	single contact
Eingangstransformator(m	input transformer
Eingehäuse-	monocarcase
Einhängedraht(m	slinging wire
Einheitsladung(f	unit charge
Einphasen-, einphasig	single-phase
Einphasen-Reihenschlussmotor(m mit Kompensationswicklung	single-phase commutator motor with series compensating winding
Einphasen-Reihenschlussmotor(m mit kurzgeschlossener Kompensationswicklung	single-phase series commutator motor with short-circuited compensating winding
Einphasen-Wechselstrommotor(m	single-phase alternat. current m.

Einphasenkommutatormotor (m	single-phase commutator motor
Einphasenmaschine (f	single-phase machine
Einphasensynchrongenerator (m	single-phase synchronous genrator
Einphasentransformator (m	single-phase transformer
einstellbarer Widerstand (m	adjustable resistor
Einstellbereich (m	range of regulation
Einstelltransformator (m	adjustable transformer
Einstellwert (m	setting
Einweg-, in 1 Richtung	one-way
Einzelkreiskontakt (m	independent contact
elektrische Arbeit (f	electrical work
elektrische Charakteristiken (pl	electrical characteristics
elektrische Heizung, Elektro-H. (f	electric heating
elektrische Kupplung (f	electric clutch
elektrischer Kontakt (m	electrical contact
elektrisches Feld (n	electric field
Elektromotor (m	electric motor
Erdkabel (n	earthing cable, grounding –
Erdkabel (n, Massekabel (n	earth lead, work lead
Erregermaschine (f	exciter

F

fahrbarer Motor (m	mobile motor
fahrbarer Transformator (m	mobile transformer
Fahrmotor (m, Triebmotor (m, Schleppmotor (m, Zugmotor (m	traction motor
Feldverdrängungsmotor (m	field-displacement motor
Ferraris-Motor (m	Ferraris motor
feste Spule (f	fixed coil
fester Leiter (m	fixed conductor
Feuchtraumschalter (m	weather proof switch
Flachriemenantrieb	flat belt drive
Flanschmotor (m	flange motor
Freilufttransformator (m	open-air transformer
Frequenz (f	frequency
frequenzabhängig	frequency-dependent
Frequenztransformator (m	frequency transformer
frequenzunabhängig	frequency-independent

G

geerdeter Transformator (m	earthing transformer, grounding transformer
Gegencompoundmotor (m, Gegenverbundmotor (m, Nichtverbundmotor (m, decompounded motor	anti-compound motor,

Gegentakttransformator (m	push-pull transformer
Gehäuse (n mit Kühlrippen	housing with cooling ribs
Generator (m	generator
Generator-Anlage (f	electricity generating set
Gesamtwiderstand (m	total resistance
geschlossener Motor (m	enclosed-type motor, protected motor
geschlossener Motor (m, ungelüfteter Motor (m	totally enclosed motor
Geschwindigkeitsbegrenzungsmotor (m	cab retarder motor, car retarder motor
gespeicherte Energie (f	stored energy
Gestellmotor (m, aufgehängter Motor (m	frame supended motor, suspended motor
getriebeloser Motor (m	gearless motor
Getriebemotor (m	Gear motor
Gewölbetransformator (m	vault type transformer
Gleichrichteranode (f	rectifier anode
Gleichrichtertransformator (m	rectifier transformer
Gleichrichtwert (m	rectified value
Gleichstrom (m	direct current
Gleichstrom-Generator (m	direct current generator
Gleichstrom-Schweissgenerator (m	D.C. welding generator
Gleichstrom-Spannungswandler (m	direct current voltage transformer
Gleichstrommaschine (f	direct-current machine
Gleichstrommotor (m	direct current motor, D.C. motor
Gleitkontakt, Schleifkontakt (m	sliding contact
Grundlast (f	base load
Grundstellung (f	normal position
Gruppe (f, Satz (m	group, set
Gruppenschaltung (f	multiple connection

H

Haupterregermaschine (f	main exciter
Hauptgenerator (m	main generator
Hauptkontakt (m	main contact
Hauptschalter (m	master switch
Hauptschlusswechselstrommotor (m	alternating-current series motor
Hilfserregermaschine (f	pilot exciter
Hilfswiderstand (m	auxiliary resistor
Hochfrequenz (f	high frequency
Hochfrequenztransformator (m	radio-frequency transformer, R.F. transformer

Hochspannung(f	high voltage
Hochspannungs-Transformator(m	high-tension transformer, high-voltage transformer
Höchstbelastung(f	peak load
höchster Kurzschlussstrom(m	rated short circuit current
Homopolarmaschine(f, Gleichpolm.	homopolar machine
Hysteresismotor(m	hysteresis motor

I

idealer Transformator(m	ideal transformer
Impedanzwandler(m	impedance transformer
Impulsgenerator(m, Stossgenerator(m	impulse generator, surge generator
Induktionsgenerator(m, Asynchrongenerator(m	induction generator
Induktionsmaschine(f	induction machine
Induktionsmotor(m	induction motor
Induktivität(f	inductance
Induktorgenerator(m	inductor generator
Induktormaschine(f	inductor machine
induzierte Spannung(f	induced voltage
Innenraumtransformator(m	indoor transformer
innere Leistung(f	internal power
innerer Zylinder(m	inner cylinder
Instrumentenlampe(f	instrument lamp
Isoliertransformator(m, Topfwandler(m	insulator type transformer

K

Kabelrohreingang(m	duct entrance
Kabelstromwandler(m	cable current transformer, slip over current transformer
Kabeltrommel(f	cable drum, extension reel
Kabelverbindungsstelle(f	cable joint, splice
Käfigankermotor(m, Käfigmotor(m	squirrel-cage induction motor, squirrel-cage motor
kapazitiver Spannungswandler(m	resonance capacitor transformer
Keilriemenantrieb(m	V-belt drive
kernloser Transformator(m	coreless transformer
Kleinmotor(m unterhalb einer Pferdestärke	fractional horsepower motor
Klemm(en)kasten(m	terminal box
Klemmenspannung(f	terminal voltage
Klingeltransformator(m	bell transformer
Kohleelektrode(f	carbon electrode
Kommutator(m, Stromwender(m	commutator

kompensierter Induktionsmotor(m compensated induction motor
kompensierter Messwandler(m compensated instrument
    transformer
kompensierter Motor(m compensated motor
kompensierter Repulsionsmotor(m sigle-phase commutator
    motor with self-excitation
Kondensator(m capacitor
Kondensatormotor(m capacitor motor
Konstantstrom-Transformator(m constant-current transformer
Kontaktmotor(m, Unterbrechermotor(m attraction motor,
    contact type motor, impulse motor
Koppelkondensator(m blocking capacitor
Kraftmaschine(f, Primärmaschine(f prime mover
Kraftspeiseleitung(f power feeder
Kreisfrequenz(f angular frequency
Kreiswindungen(pl circular windings(pl
Kreuzspule(f cross coil
Kurzschlussbremse(f short-circuit brake
Kurzschlussstrom(m short circuit current
Kurzschlussverlust(m short-circuit loss
Kurzschlusswicklung(f armature winding

L

Ladegleichrichter(m charging rectifier
Längsregeltransformator(m transformer for regulating in
    phase
Läufer(m, Anker(m rotor(m
läufergespeister Mehrphasen-Nebenschluss-Kommutatormotor(m
    rotorgespeicherter - - - shunt-characteristic polyphas
    commutator motor with double set of brushes
läuferpespeister kompensierter Induktionsmotor(m,
    rotorgespeister - - self-compensated motor with
    primary rotor
Lagenwicklung(f layer winding
Lagerschild(n bracket
Latour-Motor(m Latour motor
Leerlaufspannung(f open circuit voltage
Leistungstransformator(m power transformer
Leiterstromstärke(f line current
Leiterwiderstand(m resistance of conductor
Leiterzahl(f number of conductors
Leitfähigkeit(f conductivity
Leitungsübertrager(m line transformer
Lichtbogen-Schweisstransformator(m arc-welding transformer
Lüfter(m, Ventilator(m fan

Lüfterhaube(f	fan housing
luftgekühlter Transformator(m, Lufttransformator, Trockentransformator	air-cooled transformer
Luftspalttransformator(m	air-gap transformer

M

magnetischer Widerstand(m	reluctance
Magnetismus(m	magnetism
Magnetnadel(f	magnetic needle
Magnetpol(m	magnetic pole
Manteltransformator(m	shell-type transformer
Maschine(f mit konischem Läufer	conical rotor machine
Massivpol-Synchronmotor(m	solid pole synchronous motor
Masttransformator(m	pole-type transformer
mechanische Leistung(f	mechanical power
Mehrgeschwindigkeitenmotor(m	single-winding multispeed motor
Mehrphasen-Kommutatormotor(m	polyphase commutator motor
Mehrphasen-Nebenschlussmotor(m mit Begrenzung der Leerlaufdrehzahl	polyphase compound commutator motor
Mehrphasen-Reihenschlussmotor(m	polyphase series commutator motor
Mehrphasen-Synchronmaschine(f	polyphase synchronous generator
Mehrphasen-Transformator(m	polyphase transformer
Mehrphasenmaschine(f	polyphase machine
Mehrstromgenerator(m	multiple current generator
Messwandler(m	instrument transformer
Metadyngenerator(m	metadyne generator
metallbandumwickelt	metal wrapped
mit Wechselstrom erregter Synchron-Generator(m	reaction alternating-current generator
Motor(m mit Anlassdrossel	reactor-start motor
Motor(m mit Anlasswiderstand	resistance-start motor
Motor(m mit Anlaufkondensator	capacitor-start motor
Motor(m mit Drehzahländerung, Motor(m mit veränderlicher Drehzahl	change-speed motor, varying-speed motor
Motor(m mit Drehzalregelung	adjustable-speed motor, variable-speed motor
Motor(m mit durchgelüfteten Fahnen	ventilated commutator riser motor, ventilated riser motor
Motor(m mit Eigenbelüftung, selbstbelüftender Motor(m	self-ventilated motor
Motor(m mit einstellbarer Drehzahlregelung	adjustable-variable-speed motor

Motor(m mit Fremdbelüftung   separatly ventilated motor
Motor(m mit Fremdbelüftung, fremdbelüfteter Motor(m
    forced-ventilated motor
Motor(m mit gemischter Belüftung, Motor mit Eigen- und
    Fremdbelüftung(f   motor with combined
    ventilation
Motor(m mit konstanter Drehzahl constant-speed motor
Motor(m mit Kurzschlusswicklung shaded-pole motor
Motor(m mit Mantelkühlung   ventilated totally-enclosed
    motor
Motor(m mit mehreren Drehzahlstufen multiple-speed motor,
    multispeed motor
Motor(m mit Nebenschlussverhalten(n motor with shunt
    characteristic
Motor(m mit Reihenschlussverhalten(n motor with series
    characteristic
Motorschutz-Schalter(m   overload switch
Mutatormotor(m   mutator motor
Mutatortransformator(m   mutator transformer

N

nasenaufgehängter Motor(m, Tatzlagermotor(m axle-hung
    motor, nose suspension motor
Nebenschlussgenerator(m   shunt dynamo
Nebenschlussmotor(m   shunt motor
Nebenschlusswicklung(f   shunt winding
negative Polung(f   reversed polarity, straight -
Netztransformator(m   mains transformer
Niederfrequenztransformator(m audio-frequency transformer
Niederspannungs-Transformator(m law-tension transformer,
    low-voltage transformer
niedrige Spannung(f   low voltage
Nockenfahrschalter(m   cam controller
Notausschalter(m   emergency stop switch
Notstromaggregat(n   emergency set
Nullleiter(m   neutral conductor
Nullpunkttransformator(m   neutral-point transformer

O

ölgekühlter Transformator(m, Öltransformator(m oil-cooled
    transformer
Öltransformator(m mit Druckluftkühlung oil-immersed forced
    air-cooled transformer
Öltransformator(m mit Ölumlaufkühlung oil-immersed forced
    oil-cooled transformer

Öltransformator(m mit Selbstlürtung oil-immersed natural cooling transformer, oil-immersed self-cooler transformer

P

Parallelschaltung(f	parallel connection
Pausendauer(f, Leerlaufzeit(f	off-time
Periode(f, Periodendauer(f	period
Phasenverschiebung(f	phase shift
Phasenzahl-Differenzstromwandler(m	phase-number transformer
Plattenfläche(f	plate area
Plattenschweissgleichrichter(m	metal rectifier welding set
Polumschalter(m, Umpoler(m	pole reverser
Polung(f	polarity
positive Polung(f	straight polarity, reversed -
Prüftransformator(m	testing transformer

Q

Quartztransformator(m, quartzgekühlter Transformator(m quartz cooled transformer

Querfeldgenerator(m	cross-field generator, Rosenberg generator
Querregeltransformator(m	transformer for regulating in quadrature

R

Reaktanztransformator(m	reactance transformer
Reaktionsgenerator(m	reluctance generator
Reaktionsmotor(m	reaction motor
Regeltransformator(m	regulating transformer
Regeltransformator(m für Niederspannungssteuerung	low-tension regulating transformer
Reihenschlussmotor(m	series motor
Reihenschlussmotor(m mit Gegennebenschlusserregung	diffenrential shunt motor
relative Belastung(f	utilisation factor
relative Einschaltdauer(f	time factor, duty cycle
Reluktanzmotor(m	reluctance motor
Repulsionsmotor(m	repulsion motor
Repulsionsmotor(m mit Doppelbürstensatz	repulsion motor with double set of brushes
Resonanztransformator(m	resonance transformer, tuned transformer
Ringspule(f	toroidal coil
Ringtransformator(m, Toroidtransformator(m	ring-type transformer

Ringwicklung (f	ring winding, toroidal winding
rotierend	rotary
rotierende Maschine (f	rotating machine

S

Säulentransformator (m, Kerntransformator (m	column-type transformer, core-type transformer
Saugtransformator (m	draining transformer
Schaltbild (n	symbol
Schalter (m	switch
Schaltgruppe (f	switch group
Schaltraum (m	control room
Scheitelwert (m, Höchstwert (m	peak value
Schienenbremsung (f	track braking
Schienenstromwandler (m	rail-current-transformer
Schienenstromwandler (m, Stabwandler (m	bar-type transformer
Schleifkontakt (m	sliding contact
Schleifringmotor (m	slip-ring motor, wound-rotor induction motor
Schrage-Motor (m	Schrage motor
Schrankenantrieb (m	level-crossing-gate motor
Schrittschaltmotor (m	step-by-step motor
Schubtransformator (m	shifting transformer
Schutztransformator (m	safety transformer
Schutztransformator (m, Schutzwandler (m	protective transformer
Schweissgenerator (m mit veränderlicher Spannung	variable-voltage welding source
Schweissgleichrichter (m	rectifier welding set
Schweisskabel (n, -leitung (f	welding cable
Schweissstrom (m	welding current
Schweissstromstärke (f	value of welding current
Schweisstransformator (m	welding transformator
Schwingmotor (m	motor with reciprocating movement
Schwungradgenerator (m	flywheel generator
Scottscher Transformator (m	main transformer, scott transformer, teaser transformer
selbstanlassender Synchronmotor (m	self-starting synchronous motor
selbsterregender Wechselstromgenerator (m mit umlaufender Kommutatorwicklung	self-excited alternating-current generator with revolving armature
Selbsterregermotor (m	self-exciting motor
selbstregelnd	self adjusting
selbstregelnder Gleichstrom-Schweissgenerator (m	self-regulating D.C. welding generator

selbstregelnder Lichtbogenschweissumspanner(m	self-regulating arc-welding transformer
Serienschaltung(f	series connection
Shunt-Motor(m	shunt-wound motor
Signalantrieb(m	signal machine, signal mechanisme
Signalantrieb(m mit Kupplung	signal machine with disengager, signal mechanism with disengager
Sonderzweckmotor(m	special purpose motor
Spannung(f	voltage
Spannungsbegrenzer(m	voltage limiter
Spannungsmesser(m, Voltmeter(n	voltmeter
Spannungsmessung(f	voltage measuring
Spannungsregler(m	voltage regulator
Spannungsrelais(n	voltage relay
Spannungstransformator(m, Spannungswandler(m	potential transformer, voltage transformer
Sperrkreis(m	wave trap
spezifischer Widerstand(m	resistivity
Spitzenwert(m	crest factor, peak value
Spulenbreite(f	width of coil
Stabilisierungsdrossel(f	stabilising inductance
ständergespeister Mehrphasen-Nebenschlussmotor(m, statorgespeister - -	double-feed polyphase shunt commutator motor
Ständerwicklung(f	stator windings
Standmotor(m	fixed electric motor
Stangenstromwandler(m	bar-current-transformer
Stator(m, Ständer(m	stator
Steckdose(f	power socket
Stecker(m	plug
Stecktransformator(m, Steckertransformator(m	plug-in transformer
Stern-Dreieck-Einschaltung(f	star-delta starting circuit
Stern-Dreieck-Schaltung(f	star-delta connection
Sternschaltung(f	star-circuit
Steuerapparat(m	control-circuit transformer
Stossstrom(m	impulse current
Strangspannung(f	phase voltage
Streutransformator(m	leakage transformer
Stromabnehmerkopf(m	trolley head
Stromkreis(m	electric circuit
Strommesser(m, Amperemeter(n	ammeter
Stromstärke(f	current, intensity of current
Stromtransformator(m, Stromwandler(m	current tranformer
Stromwandler(m mit stromproportionaler Zusatzmagnetisierung	auto-compounded current transformer

Stromwandler(m mit Zusatzmagnetisierung compound-wound
   current transformer
Subsynchronreaktionsmotor(m   subsynchronous reluctance
   motor
Symmetriertopf(m, Symmetriertransformator(m
   balanced-unbalanced transformer, balun
Synchrondrehzahl(f   synchronous speed
Synchrongenerator(m   synchronous generator
synchronisierter Induktionsmotor(m synchronous induction
   motor
Synchronmotor(m   cynchronous motor
Synchronmotor(m mit Dämpferkäfig cage synchronous motor

T
Tandemmotor(m, Doppelmotor(m tandem motor
Tesla-Transformator(m   Tesla transformer
Totalwiderstand(m   total resistance
tragbarer Generator, - Erzeuger(m portable generating set
Transformator(m mit elektrischer Abschirmung electrically
   screened transformer
Transformator(m mit Fremdbelüftung, - - künstlicher
   Belüftung   transformer with artificial
   cooling
Transformator(m mit Luftstromkühlung air-blast transformer
Transformator(m mit Luftumlaufkühlung transformer with
   forced air cooling
Transformator(m mit magnetischer Abschirmung(f magnetically
   screened transformer
Transformator(m mit Ölumlauf mit äusserer Wasserkühlung
   oil-immersed water-cooled transformer
Transformator(m mit Ölumlaufkühlung transformer with forced
   oil circulation
Transformator(m mit regelbarer Streuung transformer with
   adjustable leakage
Transformator(m mit regelbarer Übersetzung variable
   transformer
Transformator(m mit Selbstlüftung transformer with natural
   cooling
Transformator(m mit Verdampfungskühlung transformer with
   evaporative cooling
Transformator(m, Umspanner(m transformer
Transformatorgruppe(f   transformer group
transportable Batterie(f   portable battery
Trenntransformator(m, Isoliertransformator(m isolating
   transformer

Trommelmotor(m	drum motor
Turbogenerator(m current generator	turbine-type alternating

U

Überbrückungsfähigkeit(f	ability to bridge
Umformer(m zum Schweissen	converter for welding
Umhüllungsdicke(f	thickness of covering
umschaltbarer Spannungstransformator(m	reversible voltage transformer
Umwandlung(f elektrischer Energie, Transformierung(f	transformation of elentric energy
Umwandlung(f, Transformation(f	transformation
Unipolargenerator(m	unipolar generator
Universalmotor, Lichtstrommotor(m	universal motor

V

veränderliche Verluste(pl	variable losses
Verlängerungsschnur(f	extension line, - cable, - cord
Verlustwinkel(m	loss angle
Verteilerschrank(m	kiosk
vom Flugzeumotor angetriebener Generator(m	engine-driven generator
Vorverstärkertransformator(m	pre-amplifier transformer, driver-transformer

W

Wanderfeldmotor(m	linear induction motor
wasserdichter Transformator(m	submersible transformer, subway type transformer
Wechselstrokommutatormotor(m	alternating-current commutator motor
Wechselstrom-Generator(m	alternating current generator
Wechselstrom-Schweissgenerator(m	welding alternator
Wechselstrombrücke(f	alternating-current bridge
Wechselstromkreis(m	alternating-current circuit
Wechselstrommotor(m	alternating current motor
Weichenantrieb(m mit Kurbel	point machine with hand crank, point mechanism with hand crank
Weichenantrieb(m mit Umstellhebel(m	point machine with long lever, point mechanisme with long lever
Weichenantrieb(m, Weichenmotor(m	point machine, point mechanism, point motor, switch motor
Weichenmechanismus(m	switch machine, point mechanism
Werkstückklemme(f	earth clamp, ground clamp

Wicklung(f	coiling, winding
Wicklungsdicke(f	thickness of winding
Wicklungsquerschnitt(m	coil cross section
Widerstand(m	resistance
Windgenrator(m	wind-driven generator
Windungslänge(f	length of winding
Windungszahl(f	numbre of turns

Z

Zangenstromwandler(m   prong-type instrument
    transformer, tongs-current-transformer
Zündspannung(f   striking voltage
Zündtransformator(m   ignition transformer
Zusammenschalten(n   electrical interconnecting
Zusatztransformator(m für Gegenschaltung booster
    transformer, step-down transformer
Zusatztransformator(m für Zuschaltung booster transformer,
    step-up transformer
zweiadriges Kabel(n   twin cable
Zweiphasen-, zweiphasig   two-phase
Zweiphasen-Schweissgerät(n   twin arc welding set
zweipolige Maschine(f   bipolar machine
Zweiwicklungs-Synchrongenerator(m double wound synchronous
    generator

**conventional and
alternative energy**

A

above ground	oberirdisch
absolute peak	Jahresspitze(f
absorber plate	Absorberplatte(f
acid liquid separator	Schwelwasserabscheider(m
addition of organic matter	Einwurf(m organischer Stoffe
aerial	Luft-
aerial cable	Luftkabel(n
air collector	Luftkollektor(m
air mattress collector	Luftmatratzenkollektor(m
air stream	Luftstrom(m
air/air HPI	Luft/Luft-WPA
air/water HPI	Luft/wasser-WPA
alcohol engine	Alkoholmotor(m
alternative energy	alternative Energie(f
amount of substance	Stoffmenge(f

anaerobic bio-degrading of organic matter anaerobe
    Zerlegung(f, Abbau(m organischer Stoffe

anchor support	Abspannmast(m
anemometer	Windmesser(m
angle of protection	Schutzwinkel(m
angle support	Winkelstütze(f

annual average temperatur
    Jahresdurchschnitts-Temperatur(f

armour	Panzerung(f, Bewehrung(f
armoured cable	Panzerkabel(n, armiertes Kabel(n
automatic adjustment	automatische Verstellung(f

B

base load	Niedriglast(f, Grundlast(f
base load	Grundlast(f
bending due to heat	Wärme-Ausbiegung(f
bio matter, bio mass	Biomasse(f
bio-alcohol	Bioalkohol(m
bio-energy	Bioenergie(f
bio-gas plant	Biogasanlage(f

bio-gas-alternating tank system
    Biogas-Wechselbehälter-System(n

biogas	Biogas(n
biogas prodution	Biogaserzeugung(f
biogas supply	Biogaszuleitung(f
biological	biologisch
bland energy	sanfte Energie(f
box collector	Kastenkollektor(m
bracket	Ausleger(m
braiding	Umflechtung(f, Umspinnung(f
brake vane	Bremsflügel(m
branch	Abzweigleitung(f
brown coal, lignite	Braunkohle(f
butt joint	Stossfuge(f, Stossnaht(f

C

cable	Kabel(n
cable terminal joint	Endverschluss(m(m
carbon	Kohlenstoff(m
carbon dioxide	Kohlendioxyd(n
cell	Schaltzelle(f
centigrade scale	Celsius-Skala(f
central pump	Zentralpumpe(f mit Verteiler
cetane number	Cetanzahl(f
circulation collector-accumulator	
Kollektor-Speicherkreislauf(m	
classical system	klassisches System(n
clear plastic sheat	glasklare Lichtplatte(f
cloud point	Trübungspunkt(m
coal	Kohle(f
coefficient of expansion	Ausdehnungskoeffizient(m
coincidence factor	Gleichzeitigkeitsfaktor(m
cold water	Kaltwasser(n
cold water inlet	Kaltwasserzuleitung(f
colector	Sammler(m
collecting strip	Sammelschiene(f
collecting tunnel	Sammelkanal(m
collector	Kollektor(m
collector control	Kollektorsteuerung(f
combustion power	Verbrennungskraft(f
compact construction	Kompaktbauweise(f
compressed gas cylinder store	Druckflaschen-Lager(n
compressing of biogas	Verdichten(n von Biogas
compressor	Kompressor(m
conductor	Leiter(m
conductor (of a cable)	Leiterdraht(m
conductor joint	Seilverbinder(m
connecting (sub)station	
Kuppelstation(f, Kuppelstelle(f	

consumption	Verbrauch(m
contact strip	Kontaktfinger(m
control cable	Hilfskabel(n
control room	Kommandoraum(m, Schaltwarte(f
control valve	Steuerventil(n
conventional energy	konventionelle Energie(f
conversion of gas into electricity + heat	Umwandlung(f von Gas in Strom + Wärem
conversion of solar energy to hot air	Umwandlung(f von Sonnenenergie in Warmluft
cooling water	Kühlwasser(n
corrosion resistant	korrosionsbeständig
counter flow	Gegenstrom(m
coupler, coupling	Muffe(f
cropping, crop growing	gewerblicher Anbau(m
cross brace	Traverse(f, Querriegel(m
cross flow	Kreuzstrom(m
crude oil	Rohöl(n
cubic expansion	Raumdehnung(f, räumliche Dehnung
cultivation of energy producing	Anbau(m von Energiepflanzen(pl

D

days of sunshine	Sonnen(schein)tage(pl
demand factor	Verbrauchsfaktor(m
density of heat flow	Wärmestromdichte(f
Diesel fuel	Dieselöl(n
diesel/wood gas producer plant	Diesel/Holzgas-Anlage(f
direct radiation	direkte Einstrahlung(f
direct transformation of solar energy to electricity	direkte Umwandlung(f von Sonnenenergie in Elektrizität
distribution of energy	Stromverteilung, Energie-
distribution pillar, link box	Schaltsäule(f, Verteilkasten(m
distribution substation	Verteileranlage(f, Netzstation(f
distributor	Verteiler(m
disturbance	Störung(f
disulphurating	Entschwefelung(f
dividing box	Kabelendverschluss(m
double circuit line	Doppelleitung(f
double conductor, twin -	Zweierbündel(n
double-panel collector	Zweischeibenkollektor(m
drain pipe	Dränrohr(n
dry matter content	Trockensubstanz(f

E

earth electrode	Erdelektrode(f, Erder(m

earth terminal	Erd(ungs)klemme(f
earthed system	geerdetes Netz(n
earthing cable, grounding	Erdkabel(n
electric line	elektrische Leitung(f
electrical equipment	elektrische Ausrüstung(f
electrical installation	elektrische Anlage(f
electricity generation	Stromerzeugung(f
electricity supply	Stromversorgung(f
electro-solar cell	Elektro-Solarzelle(f
emptying duct	Überlaufrohr(n
equation of state	Zustandsgleichung(f
equipment	Ausrüstung(f
ethano	Äthanol(n, Ethanol(n
ethyl alcohol	Äthylalkohol(m
expansion	Ausdehnung(f
expension valve	Expensionsventil(n
external pressure	Aussendruck(m

F

feed pipe to gas holder	Gasleitung(f zum Gasometer
feed point	Speisepunkt(m
feed syphon	Zulaufsyphon(m
feeder line	Speiseleitung(f
fence absorber, grid collector	Energiezaun(m
fermentation	Gärprozess(m, Faulprozess(m
fermentation chamber	Faulraum(m
fermentation silo	Faulsilo(m
fermentation tank	Gärbehälter(m
fermentation temperature	Gärtemperatur(f
fermented material, residue	ausgefaulte Masse(f
filler, filler funnel	Einfülltrichter(m
fillers of a cabel	Kabelbeilauf(m, Kabelpackung(f
filling point	Füllstation(f
filling pump	Füllpumpe(f
finned heat exchanger	Lamellenaustauscher(m
finned tube	Rippenrohr(n
fittings	Armatur(f
fittings of an insulator	Freileitungs-Armatur(f
floating layer	Schwimmschicht(f
floating valve	Schwimmerventil(n
flow principles	Strömungsprinzip(n
fossil fuels	fossile Treibstoffe(pl
foundation, footing	Fundament(n, Gründung(f
fully impregnated	vollimprägniert

G

gas (extraction) pipe	Gasleitung(f
gas engine	Gasmotor(m
gas holder, crown of the gas holder	Gasglocke(f

gas lock	Gassperre(f
gas oil	Gasöl(n
gas storage	Gasometer(m, Gasbehälter(m
gas yield	Gasausbeute(f
gas-pressure cable	Gasdruckkabel(n
gas-proof	gasdicht
gas-proof silo	gasdichter Faulsilo(m
gas/water heat changer	Wärmetauscher(m Gas/Wasser
gaseous fuels	gasförmige Stoffe(pl
geothermal power station	Erdwärmekraftwerk, geothermisches
geothermic energy	geothermische Energie(f
glass panel	Glasscheibe(f
gravel store	Kiesspeicher(m

H

heat containing substance	Wärmeträgermedium(n
heat direct from the environment	Wärme(f direkt aus der Umluft
heat exchanger	Wärme(aus)tauscher(m
heat flow, heat current	Wärmestrom(m
heat of engine	Motorwärme(f
heat of fusion	Schmelzwärme(f
heat of sublimation	Sublimationswärme(f
heat of vapourisation	Verdampfungswärme(f
heat per unit mass	massebezogene Wärme(f
heat pump	Wärmepumpe(f
heat pump installation, HPI	Wärmepumpanlage(f, WPA
heat recovery and generating set	Wärmekraft-Kupplungsaggregat(n
heat recovery efficiency	Rückwärmezahl(f
heat transfer	Wärmeabstrahlung(f
heat value, calorific -	Heizwert(m
heat, termal energy	Wärme(f, Wärmeenergie(f
heated	beheizt
heating coil	Rohrschlange(f, Rohrspirale(f
heating oil	Heizöl(n
heliostat	Heliostat(m
heliothermic generation of electricity	Stromerzeugung(f durch Sonnenenrgie
hermetically sealed	luftdicht
high-pressure gasometer	Hochdruckspeicher(m, Hochdruckbehälter(m
high-value organic fertilizer	biologisch hochwertiger Dünger(m
hinge clamp	Gelenkklemme(f, Gelenkklemme(f
hollow conductor	Hohlleiter(m, Hohlseil(n
hot air	Warmluft(f, warme Luft(f

hot air collector	Warmluftkollektor(m
hot air generation	Warmlufterzeugung(f
hot water	Warmwasser(n
hot water	Heisswasser(n, heisses Wasser(n
hot water circuit	Heizwasserkreislauf(m
hot water generation	Warmwasser-Erzeugung(f
hot water outlet	Heisswasserauslauf(m
hot water pipe	Warmwasserleitung(f
hot water storage unit	Warmwasserspeicher(m
hours of sunshine	Sonnenstunden(pl
HPI, heat pump installation	WPA, Wärmepumpanlage(f
hydrogen sulphide, hydrosulphuric acid	Schwefelwasserstoffspuren(pl
hydrogen traces	Wasserstoff-Spuren(pl

I

incident radiation	Sonneneinstrahlung(f
inflow from collector	vom Kollektor(m
ingnition quality	Zündwilligkeit(f
injection pump	Einspritzpumpe(f
inlet, feed duct	Zulauf(m
installed capacity	installierte Leistung(f
insulated cable	isoliertes Kabel(n
insulation	Isolierung(f, Isolation(f, Dämmung(f
insulation	Isolation(f
insulation level	Isolationspegel(m
insulation of a cable	Kabelisolierung(f, -isolation(f
interconnection	Netzverbund(m, Netzkupplung(f
internal pressure	Innendruck(m
iron hydroxide	Eisenhydroxid(n
joint box	Kabelmuffe(f

J

jumper	Schlaufe(f, Stromschlaufe(f

K

Kelvin scale	Kelvin-Skala(f
kerosine	Petroleum(n
kiosk	Blechstation(f, Verteilkabine(f
knock-resistance	Klopffestigkeit(f

L

latent heat	latente Wärme(f
lattice tower, pylon	Gittermast(m
lead-in insulator	Durchführungsisolator(m
lee	Windschatten(m

length of a span, span length	Spannweite(f
linear expansion	Längenausdehnung(f
liquefied	verflüssigt
liquid body	flüssiger Körper(m
liquid collector, fluid -	Flüssigkeitskollektor(m
liquid fuels	flüssige Brennstoffe(pl
load	Last(f, Belastung(f
load curve	Belastungskurve(f
loss of heat	Wärmeverlust(m
low-pressure gasometer	Niederdruckspeicher(m, Niederdruckbehälter(m
LPG, liquefied petroleum gas	Flüssiggas(n

M

mass-impregnated insulation	Masseisolation(f, -isolierung(f
mast with access ladder	Mast(m mit Leiter
mean producibility	mittleres Arbeitsvermögen(n
mean production	mittlere Erzeugung(f
medium-pressure gasometer	Mitteldruckspeicher(m, Mitteldruckbehälter(m
meshed network	Maschennetz(n
mesophillic	mesophil
metallic layer	Metallschicht(f
methane	Methan(n
methanisation	Methanisierung(f
methanol from coal	Methanol(m aus Biomasse
methanol, methyl alcohol	Methanol(n, Methylalkohol(m
middle wire	Mittelleiter(m
mineral oil	Mineralöl(n
mixing and filling pump	Mix- und Füllpumpe(f
mobile	ortsveränderlich, mobil, fahrbar
molecular volume	molares Volumen(n
motor oil	Motor(en)öl(n
multi source	multivalent
multicore	mehradrig
multicore cable	mehradriges Kabel(n
multiple conductor, bundle -	Bündelleiter(m

N

natural gas	Erdgas(n
negative silicon (layer)	Silizium(n negativ
network, electrical system	Stromnetz(n, Netz(n
neutral conductor	Nulleiter(m
neutre(m	Nullpunkt(m, Mittelpunkt(m
nitrogen	Stickstoff(m

nuclear energy	Atomenergie(f
nuclear power station	Kernkraftwerk(n, Atomkraftwerk(n
number of vanes, - - blades	Flügelzahl(f

O

octane number, ON	Oktanzahl(f, OZ
odour reduction	Geruchsminderung(f
off-peak periods(pl	Schwachlastzeiten(pl
oil-filled cable	Öl(druck)kabel(n
oil/water heat changer	Wärmetauscher(m Öl/Wasser
open collector	offener Kollektor(m
operating time	Betriebsdauer(f, Laufzeit(f
organic	organisch
organic matter	organisch Stoffe(m
organic matter / ha	Biomasse(f je ha
outdoor equipment	Freiluftanlage(f
outflow	Vorlauf(m
output	abgegebene Leistung(f, Leistung(f
overflow	Überlauf(m
overhead line	Freileitung(f
overload	Überlast(f, Überlastung(f

P

parabolic mirror collector	Parabolspiegel-Kollektor(m
parallel flow	Parallelstrom(m, Gleichstrom(m
parallel tube collector	Parallelrohrkollektor(m
peak load	Belastungsspitze(f, Lastspitze(f
peat	Torf(m
petrol, gasoline	Benzin(n
petroleum	Erdöl(n
photo-voltaic	photovoltaisch
photo-voltaic cell	photovoltaische Zelle(f
photo-voltaic cell	Solarzelle(f zur photovoltaischen Umwandlung
photo-voltaic panel	photovoltaisches Paneel(n
pin insulator	Stützisolator(m
pipe collector	Röhrenkollektor(m
pipe for fermented matter	Leitung(f für ausgefaulte Düngeschlamm-Masse
plant for energy production	Energiepflanze(f, Pflanze(f zur Energieproduktion
plant residues	pflanzliche Abfälle(pl
plastic gas holder	Plastikgasometer(m, Plastikgasbehälter(m, Ballongasometer(m
plastic pipe	Plastikrohr(n
plate collector	Plattenkollektor(m

plate type heat exchanger	Plattenaustauscher(m
platform	Arbeitsbühne(f
pole	Leitungsmast(m
portal structure	Portalmast(m
positive silicon (layer)	Silizium(n positiv
poste de sectionnement	Trennschalter-Station(f
potential peak periods	Spitzenzeiten(pl
pour point	Stockpunkt(m
power requirement	Energiebedarf(m
power station	Elektrizitätswerk(n
power station	Kraftwerk(n
power station using coal	Kohlekraftwerk(n
power station with reservoir	Speicher(wasser)kraftwerk(n
power transformer	Netztransformator(m
pre-impregnated	vorimprägniert
pressure cable	Druckkabel(n
producibility	Arbeitsvermögen(n
producibility	Regelarbeitsvermögen(n
production of energy	Energieerzeugung(f, Energieproduktion(f
protection level	Schutzniveau(n, Schutzpegel(m
protective covering	Schutzhülle(f, Schutzschicht(f
psychrophillic	psychrophil
pump drive gear	Pumpengetriebe(n
putrefaction of organic matter	Ausfaulen(n organischer Stoffe
putrefaction, decay	Ausfaulen(n

R

radial	strahlenförmig, radial
radial circuit	Stichleitung(f
radial network	Strahlennetz(n
radiation heat loss	Wärmeverlust(m durch Abstrahlung
radiator	Heizkörper(m
radiator	Radiator(M
rake angle	Windanstellwinkel(m
rate of decomposition	Umsetz(ungs)geschwindigkeit(f
rated burden	Nennleistung(f
recirculating pump	Umwälzpumpe(f
recycling of heat	Wärmerückgewinnung(f
reflection	Reflexion(f
refrigerant circuit	Kältemittelkreislauf(m
regfrigerant vapour	Kältemitteldampf(m
renewable energy	erneuerbare Energie(f
replaceable energyy	ersetzbare Energie(f
reserve bars	Reserve-Sammelschienen(pl

residence period	Verweilzeit(f
resonant earthed system	gelöschtes Netz, kompensiertes Netz(n
return flow to collector	zurück zum Kollektor(m
returnflow	Rücklauf(m
ring circuit	Ringleitung(f
ringed network	Ringnetz(n
rising main	Steigleitung(f
roof collector	Dachkollektor(m
rotational speed of vanes	Drehzahl(f der Flügel
rotor blads	Windrad(n
rotor, blades	Windflügel(m
routine tests	Stückprüfung(f, Einzelprüfung(f
run-of-river power station	Lauf(wasser)kraftwerk(n

S

sag	Durchhang(m
screened cable	Metallschirmkabel(n, M-Kabel(n
secomd glass pan	zweite Glasscheibe(f
sediment, dung slurry	Sinkschicht(f, Bodenschlamm(m
self-supporting	selbsttragend
separately leaded cable	Mehrbleimantelkabel(n
separating layer, separator layer	Grenzschicht(f
series system of distribution	Konstantstromnetz(n
serpentine collector	Serpentinkollektor(m
service capacity	Nutzleistung(f
service line	Anschlussleitung(f, Abnehmerltg.
shaped conductor	Profildraht(m, Profilleiter(m
sheath of a cable	Kabelmantel(m
silage maize, forage maize	Silomais(m, Grünmais(m
silicon solar cell	Silizium-Solarzelle(f
simple tube foil	einfache Schlauchfolie(f
single circuit collector	Einkreiskollektor(m
single circuit line	Einfachleitung(f, einsystemige Leitung(f
single core cable	einadriges Kabel(n
single source	monovalent
slip clamp	Rutschklemme(f
slurry silo	Güllesilo(n
slurry, manure	Schlamm(m, Dünger(m
small support	Dachständer(m, Ständer(m
soil collector	Erdkollektor(m
soil/air heat pump installation, - - HPI	Erdreich/Luft-Wärmepumpanlage(f, - - WPA
soil/water heat pump installation, - - HPI	Erdreich/Wasser-Wärmepumpanlage(f, - - WPA

solar air collectiong plant	Luftkollektoranlage(f
solar cell	Solarzelle(f
solar control	Solarsteuerung(f
solar cooling	Solarkühlung(f
solar energy	Sonnenenergie(f, Solarenergie(f
solar energy installation	Solarenergieanlage(f
solar engineering, - technology	Solartechnik(f
solar heat	Sonnenwärme(f
solar heat store	Solarspeicher(m
solar heating plant	Sonnenheizungsanlage(f
solar hot water plant	Solar-Warmwasseranlage(f
solar power station	Solarkraftwerk(n
solar power station	Sonnenkraftwerk(n
solar tower	Solarturm(m
solarimeter	Solarimeter(n
soldering lug	Lötfahne(f
soldering lug, negative	Lötfahne(f negativ
soldering lug, positive	Lötfahne(f positiv
solid body	fester Körper(m
solid conductor	massiver Leiter(m
solid fuels	feste Brennstoffe(pl
specific heat	spezifische Wärmekapazität(f
specific volume	spezifisches Volumen(n
splicing sleeve	Verbindungsmuffe(f
stationary	ortsfest
stay	Ankerseil(n
steam power	Dampfkraft(f
stop joint	Sperrmuffe(f
storage	Speicherung(f
storage pit	Sammelbecken(n
storage plant, storage system	Speicheranlage(f, Speichersystem(n
storage tank	Vorratsbehälter(m
storm rigging	Sturmsicherung(f
straight-line support	Tragmast(m
straight-through joint	Durchgangsmuffe(f
strand	Litze(f
stranded conductor	Litzendraht(m, Leiterseil(n
stub (of a tower)	Befestigungsplatte(f
submarine	Unterwasser-
submarine line	Unterwasserkabel(n
substation	Unterwerk(n
sunlight detector	Sonnenscheinmesser(m
sunny side	Sonnenseite(f
sunshine duration	Sonnenscheindauer(f

super grade petrol, - - gasoline	Superkraftstoff(m
supplementary heating	Zusatzheizung(f, Nacherwärmung(f
supply terminals	Hausanschluss(m, Übergabestelle(f
suspension insulator	Tragisolator(m
switch bay	Schaltfeld(n
synchronize and close	Parallelschalten(n
system with the same voltage	Konstantspannungsnetz(n

T

tee joint	Abzweigungsmuffe(f, T-Muffe(f
temperature	Temperatur(f
temperature change	Temperatur-Änderung(f
temperature difference	Temperaturdifferenz(f
tension insulator	Abspannisolator(m
terminal support	Endstütze(f, Endmast(m
terrestrial heat, geothermal energy	Erdwärme(f, geothermische Wärme(f
thermal	thermisch, Thermo-, Wärme-
thermal conduction	Wärmeleitzahl(f
thermal conductivity	Wärmeleitfähigkeit(f
thermal state	thermischer Zustand(m
thermophillic	thermophil
through-flow collector	Durchlaufkollektor(m
through-flow system	Durchflussverfahren(n, Direktflussverfahren(n
tip speed of vanes	Umfangsgeschwindigkeit(f
TOTEM, total energy module	TOTEM, Total-Energie-Modul(m
tower body	Mastschaft(m
tower heigh	Turmhöhe(f
town gas	Stadtgas(n
traction substation	Bahn-Unterwerk(n
transfer bars	Umgehungsschiene, Hilfsschiene(f
transforming station	Transformatorenstation(f
transmission line	Übertragungsleitung(f
transparent film	Film(m, Folie(f
traverse	Querträger(m
trifurcating joint	Verzweigungsmuffe(f
troughing	Kabelkanal(m
tube foil, tube film	Schlauchfolie(f
tube, pipe, duct	Kabelschutzrohr(n
tubular exchanger	Röhrentauscher(m
turntable	Drehkranz(m
twin cable	zweiadriges Kabel(n, Zweileiter-

twin circuit collector	Zweikreis-Kollektor(m
twin source	bivalent
two bladed	Zweiflügel-
two-stage rotor	zweistufiger Rotor(m

U

under-floor heating	Bodenheizung(f
underground	erdverlegt, eingegraben
underground	unterirdisch
underground link box	unterirdischer Verteilerkasten(m
unheated	unbeheizt
upright collector	Fassadenkollektor(m
utilisation factor	Ausnutzungsfaktor(m
utilization	Nutzung(f
utilization period	Ausnutzungsdauer(f

V

vanes adjustment	Flügelverstellung(f
variable of state	Zustandsgrösse(f
veined air bubble film	Luftbläschen-Schlauchfolie(f

W

waste oil	Altöl(n
water circulation	Wasserkreislauf(m
water power, hydraulic -	Wasserkraft(f
water tank	Wassertank(m
water/water heat changer	Wärmetauscher(m Wasser/Wasser
water/water HPI	Wasser/Wasser-WPA
weather vane control	Windfahnensteuerung(f
weathercock	Windfahne(f
wind direction	Windrichtung(f
wind driven pump	Wind(kraft)pumpe(f
wind energy	Windenergie(f
wind generator	Windgenerator(m
wind mill	Windmühle(f
wind motor	Windmotor(m
wind power plant	Windkraftanlage(f
wind pressure	Winddruck(m
wind strength	Windstärke(f
wind turbine	Windturbine(f
wind velocity	Windgeschwindigkeit(f

**konventionelle und
alternative Energie**

A

abgegebene Leistung(f, Leistung(f	output
Absorberplatte(f	absorber plate
Abspannisolator(m	tension insulator
Abspannmast(m	anchor support
Abzweigleitung(f	branch
Abzweigungsmuffe(f, T-Muffe(f	tee joint
Äthanol(n; Ethanol(n	ethano
Äthylalkohol(m	ethyl alcohol
Alkoholmotor(m	alcohol engine
alternative Energie(f	alternative energy
Altöl(n	waste oil

anaerobe Zerlegung(f, Abbau(m organischer Stoffe anaerobic bio-degrading of organic matter
Anbau(m von Energiepflanzen(pl cultivation of energy producing

Ankerseil(n	stay
Anschlussleitung(f, Abnehmerltg.	service line
Arbeitsbühne(f	platform
Arbeitsvermögen(n	producibility
Armatur(f	fittings
Atomenergie(f	nuclear energy
Ausdehnung(f	expansion
Ausdehnungskoeffizient(m	coefficient of expansion
Ausfaulen(n	putrefaction, decay

Ausfaulen(n organischer Stoffe putrefaction of organic matter

ausgefaulte Masse(f	fermented material, residue
Ausleger(m	bracket
Ausnutzungsdauer(f	utilization period
Ausnutzungsfaktor(m	utilisation factor
Ausrüstung(f	equipment
Aussendruck(m	external pressure
automatische Verstellung(f	automatic adjustment

B

Bahn-Unterwerk(n	traction substation
Befestigungsplatte(f	stub (of a tower)
beheizt	heated

Belastungskurve(f	load curve
Belastungsspitze(f, Lastspitze(f	peak load
Benzin(n	petrol, gasoline
Betriebsdauer(f, Laufzeit(f	operating time
Bioalkohol(m	bio-alcohol
Bioenergie(f	bio-energy
Biogas(n	biogas
Biogas-Wechselbehälter-System(n	bio-gas-alternating tank system
Biogasanlage(f	bio-gas plant
Biogaserzeugung(f	biogas production
Biogaszuleitung(f	biogas supply
biologisch	biological
biologisch hochwertiger Dünger(m	high-value organic fertilizer
Biomasse(f	bio matter, bio mass
Biomasse(f je ha	organic matter / ha
bivalent	twin source
Blechstation(f, Verteilkabine(f	kiosk
Bodenheizung(f	under-floor heating
Braunkohle(f	brown coal, lignite
Bremsflügel(m	brake vane
Bündelleiter(m	multiple conductor, bundle -

C

Celsius-Skala(f	centigrade scale
Cetanzahl(f	cetane number

D

Dachkollektor(m	roof collector
Dachständer(m, Ständer(m	small support
Dampfkraft(f	steam power
Diesel/Holzgas-Anlage(f	diesel/wood gas producer plant
Dieselöl(n	Diesel fuel
direkte Einstrahlung(f	direct radiation
direkte Umwandlung(f von Sonnenenergie in Elektrizität	direct transformation of solar energy to electricity
Doppelleitung(f	double circuit line
Dränrohr(n	drain pipe
Drehkranz(m	turntable
Drehzahl(f der Flügel	rotational speed of vanes
Druckflaschen-Lager(n	compressed gas cylinder store
Druckkabel(n	pressure cable
Durchflussverfahren(n, Direktflussverfahren(n	through-flow system
Durchführungsisolator(m	lead-in insulator
Durchgangsmuffe(f	straight-through joint
Durchhang(m	sag

Durchlaufkollektor(m	through-flow collector

E

einadriges Kabel(n	single core cable
einfache Schlauchfolie(f	simple tube foil
Einfachleitung(f, einsystemige L.	single circuit line
Einfülltrichter(m	filler, filler funnel
Einkreiskollektor(m	single circuit collector
Einspritzpumpe(f	injection pump
Einwurf(m organischer Stoffe	addition of organic matter
Eisenhydroxid(n	iron hydroxide
elektrische Anlage(f	electrical installation
elektrische Ausrüstung(f	electrical equipment
elektrische Leitung(f	electric line
Elektrizitätswerk(n	power station
Elektro-Solarzelle(f	electro-solar cell
Endstütze(f, Endmast(m	terminal support
Endverschluss(m(m	cable terminal joint
Energiebedarf(m	power requirement
Energieerzeugung(f, Energieproduktion(f	production of energy
Energiepflanze(f, Pflanze(f zur Energieproduktion	plant for energy production
Energiezaun(m	fence absorber, grid collector
Entschwefelung(f	disulphurating
Erd(ungs)klemme(f	earth terminal
Erdelektrode(f, Erder(m	earth electrode
Erdgas(n	natural gas
Erdkabel(n	earthing cable, grounding -
Erdkollektor(m	soil collector
Erdöl(n	petroleum
Erdreich/Luft-Wärmepumpanlage(f, - - WPA	soil/air heat pump installation, - - HPI
Erdreich/Wasser-Wärmepumpanlage(f, - - WPA	soil/water heat pump installation, - - HPI
erdverlegt, eingegraben	underground
Erdwärme(f, geothermische Wärme(f	terrestrial heat, geothermal energy
Erdwärmekraftwerk, geothermisches	geothermal power station
erneuerbare Energie(f	renewable energy
ersetzbare Energie(f	replaceable energyy
Expensionsventil(n	expension valve

F

Fassadenkollektor(m	upright collector
Faulraum(m	fermentation chamber
Faulsilo(m	fermentation silo
feste Brennstoffe(pl	solid fuels

fester Körper(m	solid body
Film(m, Folie(f	transparent film
Flügelverstellung(f	vanes adjustment
Flügelzahl(f	number of vanes, - - blades
flüssige Brennstoffe(pl	liquid fuels
flüssiger Körper(m	liquid body
Flüssiggas(n	LPG, liquefied petroleum gas
Flüssigkeitskollektor(m	liquid collector, fluid -
fossile Treibstoffe(pl	fossil fuels
Freileitung(f	overhead line
Freileitungs-Armatur(f	fittings of an insulator
Freiluftanlage(f	outdoor equipment
Füllpumpe(f	filling pump
Füllstation(f	filling point
Fundament(n, Gründung(f	foundation, footing

G

Gärbehälter(m	fermentation tank
Gärprozess(m, Faulprozess(m	fermentation
Gärtemperatur(f	fermentation temperature
Gasausbeute(f	gas yield
gasdicht	gas-proof
gasdichter Faulsilo(m	gas-proof silo
Gasdruckkabel(n	gas-pressure cable
gasförmige Stoffe(pl	gaseous fuels
Gasglocke(f	gas holder, crown of the gas holder
Gasleitung(f	gas (extraction) pipe
Gasleitung(f zum Gasometer	feed pipe to gas holder
Gasmotor(m	gas engine
Gasöl(n	gas oil
Gasometer(m, Gasbehälter(m	gas storage
Gassperre(f	gas lock
geerdetes Netz(n	earthed system
Gegenstrom(m	counter flow
Gelenkklemme(f, Gelenkklemme(f	hinge clamp
gelöschtes Netz, kompensiertes	- resonant earthed system
geothermische Energie(f	geothermic energy
Geruchsminderung(f	odour reduction
gewerblicher Anbau(m	cropping, crop growing
Gittermast(m	lattice tower, pylon
glasklare Lichtplatte(f	clear plastic sheat
Glasscheibe(f	glass panel
Gleichzeitigkeitsfaktor(m	coincidence factor
Grenzschicht(f	separating layer, separator layer
Grundlast(f	base load
Güllesilo(n	slurry silo

H

Hausanschluss(m, Übergabestelle(f	supply terminals
Heisswasser(n, heisses Wasser(n	hot water
Heisswasserauslauf(m	hot water outlet
Heizkörper(m	radiator
Heizöl(n	heating oil
Heizwasserkreislauf(m	hot water circuit
Heizwert(m	heat value, calorific -
Heliostat(m	heliostat
Hilfskabel(n	control cable
Hochdruckspeicher(m, Hochdruckbehälter(m	high-pressure gasometer
Hohlleiter(m, Hohlseil(n	hollow conductor

I

Innendruck(m	internal pressure
installierte Leistung(f	installed capacity
Isolation(f	insulation
Isolationspegel(m	insulation level
isoliertes Kabel(n	insulated cable
Isolierung(f, Isolation(f, Dämmung(f	insulation

J

Jahresdurchschnitts-Temperatur(f	annual average temperatur
Jahresspitze(f	absolute peak

K

Kabel(n	cable
Kabelbeilauf(m, Kabelpackung(f	fillers of a cable
Kabelendverschluss(m	dividing box
Kabelisolierung(f, -isolation(f	insulation of a cable
Kabelkanal(m	troughing
Kabelmantel(m	sheath of a cable
Kabelmuffe(f	joint box
Kabelschutzrohr(n	tube, pipe, duct
Kältemitteldampf(m	regfrigerant vapour
Kältemittelkreislauf(m	refrigerant circuit
Kaltwasser(n	cold water
Kaltwasserzuleitung(f	cold water inlet
Kastenkollektor(m	box collector
Kelvin-Skala(f	Kelvin scale
Kernkraftwerk(n, Atomkraftwerk(n	nuclear power station
Kiesspeicher(m	gravel store
klassisches System(n	classical system
Klopffestigkeit(f	knock-resistance
Kohle(f	coal
Kohlekraftwerk(n	power station using coal
Kohlendioxyd(n	carbon dioxide
Kohlenstoff(m	carbon

Kollektor (m	collector
Kollektor-Speicherkreislauf (m	circulation collector-accumulator
Kollektorsteuerung (f	collector control
Kommandoraum (m, Schaltwarte (f	control room
Kompaktbauweise (f	compact construction
Kompressor (m	compressor
Konstantspannungsnetz (n	system with the same voltage
Konstantstromnetz (n	series system of distribution
Kontaktfinger (m	contact strip
konventionelle Energie (f	conventional energy
korrosionsbeständig	corrosion resistant
Kraftwerk (n	power station
Kreuzstrom (m	cross flow
Kühlwasser (n	cooling water
Kuppelstation (f, Kuppelstelle (f	connecting (sub)station

L

Längenausdehnung (f	linear expansion
Lamellenaustauscher (m	finned heat exchanger
Last (f, Belastung (f	load
latente Wärme (f	latent heat
Lauf(wasser)kraftwerk (n	run-of-river power station
Leiter (m	conductor
Leiterdraht (m	conductor (of a cable)
Leitung (f für ausgefaulte Düngeschlamm-Masse	pipe for fermented matter
Leitungsmast (m	pole
Litze (f	strand
Litzendraht (m, Leiterseil (n	stranded conductor
Lötfahne (f	soldering lug
Lötfahne (f negativ	soldering lug, negative
Lötfahne (f positiv	soldering lug, positive
Luft-	aerial
Luft/Luft-WPA	air/air HPI
Luft/wasser-WPA	air/water HPI
Luftbläschen-Schlauchfolie (f	veined air bubble film
luftdicht	hermetically sealed
Luftkabel (n	aerial cable
Luftkollektor (m	air collector
Luftkollektoranlage (f	solar air collectiong plant
Luftmatratzenkollektor (m	air mattress collector
Luftstrom (m	air stream

M

Maschennetz (n	meshed network
massebezogene Wärme (f	heat per unit mass
Masseisolation (f, -isolierung (f	mass-impregnated insulation
massiver Leiter (m	solid conductor

Mast(m mit Leiter	mast with access ladder
Mastschaft(m	tower body
mehradrig	multicore
mehradriges Kabel(n	multicore cable
Mehrbleimantelkabel(n	separately leaded cable
mesophil	mesophillic
Metallschicht(f	metallic layer
Metallschirmkabel(n, H-Kabel(n	screened cable
Methan(n	methane
Methanisierung(f	methanisation
Methanol(m aus Biomasse	methanol from coal
Methanol(n, Methylalkohol(m	methanol, methyl alcohol
Mineralöl(n	mineral oil
Mitteldruckspeicher(m, Mitteldruckbehälter(m	
medium-pressure gasometer	
Mittelleiter(m	middle wire
mittlere Erzeugung(f	mean production
mittleres Arbeitsvermögen(n	mean producibility
Mix- und Füllpumpe(f	mixing and filling pump
molares Volumen(n	molecular volume
monovalent	single source
Motor(en)öl(n	motor oil
Motorwärme(f	heat of engine
Muffe(f	coupler, coupling
multivalent	multi source

N

Nennleistung(f	rated burden
Netztransformator(m	power transformer
Netzverbund(m, Netzkupplung(f	interconnection
Niederdruckspeicher(m, Niederdruckbehälter(m low-pressure	
gasometer	
Niedriglast(f, Grundlast(f	base load
Nullleiter(m	neutral conductor
Nullpunkt(m, Mittelpunkt(m	neutre(m
Nutzleistung(f	service capacity
Nutzung(f	utilization

O

oberirdisch	above ground
Öl(druck)kabel(n	oil-filled cable
offener Kollektor(m	open collector
Oktanzahl(f, OZ	octane number, ON
organisch	organic
organisch Stoffe(m	organic matter
ortsfest	stationary
ortsveränderlich, mobil, fahrbar	mobile

P

Panzerkabel(n, armiertes Kabel(n	armoured cable
Panzerung(f, Bewehrung(f	armour
Parabolspiegel-Kollektor(m	parabolic mirror collector
Parallelrohrkollektor(m	parallel tube collector
Parallelschalten(n	synchronize and close
Parallelstrom(m, Gleichstrom(m	parallel flow
Petroleum(n	kerosine
pflanzliche Abfälle(pl	plant residues
photovoltaisch	photo-voltaic
photovoltaische Zelle(f	photo-voltaic cell
photovoltaisches Paneel(n	photo-voltaic panel
Plastikgasometer(m, Plastikgasbehälter(m, Ballongasometer(m	
plastic gas holder	
Plastikrohr(n	plastic pipe
Plattenaustauscher(m	plate type heat exchanger
Plattenkollektor(m	plate collector
Portalmast(m	portal structure
Profildraht(m, Profilleiter(m	shaped conductor
psychrophil	psychrophillic
Pumpengetriebe(n	pump drive gear

Q

Querträger(m	traverse

R

Radiator(M	radiator
Raumdehnung(f, räumliche Dehnung	cubic expansion
Reflexion(f	reflection
Regelarbeitsvermögen(n	producibility
Reserve-Sammelschienen(pl	reserve bars
Ringleitung(f	ring circuit
Ringnetz(n	ringed network
Rippenrohr(n	finned tube
Röhrenkollektor(m	pipe collector
Röhrentauscher(m	tubular exchanger
Rohöl(n	crude oil
Rohrschlange(f, Rohrspirale(f	heating coil
Rücklauf(m	returnflow
Rückwärmezahl(f	heat recovery efficiency
Rutschklemme(f	slip clamp

S

Sammelbecken(n	storage pit
Sammelkanal(m	collecting tunnel
Sammelschiene(f	collecting strip
Sammler(m	colector
sanfte Energie(f	bland energy
Schaltfeld(n	switch bay

Schaltsäule(f, Verteilkasten(m	distribution pillar, link box
Schaltzelle(f	cell
Schlamm(m, Dünger(m	slurry, manure
Schlauchfolie(f	tube foil, tube film
Schlaufe(f, Stromschlaufe(f	jumper
Schmelzwärme(f	heat of fusion
Schutzhülle(f, Schutzschicht(f	protective covering
Schutzniveau(n, Schutzpegel(m	protection level
Schutzwinkel(m	angle of protection
Schwachlastzeiten(pl	off-peak periods(pl
Schwefelwasserstoffspuren(pl	hydrogen sulphide, hydrosulphuric acid
Schwelwasserabscheider(m	acid liquid separator
Schwimmerventil(n	floating valve
Schwimmschicht(f	floating layer
Seilverbinder(m	conductor joint
selbsttragend	self-supporting
Serpentinkollektor(m	serpentine collector
Silizium(n negativ	negative silicon (layer)
Silizium(n positiv	positive silicon (layer)
Silizium-Solarzelle(f	silicon solar cell
Silomais(m, Grünmais(m	silage maize, forage maize
Sinkschicht(f, Bodenschlamm(m	sediment, dung slurry
Solar-Warmwasseranlage(f	solar hot water plant
Solarenergieanlage(f	solar energy installation
Solarimeter(n	solarimeter
Solarkraftwerk(n	solar power station
Solarkühlung(f	solar cooling
Solarspeicher(m	solar heat store
Solarsteuerung(f	solar control
Solartechnik(f	solar engineering, - technology
Solarturm(m	solar tower
Solarzelle(f	solar cell
Solarzelle(f zur photovoltaischen Umwandlung	photo-voltaic cell
Sonnen(schein)tage(pl	days of sunshine
Sonneneinstrahlung(f	incident radiation
Sonnenenergie(f, Solarenergie(f	solar energy
Sonnenheizungsanlage(f	solar heating plant
Sonnenkraftwerk(n	solar power station
Sonnenscheindauer(f	sunshine duration
Sonnenscheinmesser(m	sunlight detector
Sonnenseite(f	sunny side
Sonnenstunden(pl	hours of sunshine
Sonnenwärme(f	solar heat
Spannweite(f	length of a span, span length

Speicher(wasser)kraftwerk(n	power station with reservoir
Speicheranlage(f, Speichersystem(n	storage plant, storage system
Speicherung(f	storage
Speiseleitung(f	feeder line
Speisepunkt(m	feed point
Sperrmuffe(f	stop joint
spezifische Wärmekapazität(f	specific heat
spezifisches Volumen(n	specific volume
Spitzenzeiten(pl	potential peak periods
Stadtgas(n	town gas
Steigleitung(f	rising main
Steuerventil(n	control valve
Stichleitung(f	radial circuit
Stickstoff(m	nitrogen
Stockpunkt(m	pour point
Störung(f	disturbance
Stoffmenge(f	amount of substance
Stossfuge(f, Stossnaht(f	butt joint
strahlenförmig, radial	radial
Strahlennetz(n	radial network
Strömungsprinzip(n	flow principles
Stromerzeugung(f	electricity generation
Stromerzeugung(f durch Sonnenenrgie	heliothermic generation of electricity
Stromnetz(n, Netz(n	network, electrical system
Stromversorgung(f	electricity supply
Stromverteilung, Energie-	distribution of energy
Stückprüfung(f, Einzelprüfung(f	routine tests
Stützisolator(m	pin insulator
Sturmsicherung(f	storm rigging
Sublimationswärme(f	heat of sublimation
Superkraftstoff(m	super grade petrol, gasoline

T

Temperatur(f	temperature
Temperatur-Änderung(f	temperature change
Temperaturdifferenz(f	temperature difference
thermisch, Thermo-, Wärme-	thermal
thermischer Zustand(m	thermal state
thermophil	thermophillic
Torf(m	peat
TOTEM, Total-Energie-Modul(m	TOTEM, total energy module
Tragisolator(m	suspension insulator
Tragmast(m	straight-line support
Transformatorenstation(f	transforming station
Traverse(f, Querriegel(m	cross brace

Trennschalter-Station(f	poste de sectionnement
Trockensubstanz(f	dry matter content
Trübungspunkt(m	cloud point
Turmhöhe(f	tower heigh

U

Überlast(f, Überlastung(f	overload
Überlauf(m	overflow
Überlaufrohr(n	emptying duct
Übertragungsleitung(f	transmission line
Umfangsgeschwindigkeit(f	tip speed of vanes
Umflechtung(f, Umspinnung(f	braiding
Umgehungsschiene, Hilfsschiene(f	transfer bars
Umsetz(ungs)geschwindigkeit(f	rate of decomposition
Umwälzpumpe(f	recirculating pump
Umwandlung(f von Gas in Strom + Wärem	conversion of gas into electricity + heat
Umwandlung(f von Sonnenenergie in Warmluft	conversion of solar energy to hot air
unbeheizt	unheated
unterirdisch	underground
unterirdischer Verteilerkasten(m	underground link box
Unterwasser-	submarine
Unterwasserkabel(n	submarine line
Unterwerk(n	substation

V

Verbindungsmuffe(f	splicing sleeve
Verbrauch(m	consumption
Verbrauchsfaktor(m	demand factor
Verbrennungskraft(f	combustion power
Verdampfungswärme(f	heat of vapourisation
Verdichten(n von Biogas	compressing of biogas
verflüssigt	liquefied
Verteiler(m	distributor
Verteileranlage(f, Netzstation(f	distribution substation
Verweilzeit(f	residence period
Verzweigungsmuffe(f	trifurcating joint
vollimprägniert	fully impregnated
vom Kollektor(m	inflow from collector
vorimprägniert	pre-impregnated
Vorlauf(m	outflow
Vorratsbehälter(m	storage tank

W

Wärme(aus)tauscher(m	heat exchanger
Wärme(f direkt aus der Umluft	heat direct from the environment

Wärme(f, Wärmeenergie(f	heat, termal energy
Wärme-Ausbiegung(f	bending due to heat
Wärmeabstrahlung(f	heat transfer
Wärmekraft-Kupplungsaggregat(n	heat recovery and generating set
Wärmeleitfähigkeit(f	thermal conductivity
Wärmeleitzahl(f	thermal conduction
Wärmepumpanlage(f, WPA	heat pump installation, HPI
Wärmepumpe(f	heat pump
Wärmerückgewinnung(f	recycling of heat
Wärmestrom(m	heat flow, heat current
Wärmestromdichte(f	density of heat flow
Wärmetauscher(m Gas/Wasser	gas/water heat changer
Wärmetauscher(m Öl/Wasser	oil/water heat changer
Wärmetauscher(m Wasser/Wasser	water/water heat changer
Wärmeträgermedium(n	heat containing substance
Wärmeverlust(m	loss of heat
Wärmeverlust(m durch Abstrahlung	radiation heat loss
Warmluft(f, warme Luft(f	hot air
Warmlufterzeugung(f	hot air generation
Warmluftkollektor(m	hot air collector
Warmwasser(n	hot water
Warmwasser-Erzeugung(f	hot water generation
Warmwasserleitung(f	hot water pipe
Warmwasserspeicher(m	hot water storage unit
Wasser/Wasser-WPA	water/water HPI
Wasserkraft(f	water power, hydraulic -
Wasserkreislauf(m	water circulation
Wasserstoff-Spuren(pl	hydrogen traces
Wassertank(m	water tank
Wind(kraft)pumpe(f	wind driven pump
Windanstellwinkel(m	rake angle
Winddruck(m	wind pressure
Windenergie(f	wind energy
Windfahne(f	weathercock
Windfahnensteuerung(f	weather vane control
Windflügel(m	rotor, blades
Windgenerator(m	wind generator
Windgeschwindigkeit(f	wind velocity
Windkraftanlage(f	wind power plant
Windmesser(m	anemometer
Windmotor(m	wind motor
Windmühle(f	wind mill
Windrad(n	rotor blads
Windrichtung(f	wind direction
Windschatten(m	lee
Windstärke(f	wind strength

Windturbine(f	wind turbine
Winkelstütze(f	angle support
WPA, Wärmepumpanlage(f	HPI, heat pump installation

Z

Zentralpumpe(f mit Verteiler	central pump
Zündwilligkeit(f	ingnition quality
Zulauf(m	inlet, feed duct
Zulaufsyphon(m	feed syphon
zurück zum Kollektor(m	return flow to collector
Zusatzheizung(f, Nacherwärmung(f	supplementary heating
Zustandsgleichung(f	equation of state
Zustandsgrösse(f	variable of state
zweiaderiges Kabel(n, Zweileiter-	twin cable
Zweierbündel(n	double conductor, twin -
Zweiflügel-	two bladed
Zweikreis-Kollektor(m	twin circuit collector
Zweischeibenkollektor(m	double-panel collector
zweistufiger Rotor(m	two-stage rotor
zweite Glasscheibe(f	secomd glass pan

**Machine parts
and
vehicle parts**

A

accelerator	Beschleunigungsvorrichtung(f
accelerator	Gaspedal(n, Beschleuniger(m
adjustable squabs	verstellbare Lehne(f
adjusting screw	Einstellschraube(f
adjusting screw (Leerlauf-)	Einstellschraube(f
air brake, air pressure brake	Druckluftbremse(f
air duct, ventilation duct	Luftkanal(m
air guide	Luftführung(f, Luftleitfläche(f
air pipe	Luftleitung(f
air trunking	Luftstutzen(m
air-deflectors	Ausstellfenster(n pl
alignment	Spur(f
antenna	Antenne(f
antifogging resistance	Klarsichtwiderstand(m
arc of contact	Überdeckungsgrad(m
arm	Armlehne(f
armature	Anker(m
automatic gearbox	automatische Kupplung(f
automatic gearbox	automatisches Getriebe(n
automatic selection	automatische Schaltung(f
automatic steering	automatische Steuerung(f, automatische Lenkung(f

auxiliary shaft   Vorlegewelle(f

B
balancing   Auswuchten(n
ball bearing   Kugellager(n
ball-type safety clutch   Kugelratschkupplung(f
barring gear, turning gear   Drehvorrichtung(f
battery   Batterie(f
bearing   Lager(n, Lagerpackung(f
bearing clearance   Lagerspiel(n
bearing housing   Lagergehäuse(n
bearing liner   Lagerkörper(m
bearing lining   Lagergleitfläche(f
bearing pedestal   Lagerbock(m
bearing pressure   Lagerdruck(m
bearing shell   Lagerschale(f
belt   Riemen(m
bevel gear   Kegelrad(n
big end bearings   Pleuellager(pl
binding band   Bandage(f
blade   Wischerarm(m
bleeding the brakes   Bremsentlüftung(f
blinking light   Blinklicht(n
bolt   Bolzen(m
boot lid   Kofferraumdeckel(m
boot light   Kofferraumlampe(f
bore   Bohrung(f
box frame   Kastengehäuse(n
bracket   Federbügel(m
brake conduit   Bremsleitung(f
brake cylinder   Bremszylinder(m
brake fluid   Bremsflüssigkeit(f
brake pedal   Bremspedal(n
brake servo, servo brake   Servobremse(f
brakes   Bremsen(pl
braking device   Bremsvorrichtung(f
braking system   Bremssystem(n
bumper   Stossstange(f
bush   Bronzelager(n

C

cam	Nocke(f
camshaft	Nockenwelle(f
cartrige type bearing	Wälzlager(n
central backbone	Mittelrohr(n
centrifugal clutch	Fliehkraftkupplung(f
centrifugal pump	Schleuderpumpe, Zentrifugalpumpe(f
chain variator	Kettenwandler(m
charcoal	Kohle(f
chassis	Fahrwerk(n
choke	Starter(m
chromium plating	Verchromung(f
cigarette lighter	Zigarren-Anzünder(m
circuit cooling, circulating circuit	Kühlkreislauf(m, Kühlerkreislauf(m
closed circuit cooling	geschlossener Kühlkreislauf(m
clutch	Kupplung(f
clutch lining	Kupplungsbelag(m
clutch pedal	Kupplungspedal(n
coil spring	Schraubenfeder(f
coiled spring	gewundene Feder(f
cold water	kaltes Wasser(n
column	Lenksäule(f
connecting body	Anschlussgehäuse(n
connecting rod	Pleuelstange(f
connexions	Briden(pl, Leitungsanschlüsse(pl
control for distance	Sitzverstellung(f
control for lights	Lichtschalter(m
control for tilt of seats	Lehnenverstellung(f
control valve	Steuerventil(n
cooler, cooling apparatus, radiator	Kühler(m
core ducts	Luftschlitze(pl
coupling	Muffe(f
crankcase	Kurbelgehäuse(n
crankshaft	Kurbelwelle(f
cross member	Querträger(m
crown gear	Tellerrad(n
cylinder	Zylinder(m

D

damper	Lenkungsdämpfer(m
dashboard light	Instrumentenbeleuchtung(f
dependent circulating circuit component	abhängige Kühlvorrichtung(f, Eigenkühlung(f
depth of teeth	Zahnhöhe(f
differential casing	Differentialgehäuse(n
differential satellite	Ausgleichsatellit(m
differential spider, cage	Differentialkreuz(n
dipped beams	Abblendlicht(n
disc brake, disk brake	Scheibenbremse(f, Teilscheibenbremse(f
disengagement	Ausrückvorrichtung(f
disk (and wiper) lubricating	Ringschmierung(f, Festringschmierung(f
disk and wiper lubricated bearing	Lager(n mit Festringschmierung
distributor shaft	Antriebswelle(f
dog's movement, crab steering	Hundegang(m
door light	Türleuchte(f
double clutch, two-stage clutch	Zweifachkupplung(f, Doppelkupplung(f
drain plug	Ablassschraube(f (Öl-)
drainage tap	Ablasshahn(m
driven shaft	Abtriebswelle(f
drum brakes	Trommelbremsen(pl
dry plate clutch	Trockenkupplung(f
dumb-bell shaft, spacer shaft	Verbindungswelle(f
Duplex-type	Duplex-System(n
duplicate key	Reserveschlüssel(m
dust seal	Staubdichtung(f

E

end bracket, bearing bracket	Lagerbrücke(f
end plate	Kappenendplatte(f
end shield	Gehäuseschild(m, Lagerschild(m

end-shift frame	verschiebbares Gehäuse(n
end-winding cover	Wickelkopfabdeckung(f
engagement	Einrückvorrichtung(f
engine brake, retarder	Motorbremse(f
epicyclic gearing	Planetengetriebe(n
exhaust pipe	Auspuffrohr(n
exhaust valve	Auslassventil(n
exterior	Aussenteile(pl
external cylinder	äussere Hülse(f
extra tank	Hilfsbehälter(m

F

facia	Armaturenbrett(n
fan	Gebläserad(n
fan	Ventilator(m
fan belt	Keilriemen(m
fan housing	Gebläsegehäuse(n
fan housing	Lüftergehäuse(n
fan shroud	Lüfterkragen(m
field system	Feldsystem(n
fifth gear	fünfter Gang(m
final drive, differential gear	Ausgleichgetriebe(n, Differential(n
first gear	erster Gang(m
fixed drawbar, rigid attachement	feste Kupplung(f, Starrkupplung(f
flexible coupling	Federkupplung(f
flexible coupling	Keilnabengelenk(n
float chamber	Schwimmergehäuse(n
flood lubricated bearing	Lager(n mit Spülölschmierung
flood lubricating	Spülölschmierung(f
flywheel	Schwungrad(n
foot brake	Fussbremse(f
forced lubricating	verstärkte Spülölschmierung(f
four-wheel hydraulic pressure brake	Vierrad-Öldruckbremse(f, hydraulisch
four-wheel steering	Vierradlenkung(f, Allradlenkung(f
fourth gear	vierter Gang(m
friction clutch	Reibungskupplung(f
friction disc free-wheel clutch	Scheiben-Freilaufkupplung(f

friction lining	Belag(m
front axle	Vorderachse(f
front brake	Vorderachsbremse(f
front door	vordere Türe(f
front seat	Vordersitz(m
front sidelights	vordere Parkleuchten(pl
front-wheel steering	Vorderradlenkung(f, Frontlenkung(f
fuel pressure line	Druckleitung(f

G

gas seal	Gasdichtung(f
gear	Getriebe(n
gear lever	Getriebeschalthebel(m
gearbox	Getriebegehäuse(n
gearbox output shaft	Getriebewelle(f
gears	Zahnräder(pl
gearshift	Schaltgabel(f
glass	Scheibe(f, Glas(n
grill tube radiator	Lamellenkühler(m
guide bearing	Führungslager(n

H

hammering out	Richten(n
hand brake	Handbremse(f, Feststellbremse(f
hard top	Hardtop(m
headlamp	Scheinwerfer(m
heating control	Heizungsschalter(m
heating system	Heizungsanlage(f
heating warning light	Heizungskontrollleuchte(f
helicoid sector	Schneckensegment(n
holding pin	Haltebolzen(m
hood	Klappverdeck(n
horn	Hupe(f
horn	Horn(n
hot water	warmes Wasser(n, heisses W.
housing	Gehäuse(n
hub	Nabe(f
hub diameter	Naben-Durchmesser(m

hub length	Nabenlänge(f
hub-cap	Radkappe(f
hydraulic brakes	hydraulische Bremsen(pl
hydraulic drive	hydraulische Betätigung(f
hydraulic steering	hydraulische Lenkung(f
hydrodynamic torque converter	hydrodynamisches Getriebe(n
hydrostatic clutch	hydrostatische Kupplung(f
hydrostatic transmission	hydrostatischer Antrieb(m

I

independent circulating circuit component	unabhängige Kühlvorrichtung(f, Fremdkühlung(f
independent suspension	Einzelradaufhängung(f
insulated bearing housing	isoliertes Lagergehäuse(n
insulated bearing pedestal	isolierter Lagerbock(m
insulating bush	Isolierbuchse(f
integral circulating circuit component	eingebaute Kühlvorrichtung(f
internal cylinder	inneres Rohr(n
internal shoe brake, internal brake	Innenbackenbremse(f, Innenbremse(f
involute-tooth system	Evolventen-Verzahnung(f

J

jack shaft	Zwischenwelle(f
jet	Scheibenwasch-Spritzdüse(f
journal (of a shaft)	Wellen-Gleitersatz(m
journal bearing	Gleitlager(n

K

key	Passfeder(f (Keil)

L

laminated frame	geblechtes Gehäuse(n

laminated glass	Verbundglas(n
lead	Blei(n
leaf	Federblatt(n
leafspring	Blattfeder(f
left door	linke Türe(f
linings	Bremsbeläge(pl
live power take-off shaft	Motorzapfwelle(f
location bearing	Zentrierlager(n
locker lock	Handschuhkastenschloss(n
long member	Längsträger(m
lower swinging arm	unterer Schwingarm(m
lower toggle	unter Nocke(f
lubricating bearing, lubricated bearing	Schmierlager(n

M

main beams	Fernlicht(n
main bearings	Hauptlager(pl
main brake cylinder	Hauptbremszylinder(m
main leaf	Hauptblatt(n
main shaft	Hauptwelle(f
manual selection	Handschaltung(f
mechanical gearbox	mechanisches Getriebe(n
mileage indicator	Kilometerzähler(m
mouldings	Zierleisten(f pl
multi-plate clutch	Lamellenkupplung(f
multi-step transmission	Feinstufengetriebe(n
multiple plate brake, multiple disc brake, multiple disk brake	Vollscheibenbremse(f, Mehrscheibenbremse(f

N

neutral	Leergang(m, Leerlauf(m
nickle plating	Vernickelung(f
number plate	Kennzeichenschild(n
number plate light	Kennzeichenbeleuchtung(f

O

oil filler	Öleinfüllstutzen(m
oil grooves	Schmiernuten(pl
oil pressure gauge	Öldruckanzeiger(m
oil pressure warning light	Öldruck-Kontrollleuchte(f
oil pump	Ölpumpe(f
oil ring lubricated bearing	Ringschmierlager(n
oil seal	Öldichtung(f
oil seal, gasket	Dichtring(m, Dichtung(f
oil tank	Ölbehälter(m
oil thrower	Ölspritzring(m
one-wheel steering	Einradlenkung(f
open circuit cooling	offener Kühlkreislauf(m
outside circle	Kopfkreis(m
outwardly acting pin-type safety clutch	Sternratschkupplung(f

P

pad type bearing	Segment-Gleitlager(n
pads	Beläge(pl der Scheibenbremse
paint	Lack(m
parking brake	Parkierbremse(f
pedestal bearing	Stehlager(n
petrol cap	Benzintankdeckel(m
petrol reserve warning light	Reservetank-Kontrollleuchte(f
pin free-wheel clutch	Stiftfreilauf(m
pins	Lenkbolzen(m pl
pivotted axle, swinging axle	Pendelachse(f
planet bevel pinion	Ausgleichskegelrad(n
planetary	Planetenrad(n
plat clutch, disc clutch, disk clutch	Scheibenkupplung(f
plate	Kupplungsscheibe(f
play of pedal	Kupplungsspiel(n
plug-in type bearing	Schildlager(n
polishing	Polieren(n
polishing paste	Schleifpaste(f
polishing wax	Poliermittel(n
porcelain	Porzellan(n
portal axle, high clearance axle	Portalachse(f

power shift gear transmission	Unter-Last-Schalt-Getriebe(f
power take-off an couplings Kraftanschluss	Zapfwelle(f und
power take-off coupling	Zapfwellenkupplung(f
pressure gauge	Druckmesser(m, Manometer(n
pressure greaser	Druckschmierkopf(m
pressure lubricated bearing	Lager(n mit Druckölschmierung
pressure lubricated bearing	Lager mit Druckölschmierung(f
pressure lubricating	Druckölschmierung(f
protuberance	Stossstangenhorn(n
pulley	Schwungscheibe(f
pulley	Riemenscheibe(f

Q

quill shaft	elastische Hohlwelle(f

R

rack-and-pinion	Zahnstange(f
radio controlled steering Fernsteuerung(f	Fernlenkung(f,
rear axle housing, driving axle housing Hinterachsgehäuse(n	Hinterachsbrücke(f,
rear axle, driving axle	Hinterachse(f
rear brake	Hinterachsbremse(f
rear door	hintere Türe(f
rear mirror	Rückspiegel(m
rear seat	Sitzbank(f hinten, hintere S.
rear sidelights	hintere Parkleuchten(pl
rear window	Heckscheibe(f
reclinable squabs	umlegbare Lehne(f
red tail-light	Bremslicht(m, Stoplicht(n
register nut	Einstellmutter(f
registration pivot	Nachstellbolzen(m
registration pull rod	Nachstellzugstange(f
release spring	Rückzugfeder(f
repair	Reparatur(f
retaining ring	Tragring(m
return spring	Rückholfeder(f
reverse drive adaptation	Rückfahreinrichtung(f

reverse gear	Rückwärtsgang(m
reversing gear, back gear	Wendegetriebe(n
reversing light	Rückfahrscheinwerfer(m
revolution counter	Drehzahlmesser(m
right door	rechte Türe(f
rim	Felge(f
rocker	Kipphebel(m
rod	Kegelradtrieb(m
roller bearing	Rollenlager(n
root angle	Fusswinkel(m
root circle	Fusskreis(m
root width of tooth	Zahndicke(f
rotatable frame	drehbares Gehäuse(n
rotor	Läufer(m, Rotor(m, Laufrad(n
rotor end-winding retaining ring	Läuferkappenring(m
rubber buffer	Gummipuffer(m
rubber elements	Wischblätter(pl
rubber mat	Gummimatte(f

S

safety belt	Sicherheitsgurt(m
safety glass	Sicherheitsglas(n
safety lock	Türsicherungsstift(m
safety pin	Sicherheitsbolzen(m
sealing ring	Dichtring(m
second gear	zweiter Gang(m
segmental rim motor	Blechkettenläufer(m
self-lubricating	selbstschmierend
self-lubricating bearing	selbstschmierendes Lager(n
semi-axle	Achswelle(f
service brake	Betriebsbremse(f
servo-steering	Servolenkung(f
shackle	Federlasche(f
shaft	Welle(f
shaft diameter	Wellendurchmesser(m
shaft estension	Wellenzapfen(m
shrunk-on ring	Schrumpfring(m
simple pin-type safety clutch	Nockenratschkupplung(f
single dry plate	Einscheibentrockenkupplung(f
single wheel brake	Einzelradbremse(f

skeleton frame	Gehäusegestell(n
sleeve bearing	Ringlager(n, ungeteiltes
Ringlager(n	
slip coupling	Schiebemuffe(f
slip joint	Schiebegelenk(n
slot wedge	Nutenkeil(m
spacing of coils	Windungsabstand(m
spherically seated bearing	Lager(n mit kugeligem Sitz
spider	Armstern(m
spiral spring	Spiralfeder(f
split sleeve bearing	geteiltes Ringlager(n
spraying	Lackieren(n
spring loaded bearing	Federkugellager(n
spring retaining collar	Federteller(m
spur gear	Stirnrad(n
standby cooling, emergency cooling	Notkühlung(f
stator	Ständer(m, Stator(m
stator frame	Ständergehäuse(n
steered axle	Lenkachse(f
steering	Steuerung(f
steering cylinder	Lenkzylinder(f
steering, controlling apparatus	Lenkung(f
steering-box	Lenkgehäuse(n
stepless speed variator	stufenloses Getriebe(n, -
Drehzahlregler(m	
stoppering	Spachteln(n
straight seated bearing	Lager(n mit festem Sitz
stub axle	Achsschenkel(m
stub shaft	Flanschwelle(f
sun visor	Sonnenblende(f
suspension	Aufhängung(f
swinging drawbar	Pendelzugstange(f,
Zugpendel(n	
switch	Einstell-Knopf(m
swivel pin	Lenkschenkel(m
synchronized gearbox	Synchrongetriebe(n

T

tapered key	Querkeil-Verbindung(f

telescopic axle	Teleskopachse(f
telescoping power take-off shaft with guard	Gelenkwelle(f mit Schutz
terminal nut	Anschlussmutter(f
third gear	dritter Gang(m
three-way pipe	Dreiwegverschraubung(f
thrust bearing	Drucklager(n
thrust bearing	Axialdrucklager(n
thrust spring	Kupplungsdruckfeder(f
tilting pad bearing	Kippsegment-Gleitlager(n
toe-in	Sturz(m
tooth calculation	Zahnberechnung(f
tooth spacing	Zahnlücke(f
tooth system	Verzahnung(f
tooth wheel rim	Zahnkranzstärke(f
torque shaft	Verdrehwelle(f
total number of teeth	Zähnezahlsumme(f
touching up	Retuschieren(n
track rod	Spurstange(f
track width	Spurbreite(f
track width adjustment	Spurverstellung(f
trafficator	Richtungsanzeiger(m
trailer brake	Anhängerbremse(f
transmission brake	Getriebebremse(f, Getriebewellenbremse(f(f
transmission input shaft	Motorwelle(f, Antriebswelle(f
transmission shaft	Übertragungswelle, Gelenkwelle(f
tread	Lauffläche(f
twin camshaft	doppelt gelagerte Nockenwelle(f

U

universal joint	Kardangelenk(n
unsynchronized gear	nicht synchronisierter Gang(m
uper swinging arm	oberer Schwingarm(m
upper toggle	obere Nocke(f

V
v-belt variator   Keilriemenwandler(m

W
warning light   Kontrollleuchte(f
warning light for sidelights Standlicht-Kontrollleuchte(f
wheel   Rad(n
wick lubricated bearing   Lager(n mit Dochtschmierung
wide-angle drive shaft   Weitwinkelgelenk(n
window handle   Fensterkurbel(f
windscreen   Windschutzscheibe(f
windscreen wiper   Scheibenwischer(m
windscreen wiper switch   Scheibenwischer-Schalter(m
wing   Kotflügel(m
with of tooth   Zahnbreite(r
worm gearing   Schneckengetriebe(n
worm screw   Lenkschnecke(f

Maschinen– und Fahrzeugelemente

A

Abblendlicht(n	dipped beams
abhängige Kühlvorrichtung(f, Eigenkühlung(f	dependent circulating circuit component
Ablasshahn(m	drainage tap
Ablassschraube(f (Öl-)	drain plug
Abtriebswelle(f	driven shaft
Achsschenkel(m	stub axle
Achswelle(f	semi-axle
äussere Hülse(f	external cylinder
Anhängerbremse(f	trailer brake
Anker(m	armature
Anschlussgehäuse(n	connecting body
Anschlussmutter(f	terminal nut
Antenne(f	antenna
Antriebswelle(f	distributor shaft
Armaturenbrett(n	facia
Armlehne(f	arm
Armstern(m	spider
Aufhängung(f	suspension
Ausgleichgetriebe(n, Differential(n	final drive, differential gear
Ausgleichsatellit(m	differential satellite
Ausgleichskegelrad(n	planet bevel pinion
Auslassventil(n	exhaust valve
Auspuffrohr(n	exhaust pipe
Ausrückvorrichtung(f	disengagement

Aussenteile(pl	exterior
Ausstellfenster(n pl	air-deflectors
Auswuchten(n	balancing
automatische Kupplung(f	automatic gearbox
automatische Schaltung(f	automatic selection
automatische Steuerung(f, automatische Lenkung(f	automatic steering
automatisches Getriebe(n	automatic gearbox
Axialdrucklager(n	thrust bearing

B

Bandage(f	binding band
Batterie(f	battery
Beläge(pl.der Scheibenbremse	pads
Belag(m	friction lining
Benzintankdeckel(m	petrol cap
Beschleunigungsvorrichtung(f	accelerator
Betriebsbremse(f	service brake
Blattfeder(f	leafspring
Blechkettenläufer(m	segmental rim motor
Blei(n	lead
Blinklicht(n	blinking light
Bohrung(f	bore
Bolzen(m	bolt
Bremsbeläge(pl	linings
Bremsen(pl	brakes
Bremsentlüftung(f	bleeding the brakes
Bremsflüssigkeit(f	brake fluid
Bremsleitung(f	brake conduit
Bremslicht(m, Stoplicht(n	red tail-light
Bremspedal(n	brake pedal
Bremssystem(n	braking system
Bremsvorrichtung(f	braking device
Bremszylinder(m	brake cylinder
Briden(pl, Leitungsanschlüsse(pl	connexions
Bronzelager(n	bush

D

Dichtring(m	sealing ring
Dichtring(m, Dichtung(f	oil seal, gasket
Differentialgehäuse(n	differential casing

Differentialkreuz(n	differential spider, cage
doppelt gelagerte Nockenwelle(f	twin camshaft
drehbares Gehäuse(n	rotatable frame
Drehvorrichtung(f	barring gear, turning gear
Drehzahlmesser(m	revolution counter
Dreiwegverschraubung(f	three-way pipe
dritter Gang(m	third gear
Drucklager(n	thrust bearing
Druckleitung(f	fuel pressure line
Druckluftbremse(f	air brake, air pressure brake
Druckmesser(m, Manometer(n	pressure gauge
Druckölschmierung(f	pressure lubricating
Druckschmierkopf(m	pressure greaser
Duplex-System(n	Duplex-type

E

eingebaute Kühlvorrichtung(f	integral circulating circuit component
Einradlenkung(f	one-wheel steering
Einrückvorrichtung(f	engagement
Einscheibentrockenkupplung(f	single dry plate
Einstell-Knopf(m	switch
Einstellmutter(f	register nut
Einstellschraube(f	adjusting screw
Einstellschraube(f (Leerlauf-)	adjusting screw
Einzelradaufhängung(f	independent suspension
Einzelradbremse(f	single wheel brake
elastische Hohlwelle(f	quill shaft
erster Gang(m	first gear
Evolventen-Verzahnung(f	involute-tooth system

F

Fahrwerk(n	chassis
Federblatt(n	leaf
Federbügel(m	bracket
Federkugellager(n	spring loaded bearing
Federkupplung(f	flexible coupling
Federlasche(f	shackle
Federteller(m	spring retaining collar
Feinstufengetriebe(n	multi-step transmission
Feldsystem(n	field system

Felge(f	rim
Fensterkurbel(f	window handle
Fernlenkung(f, Fernsteuerung(f	radio controlled steering
Fernlicht(n	main beams
feste Kupplung(f, Starrkupplung(f	fixed drawbar, rigid attachement
Flanschwelle(f	stub shaft
Fliehkraftkupplung(f	centrifugal clutch
Führungslager(n	guide bearing
fünfter Gang(m	fifth gear
Fussbremse(f	foot brake
Fusskreis(m	root circle
Fusswinkel(m	root angle

G

Gasdichtung(f	gas seal
Gaspedal(n, Beschleuniger(m	accelerator
Gebläsegehäuse(n	fan housing
Gebläserad(n	fan
geblechtes Gehäuse(n	laminated frame
Gehäuse(n	housing
Gehäusegestell(n	skeleton frame
Gehäuseschild(m, Lagerschild(m	end shield
Gelenkwelle(f mit Schutz	telescoping power take-off shaft with guard
geschlossener Kühlkreislauf(m	closed circuit cooling
geteiltes Ringlager(n	split sleeve bearing
Getriebe(n	gear
Getriebebremse(f, Getriebewellenbremse(f	transmission brake
Getriebegehäuse(n	gearbox
Getriebeschalthebel(m	gear lever
Getriebewelle(f	gearbox output shaft
gewundene Feder(f	coiled spring
Gleitlager(n	journal bearing
Gummimatte(f	rubber mat
Gummipuffer(m	rubber buffer

H

Haltebolzen(m	holding pin
Handbremse(f, Feststellbremse(f	hand brake
Handschaltung(f	manual selection
Handschuhkastenschloss(n	locker lock
Hardtop(m	hard top
Hauptblatt(n	main leaf
Hauptbremszylinder(m	main brake cylinder
Hauptlager(pl	main bearings
Hauptwelle(f	main shaft
Heckscheibe(f	rear window
Heizungsanlage(f	heating system
Heizungskontrollleuchte(f	heating warning light
Heizungsschalter(m	heating control
Hilfsbehälter(m	extra tank
Hinterachsbremse(f	rear brake
Hinterachsbrücke(f, Hinterachsgehäuse(n	rear axle housing, driving axle housing
Hinterachse(f	rear axle, driving axle
hintere Parkleuchten(pl	rear sidelights
hintere Türe(f	rear door
Horn(n	horn
Hundegang(m	dog's movement, crab steering
Hupe(f	horn
hydraulische Betätigung(f	hydraulic drive
hydraulische Bremsen(pl	hydraulic brakes
hydraulische Lenkung(f	hydraulic steering
hydrodynamisches Getriebe(n	hydrodynamic torque converter
hydrostatische Kupplung(f	hydrostatic clutch
hydrostatischer Antrieb(m	hydrostatic transmission

I

Innenbackenbremse(f, Innenbremse(f	internal shoe brake, internal brake
inneres Rohr(n	internal cylinder
Instrumentenbeleuchtung(f	dashboard light
Isolierbuchse(f	insulating bush
isolierter Lagerbock(m	insulated bearing pedestal
isoliertes Lagergehäuse(n	insulated bearing housing

K

kaltes Wasser(n	cold water
Kappenendplatte(f	end plate
Kardangelenk(n	universal joint
Kastengehäuse(n	box frame
Kegelrad(n	bevel gear
Kegelradtrieb(m	rod
Keilnabengelenk(n	flexible coupling
Keilriemen(m	fan belt
Keilriemenwandler(m	v-belt variator
Kennzeichenbeleuchtung(f	number plate light
Kennzeichenschild(n	number plate
Kettenwandler(m	chain variator
Kilometerzähler(m	mileage indicator
Kipphebel(m	rocker
Kippsegment-Gleitlager(n	tilting pad bearing
Klappverdeck(n	hood
Klarsichtwiderstand(m	antifogging resistance
Kofferraumdeckel(m	boot lid
Kofferraumlampe(f	boot light
Kohle(f	charcoal
Kontrollleuchte(f	warning light
Kopfkreis(m	outside circle
Kotflügel(m	wing
Kühler(m	cooler, cooling apparatus, radiator

Kühlkreislauf(m, Kühlerkreislauf(m circuit cooling, circulating circuit

Kugellager(n	ball bearing
Kugelratschkupplung(f	ball-type safety clutch
Kupplung(f	clutch
Kupplungsbelag(m	clutch lining
Kupplungsdruckfeder(f	thrust spring
Kupplungspedal(n	clutch pedal
Kupplungsscheibe(f	plate
Kupplungsspiel(n	play of pedal
Kurbelgehäuse(n	crankcase
Kurbelwelle(f	crankshaft

L

Lack(m	paint
Lackieren(n	spraying

Längsträger(m	long member
Läufer(m, Rotor(m, Laufrad(n	rotor
Läuferkappenring(m	rotor end-winding retaining ring
Lager mit Druckölschmierung(f	pressure lubricated bearing
Lager(n mit Dochtschmierung	wick lubricated bearing
Lager(n mit Druckölschmierung	pressure lubricated bearing
Lager(n mit festem Sitz	straight seated bearing
Lager(n mit Festringschmierung	disk and wiper lubricated bearing
Lager(n mit kugeligem Sitz	spherically seated bearing
Lager(n mit Spülölschmierung	flood lubricated bearing
Lager(n, Lagerpackung(f	bearing
Lagerbock(m	bearing pedestal
Lagerbrücke(f	end bracket, bearing bracket
Lagerdruck(m	bearing pressure
Lagergehäuse(n	bearing housing
Lagergleitfläche(f	bearing lining
Lagerkörper(m	bearing liner
Lagerschale(f	bearing shell
Lagerspiel(n	bearing clearance
Lamellenkühler(m	grill tube radiator
Lamellenkupplung(f	multi-plate clutch
Lauffläche(f	tread
Leergang(m, Leerlauf(m	neutral
Lehnenverstellung(f	control for tilt of seats
Lenkachse(f	steered axle
Lenkbolzen(m pl	pins
Lenkgehäuse(n	steering-box
Lenksäule(f	column
Lenkschenkel(m	swivel pin
Lenkschnecke(f	worm screw
Lenkung(f	steering, controlling apparatus
Lenkungsdämpfer(m	damper
Lenkzylinder(f	steering cylinder
Lichtschalter(m	control for lights
linke Türe(f	left door
Lüftergehäuse(n	fan housing
Lüfterkragen(m	fan shroud
Luftführung(f, Luftleitfläche(f	air guide
Luftkanal(m	air duct, ventilation duct
Luftleitung(f	air pipe
Luftschlitze(pl	core ducts

Luftstutzen(m air trunking

M
mechanisches Getriebe(n mechanical gearbox
Mittelrohr(n central backbone
Motorbremse(f engine brake, retarder
Motorwelle(f, Antriebswelle(f transmission input shaft
Motorzapfwelle(f live power take-off shaft
Muffe(f coupling

N
Nabe(f hub
Naben-Durchmesser(m hub diameter
Nabenlänge(f hub length
Nachstellbolzen(m registration pivot
Nachstellzugstange(f registration pull rod
nicht synchronisierter Gang(m unsynchronized gear
Nocke(f cam
Nockenratschkupplung(f simple pin-type safety clutch
Nockenwelle(f camshaft
Notkühlung(f standby cooling, emergency cooling
Nutenkeil(m slot wedge

O
obere Nocke(f upper toggle
oberer Schwingarm(m uper swinging arm
Ölbehälter(m oil tank
Öldichtung(f oil seal
Öldruck-Kontrollleuchte(f oil pressure warning light
Öldruckanzeiger(m oil pressure gauge
Öleinfüllstutzen(m oil filler
Ölpumpe(f oil pump
Ölspritzring(m oil thrower
offener Kühlkreislauf(m open circuit cooling

P
Parkierbremse(f parking brake
Passfeder(f (Keil) key

Pendelachse(f	pivotted axle, swinging axle
Pendelzugstange(f, Zugpendel(n	swinging drawbar
Planetengetriebe(n	epicyclic gearing
Planetenrad(n	planetary
Pleuellager(pl	big end bearings
Pleuelstange(f	connecting rod
Polieren(n	polishing
Poliermittel(n	polishing wax
Portalachse(f	portal axle, high clearance axle
Porzellan(n	porcelain

Q

Querkeil-Verbindung(f	tapered key
Querträger(m	cross member

R

Rad(n	wheel
Radkappe(f	hub-cap
rechte Türe(f	right door
Reibungskupplung(f	friction clutch
Reparatur(f	repair
Reserveschlüssel(m	duplicate key
Reservetank-Kontrollleuchte(f	petrol reserve warning light
Retuschieren(n	touching up
Richten(n	hammering out
Richtungsanzeiger(m	trafficator
Riemen(m	belt
Riemenscheibe(f	pulley
Ringlager(n, ungeteiltes Ringlager(n	sleeve bearing
Ringschmierlager(n	oil ring lubricated bearing
Ringschmierung(f, Festringschmierung(f	disk (and wiper) lubricating
Rollenlager(n	roller bearing
Rückfahreinrichtung(f	reverse drive adaptation
Rückfahrscheinwerfer(m	reversing light
Rückholfeder(f	return spring
Rückspiegel(m	rear mirror
Rückwärtsgang(m	reverse gear
Rückzugfeder(f	release spring

S

Schaltgabel(f	gearshift
Scheibe(f, Glas(n	glass
Scheiben-Freilaufkupplung(f	friction disc free-wheel clutch
Scheibenbremse(f, Teilscheibenbremse(f	disc brake, disk brake
Scheibenkupplung(f	plat clutch, disc clutch, disk clutch
Scheibenwasch-Spritzdüse(f	jet
Scheibenwischer(m	windscreen wiper
Scheibenwischer-Schalter(m	windscreen wiper switch
Scheinwerfer(m	headlamp
Schiebegelenk(n	slip joint
Schiebemuffe(f	slip coupling
Schildlager(n	plug-in type bearing
Schleifpaste(f	polishing paste
Schleuderpumpe, Zentrifugalpumpe(f	centrifugal pump
Schmierlager(n	lubricating bearing, lubricated bearing
Schmiernuten(pl	oil grooves
Schneckengetriebe(n	worm gearing
Schneckensegment(n	helicoid sector
Schraubenfeder(f	coil spring
Schrumpfring(m	shrunk-on ring
Schwimmergehäuse(n	float chamber
Schwungrad(n	flywheel
Schwungscheibe(f	pulley
Segment-Gleitlager(n	pad type bearing
selbstschmierend	self-lubricating
selbstschmierendes Lager(n	self-lubricating bearing
Servobremse(f	brake servo, servo brake
Servolenkung(f	servo-steering
Sicherheitsbolzen(m	safety pin
Sicherheitsglas(n	safety glass
Sicherheitsgurt(m	safety belt
Sitzbank(f hinten, hintere S.	rear seat
Sitzverstellung(f	control for distance
Sonnenblende(f	sun visor
Spachteln(n	stoppering
Spiralfeder(f	spiral spring
Spülölschmierung(f	flood lubricating
Spur(f	alignment

Spurbreite(f	track width
Spurstange(f	track rod
Spurverstellung(f	track width adjustment
Ständer(m, Stator(m	stator
Ständergehäuse(n	stator frame
Standlicht-Kontrollleuchte(f	warning light for sidelights
Starter(m	choke
Staubdichtung(f	dust seal
Stehlager(n	pedestal bearing
Sternratschkupplung(f safety clutch	outwardly acting pin-type
Steuerung(f	steering
Steuerventil(n	control valve
Stiftfreilauf(m	pin free-wheel clutch
Stirnrad(n	spur gear
Stossstange(f	bumper
Stossstangenhorn(n	protuberance
stufenloses Getriebe(n, - Drehzahlregler(m stepless speed variator	
Sturz(m	toe-in
Synchrongetriebe(n	synchronized gearbox

T

Teleskopachse(f	telescopic axle
Tellerrad(n	crown gear
Tragring(m	retaining ring
Trockenkupplung(f	dry plate clutch
Trommelbremsen(pl	drum brakes
Türleuchte(f	door light
Türsicherungsstift(m	safety lock

U

Überdeckungsgrad(m	arc of contact
Übertragungswelle, Gelenkwelle(f	transmission shaft
umlegbare Lehne(f	reclinable squabs
unabhängige Kühlvorrichtung(f, Fremdkühlung(f independent circulating circuit component	
unter Nocke(f	lower toggle
Unter-Last-Schalt-Getriebe(f	power shift gear transmission
unterer Schwingarm(m	lower swinging arm

V

Ventilator(m	fan
Verbindungswelle(f	dumb-bell shaft, spacer shaft
Verbundglas(n	laminated glass
Verchromung(f	chromium plating
Verdrehwelle(f	torque shaft
Vernickelung(f	nickle plating
verschiebbares Gehäuse(n	end-shift frame
verstärkte Spülölschmierung(f	forced lubricating
verstellbare Lehne(f	adjustable squabs
Verzahnung(f	tooth system
Vierrad-Öldruckbremse(f, hydraulisch	four-wheel hydraulic pressure brake
Vierradlenkung(f, Allradlenkung(f	four-wheel steering
vierter Gang(m	fourth gear
Vollscheibenbremse(f, Mehrscheibenbremse(f	multiple plate brake, multiple disc brake, multiple disk brake
Vorderachsbremse(f	front brake
vordere Parkleuchten(pl	front sidelights
vordere Türe(f	front door
Vorderradlenkung(f, Frontlenkung(f	front-wheel steering
Vordersitz(m	front seat
Vorederachse(f	front axle
Vorlegewelle(f	auxiliary shaft

W

Wälzlager(n	cartrige type bearing
warmes Wasser(n, heisses W.	hot water
Weitwinkelgelenk(n	wide-angle drive shaft
Welle(f	shaft
Wellen-Gleitersatz(m	journal (of a shaft)
Wellendurchmesser(m	shaft diameter
Wellenzapfen(m	shaft estension
Wendegetriebe(n	reversing gear, back gear
Wickelkopfabdeckung(f	end-winding cover
Windschutzscheibe(f	windscreen
Windungsabstand(m	spacing of coils
Wischblätter(pl	rubber elements
Wischerarm(m	blade

Z

Zähnezahlsumme(f	total number of teeth
Zahnberechnung(f	tooth calculation
Zahnbreite(f	with of tooth
Zahndicke(f	root width of tooth
Zahnhöhe(f	depth of teeth
Zahnkranzstärke(f	tooth wheel rim
Zahnlücke(f	tooth spacing
Zahnräder(pl	gears
Zahnstange(f	rack-and-pinion
Zapfwelle(f und Kraftanschluss	power take-off an couplings
Zapfwellenkupplung(f	Power take-off coupling
Zentrierlager(n	location bearing
Zierleisten(f pl	mouldings
Zigarren-Anzünder(m	cigarette lighter
Zweifachkupplung(f, Doppelkupplung(f	double clutch, two-stage clutch
zweiter Gang(m	second gear
Zwischenwelle(f	jack shaft
Zylinder(m	cylinder

**Pumps,
gates
and
valves**

A

aeration valve	Belüftungsklappe(f
air bleeding valve	Entlüftungsventil(n
air inlet pipe	Belüftungsrohr(n
air intake	Belüftung(f
air pump	Luftpumpe(f
air relief cock, vent cock	Entlüftungshahn(m
air valve	Luftventil(n
air vent	Auslassventil(n
air-compression pump	Luftverdichtungspumpe(f

air-lift pump
    Druckluftwasserheber(m, Mammutpumpe(f
air-operated diaphragm valve   luftgesteuertes
    Membranventil(n

anchor bolt	Verankerungsschraube(f
angle joint	Kardangelenk(n

angle valve, corner valve, miter valve
    Eckventil(n, Winkelventil(n

annular valve	Ringventil(n
antechamber	Vorkammer(f
apron	Schwelle(f

automatic closing gear
    Schnellverschlussvorrichtung(f

automatic pumping plant   automatische Pumpanlage
automatic winch   automatischer Antrieb(m
axle lubrication pipe   Rohr(n zum Schmieren der
    Achse

B

back-pressure valve
    Rückschlagklappe(f, Rückschlagventil(n
backflow valve, check valve, reflux valve, stop valve
    Absperrventil(n
balance beam   Ausgleichsbalken(m
ball check valve   Kugelrückschlagventil(n
ball clock   Kugelhahn(m, Schwimmerhahn(m
ball cup valve, ball valve, globe valve Kugelventil(n,
    Ballventil(n
ball thrust bearing   Kugellager(n
ball valve   Kugelventil(n
bellmouth intake   Einlauftrompete(f
bevel gear   Kegelradübersetzung(f
blow-down valve
    Auslassventil(n, Abblaseventil(n
brass lining, brass bushing   Gleitrohr(n in Messing
bronze guide   Führungsleiste(f
butterfly valve   Drosselklappe(f, Regelklappe(f
by-pass pipe   Umleitungsrohr(n

C

capacity   Förderleistung(f
caststeel gate, cast st. gate leafe Stahlguss-Schütze(f
caterpillar   Raupe(f
caterpillat gate   Raupenschütze(f
centrifugal pump
    Kreiselpumpe(f, Schleuderpumpa(f, Zentrifugalpumpe(f
circular irrigation lay-out   Ringleitung(f
circulating pump   Umlaufpumpe(f, Umwälzpumpe(f
cock   Hahn(m
combined vacuum pump/compressor
    Vakuumpumpe-Verdichter-Kombination(f

compressed air chamber	Windkessel(m
compression chamber	Druckspeicher(m, Druckkammer(f
concrete pump	Betonpumpe(f
connecting bolt	Verbindungsbolzen(m
connecting cock	Verbindungshahn(m
connecting rod	Pleuelstange(f
connecting rods	Verbindungsgestänge(n
connection link	Aufhänge-Kettenglied(n
control panel	Schaltanlage(f, Schalttafel(f
control valve	Regelventil(n
control valve	Regulierventil(n
controlled-volume pump, metering pump	Pumpe(f mit regelbarer Kapazität
counterweight	Gegengewicht(n
coupling	Anschluss(m
cover, dome	Glocke(f
cradle feet	Lager(n
crankshaft	Kurbelwelle(f
cylinder	Zylinder(m

D

deep well pump	Tiefbrunnenpumpe(f
delivery valve, discharge valve	Druckventil(n
delivery valve, head valve	Steuerventil(n
diaphragm pump	Membranpumpe(f
diaphragm pump, membrane pump	Balgpumpe(f, Membranpumpe(f
diaphragm valve	Membranschleuse(f, Membranventil(n
diffusion condensation pump, diffusion pump	Diffusionspumpe(f
discharge cock, drain cock, purge cock	Ablasshahn(m, Entleerungshahn(m
discharge pipe, outlet -	Anschlussrohrleitung(f
discharge valve, outlet valve, unloading valve	Ablaufventil(n, Ablassventil(n
disk valve	Scheibenventil(n, Tellerventil(n
dismantling flange	Überwurfflansch(m
double beat valve	Gleichgewichtsventil(n
drain pipe, waste pipe	Entleerung(f des Schiebers
drain valve	Ablassventil(n

drop valve   Kegelventil(n, Pilzventil(n

E
eccentric drive   Exzenterantrieb(m
eduction valve
   Auslassventil(n, Abzugsventil(n
ejector pump
   Ejectorpumpe(f, Saugstrahlpumpe(f
electric motor pump   Elektro-Motorpumpe(f
emergency gate
   Hilfsabschluss(m, Notabschluss(m
equalizing pipe   Ausgleichsrohrleitung(f
explosion valve   Explosionsklappe(f

F
feed pipe   Speiserohr(n
feed pump   Beschickungspumpe(f
feed slide   Dosierschieber(m
feed valve, filling valve   Füllventil(n
female end   Mutterteil(m
field pump   Freiluft-Pumpstation(f
filling conduit   Füllleitung(f
filling valve   Füllschieber(m
fittings   Formteile(pl
fixed housing   festes Gehäuse(f
fixed needle   feste Nadel(f
flab, hinged flash gate   absenkbare Klappe(f
flap valve, tilting disk check valve
   Klappenventil(n, Verschlussklappe(f
flat stopcock   Flachhahn(m
flexible plate   Federblech(n
float   Schwimmer(m
float valve   Schwimmabsperrventil(n
flywheel pump   Schwungradpumpe(f
foot valve   Saugventil(n
force pump, pressure pump   Druckpumpe(f

G

gage cock, gauge cock, pet cock, test cock	Probierhahn(m, Wasserstandshahn(m
gate arm	Segmentarm(m
gate beams, cross beams	Vertsteifungsbalken d. Schützentafel
gate pivot	Klappenachse(f
gate valve, straight-way valve	Durchgangsventil(n
gate, gate valve, sluice valve	Absperrschieber(m, Abzugschieber(m
gear box	Getriebekasten(m
gear pump	Zahnradpumpe(f
groove, gate guide	Nut(f, Nische(f
guide piston	Führungskolben(m
guide pulley	Führungsrolle(f
guide rail, side guide	Führungsschiene(f
guide roller, side guide wheel	Führungsrolle(f
guide wheel, guide roller	Leitrolle(f

H

hand lifting winch	Handaufzugswinde(f
handwheel	Handrad(n
handwheel	Handrad(n
hardened (steel) roller	Stahlrolle(f
heat pump	Wärmepumpe(f
heavy duty pump	Hochleistungspumpe(f
hoist motor	Hubmotor(m
holding ring	Einsatzring(m
horizontal beam	horizontaler Balken(m
hydraulic jack	hydraulische Winde(f
hydraulic tripping device	hydraulischer Auslöseapparat(m

I

immersion pump
    Tauchpumpe(f, Unterwasserpumpe(f
inclined seat valve   Schrägsitzventil(n
injection pump, grout pump   Injektionspumpe(f
inlet   Einlass(m
inlet valve
    Einlassschieber(m, Eintrittsventil(n
inlet valve   Einlassventil(n
intake sluice valve   Entnahmeschieber(m
intake tunnel   Entnahmetunnel(m
irrigation pump   Beregnungspumpe(f

J

jet pump   Strahlpumpe(f

L

leather seal plate backing   Ledermanschette(f
leather sealing strip   Dichtungsleder(n
lever   Hebel(m
lever safety valve   Hebersicherheitsventil(n
lifting chain   Aufzugskette(f
lifting eye, - bolt, - ring   Aufhängeöse(f
lifting hook, hoisting hook   Aufhängehaken(m
lintol seating   oberer Dichtungsbalken(m

M

machined plate, - sealing strip   gehobeltes Blech(n
machined rib   gehobelte Rippe(f
main operating rod   Aufhängestange(f
main pivot   Drehachse(f

male end	Vorderteil(m
manhole	Mannloch(n
manometer	Manometer(n
maximum pressure	Höchstdruck(m
mechanical lock	mechanische Verklinkung(f
membrane, diaphragm	Membrane(f
mercury check valve	Quecksilberdruckventil(n
mobile pump unit	fahrbarer Pumpensatz(m
moving member	Drehkörper(m
moving roller path	bewegliche Schiene(f
mud pump	Schlammpumpe(f
mud water pump	Schlammwasserpumpe(f
multiple-stage centrifugal pump	Mehrstufenkreiselpumpe(f
mushroom spindle, needle stem	Führungsstange(f

N

needle	Abschlussnadel(f
needle seat(ing), valve seat	Sitz(m der Abschlussnadel
needle valve	Nadelventil(n
non-return valve	Rückschlagventil(n

O

oil bath	Ölbad(n
oil diffusion pump	Öldiffusionspumpe(f
oil feed pipe	Ölzuleitung(f
oil vapor-jet pump, oil vapour-jet pump	Öldampfstrahlpumpe(f
operating lever	Schwenkhebel(m
operating screw, - spindle	Betätigungsspindel(m
operation piston	Antriebskolben(m
outlet bellmouth	Auslaufkonus(m
outlet valve	Auslassventil(n
overflow line	Überlaufleitung(f
overflow valve	Überlaufventil(n

P

packing flange	Verschlussflansch(m
packing gland	Manschette(f
passage valve, running valve	Durchlaufventil(n
pier	Pfeiler(m
pilot valve, relay valve	Steuerventil(n
pipe	Rohr(n
pipe coupling	Rohrkupplung(f
piston head	Kolbenkopf(m
piston pump	Kolbenpumpe(f
piston rod	Kolbenstange(f
piston wall	Kolbenwandung(f
pop valve	Sicherheitsventil(n
power pump	Motorpumpe(f
power requirement	Kraftbedarf(m
power shaft	Zapfwelle(f, Kraftwelle(f
prefill valve	Vorfüllventil(n
pressed-steel pipe	Bandstahlrohr(n

pressure adapter, pressure control valve, pressure govrenor, pressure regulator
    Druckregulierventil(n, Druckregler(m

pressure connection	Druckanschluss(m

pressure reducing valve, reducing valve
    Druckreduzierventil(n, Reduzierventil(n

pressure relief valve	Überdruckventil(n
pressure stroke	Drucktakt(m
pressure tank	Druckkessel(m
proportioning pump	Dosierpumpe(f
pulp water pump	Schnitzelwasserpumpe(f
pump housing	Pumpengehäuse(n
pump valve	Pumpenventil(n, Pumpventil(n
pumpcylinder	Pumpenzylinder(m
pumping station	Pumpstation(f

Q

quick coupling	Schnellkupplung(f

R

rack rail, gate track rack	Zahnstange(f
recirculating pump	kontinuierliche Umlaufpumpe(f
rectangular opening	rechteckige Öffnung(f
reduction gear	Übersetzung(f
reduction gear	Untersetzungsgetriebe(n
regulating tap	Regulierhahn(m
relief valve	Druckreduktionsventil(n, Entlastungsventil(n
remote controlled	ferngesteuert
return line	Rücklaufleitung(f
rocker support	Auflagergelenk(n
roller	Laufwalze(f
roller	Walze(f
roller box, side frame	Rollenkasten(m
roller drum gate	Walzenwehr(n
roller gate shield	Schnabel(m der Walze
roller path	feste Schiene(f
roller path, roller track, track	Laufschiene(f
roller pin	Rollenachse(f
roller pump	Rollenpumpe(f
roller train	Walzenwagen(m
roller train side plate	Führungsblech(n des Walzenwagens
rorary slide valve	Drehschieber(m
rotary piston	Drehkolben(m
rotary piston drive	Drehkolbenantrieb(m
rotary pump	Umlaufpumpe(f
rotary segment pump	Segmentpumpe(f
rotary vacuum pump	Umlaufvakuumpumpe(f
rotary valve	Drehventil(n
rotary vane pump	Flügelpumpe(f
rubber collar	Gummimanschette(f

S

safety valve	Sicherheitsventil(n
scavenging pump	Spülpumpe(f
screen rake, trash rack rake	Rechenreiniger(m
screen, trash rack	Rechen(m

screwcapstan	Schneckengetriebe(n
sealing ring	Dichtungsring(m
sealing ring, packing gland	Stopfbüchse(f
sealing rod, standing rod	Dichtungsstab(m
seat, seating	Sitz(m
sector	Sektor(m
semi-rotary pump, vane pump	Allweilerpumpe(f, Flügelpumpe(f
sewage pump	Abwasserpumpe(f
shaft, trunnion	Welle(f, Baum(m
shield	Schild(m
shifting eye, shifting bolt	Zugring(m
shut-off valve	Absperrventil(n
shut-off valve	Absperrventil(n, Verschlussventil(n
side frame of gate (leaf)	Träger(m des Rahmens der Schütze
side opening	seitliche Öffnung(f
side seal(ing)	seitliche Dichtung(f
side valve	seitengesteuertes Ventil(n
sill	Schwelle(f
skin plating, skin plate	Stahlblech(n der Schützentafel
skin plating, shell skin plate	Blechabdeckung(f
sleeve valve, socket valve	Muffenventil(n, Ventilschieber(m
slide gate	Gleitschütze(f
slide gate, slide valve	Schieberventil(n
slide valve	Steuerschieber(m
sliding housing	bewegliches Gehäuse(n
sliding pump	Schieberpumpe(f
slip joint	Ausbaurohr(n
sludge gate	Schlammschleuse(f, Schlammschieber(m
sludge valve	Schlammventil(n
spill valve	Überströmventil(n, Überlaufventil(n
sprocket winch, lifting gear	Aufzugsritzel(m
steam air pump, steam pump	Dampfpumpe(f, Dampfluftpumpe(f
stem bearing	Führung(f der Spindelstange
stiffener, stiffening plate	Versteifungsblech(n
Stoney gate	Stoney-Schütze(f

stop cock, stop tap	Absperrhahn(m
stop valve, backflow valve, check valve, reflux valve	
Absperrventil(n, Sperrventil(n	
stuffing gland	Stopfbüchse(f
suction chamber	Saugkammer(f
suction connection	Sauganschluss(m
suction hose	Saugschlauch(m
suction pump	Saugpumpe(f
suction stroke	Saugtakt(m
suction valve	Ansaugventil(n
sump	Pumpensumpf(m
support	Stützfuss(m
suspension pin, - shaft	Aufhängebolzen(m

T

testing pump	Probierpumpe(f, Testpumpe(f
threaded operating spindle	Schwenkspindel(m
three-way cock	Dreiweghahn(m
throttle valve	
Drosselventil(n, Dampfabsperrventil(n	
timber planking	Holzabdeckung(f
timber seal	Dichtungsholz(n
timber sill, wooden sill	Holzschwelle(f
toothed wheel, gear segment	Zahnrad(n
top frame	obere Traverse(f
trip paddle	Staupendel(n
twin pump	Zwillingspumpe(f
two-way cock	Zweiweghahn(m
two-way valve	
Wechselventil(m, Zweiwegventil(n	

U
underground line	Unterflurleitung(f

V
vacuum breaker	Rückschlagventil(n gegen Vakuum
vacuum pump	Vakuumpumpe(f
vacuum tap	Vakuumhahn(m
valve	Ventil(n
valve body	Schiebergehäuse(n
variable delivering pump	Pumpe(f mit variabler Förderleistung
vent pipe	Belüftungsrohr(n
vertical immersion pump, verical wet-pit pump	stehende Unterwasserpumpe(f, Tauchpumpe(f
vertical side plate, keeper	vertikales Führungsblech(n

W
water jet pump, water pressure pump	Wasserstrahlpumpe(f
wheel, roller	Rolle(f, Rad(n
worm gear drive	Schneckenantrieb(m

**Pumpen,
Schützen
und
Ventile**

A

Ablasshahn(m, Entleerungshahn(m discharge cock, drain cock, purge cock
Ablassventil(n   drain valve
Ablaufventil(n, Ablassventil(n   discharge valve, outlet valve, unloading valve
Abschlussnadel(f   needle
absenkbare Klappe(f   flab, hinged flash gate
Absperrhahn(m   stop cock, stop tap
Absperrschieber(m, Abzugschieber(m gate, gate valve, sluice valve
Absperrventil(n   shut-off valve
Absperrventil(n   backflow valve, check valve, reflux valve, stop valve
Absperrventil(n, Sperrventil(n   stop valve, backflow valve, check valve, reflux valve
Absperrventil(n, Verschlussventil(n shut-off valve
Abwasserpumpe(f   sewage pump
Allweilerpumpe(f, Flügelpumpe(f   semi-rotary pump, vane pumo
Ansaugventil(n   suction valve
Anschluss(m   coupling
Anschlussrohrleitung(f   discharge pipe, outlet -

Antriebskolben(m	operation piston
Aufhänge-Kettenglied(n	connection link
Aufhängebolzen(m	suspension pin, – shaft
Aufhängehaken(m	lifting hook, hoisting hook
Aufhängeöse(f	lifting eye, – bolt, – ring
Aufhängestange(f	main operating rod
Auflagergelenk(n	rocker support
Aufzugskette(f	lifting chain
Aufzugsritzel(m	sprocket winch, lifting gear
Ausbaurohr(n	slip joint
Ausgleichsbalken(m	balance beam
Ausgleichsrohrleitung(f	equalizing pipe
Auslassventil(n	outlet valve
Auslassventil(n	air vent
Auslassventil(n, Abblaseventil(n	blow-down valve
Auslassventil(n, Abzugsventil(n	eduction valve
Auslaufkonus(m	outlet bellmouth
automatische Pumpanlage	automatic pumping plant
automatischer Antrieb(m	automatic winch

B

Balgpumpe(f, Membranpumpe(f	diaphragm pump, membrane pump
Bandstahlrohr(n	pressed-steel pipe
Belüftung(f	air intake
Belüftungsklappe(f	aeration valve
Belüftungsrohr(n	air inlet pipe
Belüftungsrohr(n	vent pipe
Beregnungspumpe(f	irrigation pump
Beschickungspumpe(f	feed pump
Betätigungsspindel(m	operating screw, – spindle
Betonpumpe(f	concrete pump
bewegliche Schiene(f	moving roller path
bewegliches Gehäuse(n	sliding housing
Blechabdeckung(f	skin plating, shell skin plate

D

Dampfpumpe(f, Dampfluftpumpe(f	steam air pump, steam pump
Dichtungsholz(n	timber seal
Dichtungsleder(n	leather sealing strip
Dichtungsring(m	sealing ring
Dichtungsstab(m	sealing rod, standing rod
Diffusionspumpe(f	diffusion condensation pump, diffusion pump
Dosierpumpe(f	proportioning pump
Dosierschieber(m	feed slide
Drehachse(f	main pivot
Drehkörper(m	moving member
Drehkolben(m	rotary piston
Drehkolbenantrieb(m	rotary piston drive
Drehschieber(m	rorary slide valve
Drehventil(n	rotary valve
Dreiweghahn(m	three-way cock
Drosselklappe(f, Regelklappe(f	butterfly valve
Drosselventil(n, Dampfabsperrventil(n	throttle valve
Druckanschluss(m	pressure connection
Druckkessel(m	pressure tank
Druckluftwasserheber(m, Mammutpumpe(f	air-lift pump
Druckpumpe(f	force pump, pressure pump
Druckreduktionsventil(n, Entlastungsventil(n	relief valve
Druckreduzierventil(n, Reduzierventil(n	pressure reducing valve, reducing valve
Druckregulierventil(n, Druckregler(m	pressure adapter, pressure control valve, pressure govrenor, pressure regulator
Druckspeicher(m, Druckkammer(f	compression chamber
Drucktakt(m	pressure stroke
Druckventil(n	delivery valve, discharge valve
Durchgangsventil(n	gate valve, straight-way valve
Durchlaufventil(n	passage valve, running valve

E

Eckventil(n, Winkelventil(n	angle valve, corner valve, miter valve

Einlass(m	inlet
Einlassschieber(m, Eintrittsventil(n	inlet valve
Einlassventil(n	inlet valve
Einlauftrompete(f	bellmouth intake
Einsatzring(m	holding ring
Ejectorpumpe(f, Saugstrahlpumpe(f	ejector pump
Elektro-Motorpumpe(f	electric motor pump
Entleerung(f des Schiebers	drain pipe, waste pipe
Entlüftungshahn(m	air relief cock, vent cock
Entlüftungsventil(n	air bleeding valve
Entnahmeschieber(m	intake sluice valve
Entnahmetunnel(m	intake tunnel
Explosionsklappe(f	explosion valve
Exzenterantrieb(m	eccentric drive

F

fahrbarer Pumpensatz(m	mobile pump unit
Federblech(n	flexible plate
ferngesteuert	remote controlled
feste Nadel(f	fixed needle
feste Schiene(f	roller path
festes Gehäuse(f	fixed housing
Flachhahn(m	flat stopcock
Flügelpumpe(f	rotary vane pump
Förderleistung(f	capacity
Formteile(pl	fittings
Freiluft-Pumpstation(f	field pump
Führung(f der Spindelstange	stem bearing
Führungsblech(n des Walzenwagens	roller train side plate
Führungskolben(m	guide piston
Führungsleiste(f	bronze guide
Führungsrolle(f wheel	guide roller, side guide
Führungsrolle(f	guide pulley
Führungsschiene(f	guide rail, side guide
Führungsstange(f	mushroom spindle, needle stem
Füllleitung(f	filling conduit
Füllschieber(m	filling valve
Füllventil(n	feed valve, filling valve

G

Gegengewicht(n	counterweight
gehobelte Rippe(f	machined rib
gehobeltes Blech(n strip	machined plate, - sealing
Getriebekasten(m	gear box
Gleichgewichtsventil(n	double beat valve
Gleitrohr(n in Messing	brass lining, brass bushing
Gleitschütze(f	slide gate
Glocke(f	cover, dome
Gummimanschette(f	rubber collar

H

Hahn(m	cock
Handaufzugswinde(f	hand lifting winch
Handrad(n	handwheel
Handrad(n	handwheel
Hebel(m	lever
Hebersicherheitsventil(n	lever safety valve
Hilfsabschluss(m, Notabschluss(m	emergency gate
Hochleistungspumpe(f	heavy duty pump
Höchstdruck(m	maximum pressure
Holzabdeckung(f	timber planking
Holzschwelle(f	timber sill, wooden sill
horizontaler Balken(m	horizontal beam
Hubmotor(m	hoist motor
hydraulische Winde(f	hydraulic jack
hydraulischer Auslöseapparat(m	hydraulic tripping device

I

Injektionspumpe(f	injection pump, grout pump

K

Kardangelenk(n	angle joint
Kegelradübersetzung(f	bevel gear
Kegelventil(n, Pilzventil(n	drop valve
Klappenachse(f	gate pivot
Klappenventil(n, Verschlussklappe(f	flap valve, tilting disk check valve
Kolbenkopf(m	piston head
Kolbenpumpe(f	piston pump
Kolbenstange(f	piston rod
Kolbenwandung(f	piston wall
kontinuierliche Umlaufpumpe(f	recirculating pump
Kraftbedarf(m	power requirement
Kreiselpumpe(f, Schleuderpumpa(f, Zentrifugalpumpe(f	centrifugal pump
Kugelhahn(m, Schwimmerhahn(m	ball clock
Kugellager(n	ball thrust bearing
Kugelrückschlagventil(n	ball check valve
Kugelventil(n	ball valve
Kugelventil(n, Ballventil(n	ball cup valve, ball valve, globe valve
Kurbelwelle(f	crankshaft

L

Lager(n	cradle feet
Laufschiene(f	roller path, roller track, track
Laufwalze(f	roller
Ledermanschette(f	leather seal plate backing
Leitrolle(f	guide wheel, guide roller
luftgesteuertes Membranventil(n	air-operated diaphragm valve
Luftpumpe(f	air pump
Luftventil(n	air valve
Luftverdichtungspumpe(f	air-compression pump

M

Mannloch(n	manhole
Manometer(n	manometer
Manschette(f	packing gland
mechanische Verklinkung(f	mechanical lock
Mehrstufenkreiselpumpe(f	multiple-stage centrifugal pump
Membrane(f	membrane, diaphragm
Membranpumpe(f	diaphragm pump
Membranschleuse(f, Membranventil(n	diaphragm valve
Motorpumpe(f	power pump
Muffenventil(n, Ventilschieber(m	sleeve valve, socket valve
Mutterteil(m	female end

N

Nadelventil(n	needle valve
Nut(f, Nische(f	groove, gate guide

O

obere Traverse(f	top frame
oberer Dichtungsbalken(m	lintol seating
oberirdische Leitung(f	above-ground pipe line
Ölbad(n	oil bath
Öldampfstrahlpumpe(f	oil vapor-jet pump, oil vapour-jet pump
Öldiffusionspumpe(f	oil diffussion pump
Ölzuleitung(f	oil feed pipe

P

Pfeiler (m	pier
Pleuelstange (f	connecting rod
Probierhahn (m, Wasserstandshahn (m	gage cock, gauge cock, pet cock, test cock
Probierpumpe (f, Testpumpe (f	testing pump
Pumpe (f mit regelbarer Kapazität	controlled-volume pump, metering pump
Pumpe (f mit variabler Förderleistung	variable delivering pump
Pumpengehäuse (n	pump housing
Pumpensumpf (m	sump
Pumpenventil (n, Pumpventil (n	pump valve
Pumpenzylinder (m	pumpcylinder
Pumpstation (f	pumping station

Q

Quecksilberdruckventil (n	mercury check valve

R

Raupe (f	caterpillar
Raupenschütze (f	caterpillat gate
Rechen (m	screen, trash rack
Rechenreiniger (m	screen rake, trash rack rake
rechteckige Öffnung (f	rectangular opening
Regelventil (n	control valve
Regulierhahn (m	regulating tap
Regulierventil (n	control valve
Ringleitung (f	circular irrigation lay-out
Ringventil (n	annular valve
Rohr (n	pipe
Rohr (n zum Schmieren der Achse	axle lubrication pipe
Rohrkupplung (f	pipe coupling
Rolle (f, Rad (n	wheel, roller
Rollenachse (f	roller pin

Rollenkasten(m	roller box, side frame
Rollenpumpe(f	roller pump
Rücklaufleitung(f	return line
Rückschlagklappe(f, Rückschlagventil(n	back-pressure valve
Rückschlagventil(n	non-return valve
Rückschlagventil(n gegen Vakuum	vacuum breaker

S

Sauganschluss(m	suction connection
Saugkammer(f	suction chamber
Saugpumpe(f	suction pump
Saugschlauch(m	suction hose
Saugtakt(m	suction stroke
Saugventil(n	foot valve
Schaltanlage(f, Schalttafel(f	control panel
Scheibenventil(n, Tellerventil(n	disk valve
Schiebergehäuse(n	valve body
Schieberpumpe(f	sliding pump
Schieberventil(n	slide gate, slide valve
Schild(m	shield
Schlammpumpe(f	mud pump
Schlammschleuse(f, Schlammschieber(m	sludge gate
Schlammventil(n	sludge valve
Schlammwasserpumpe(f	mud water pump
Schnabel(m der Walze	roller gate shield
Schneckenantrieb(m	worm gear drive
Schneckengetriebe(n	screwcapstan
Schnellkupplung(f	quick coupling
Schnellverschlussvorrichtung(f	automatic closing gear
Schnitzelwasserpumpe(f	pulp water pump
Schrägsitzventil(n	inclined seat valve
Schwelle(f	apron
Schwelle(f	sill
Schwenkhebel(m	operating lever
Schwenkspindel(m	threaded operating spindle
Schwimmabsperrventil(n	float valve
Schwimmer(m	float
Schwungradpumpe(f	flywheel pump
Segmentarm(m	gate arm
Segmentpumpe(f	rotary segment pump

seitengesteuertes Ventil(n	side valve
seitliche Dichtung(f	side seal(ing)
seitliche Öffnung(f	side opening
Sektor(m	sector
Sicherheitsventil(n	safety valve
Sicherheitsventil(n	pop valve
Sitz(m	seat, seating
Sitz(m der Abschlussnadel	needle seat(ing), valve seat
Speiserohr(n	feed pipe
Spülpumpe(f	scavenging pump
Stahlblech(n der Schützentafel	skin plating, skin plate
Stahlguss-Schütze(f	caststeel gate, cast st. gate leafe
Stahlrolle(f	hardened (steel) roller
Staupendel(n	trip paddle
stehende Unterwasserpumpe(f, Tauchpumpe(f	vertical immersion pump, verical wet-pit pump
Steuerschieber(m	slide valve
Steuerventil(n	pilot valve, relay valve
Steuerventil(n	delivery valve, head valve
Stoney-Schütze(f	Stoney gate
Stopfbüchse(f	stuffing gland
Stopfbüchse(f	sealing ring, packing gland
Strahlpumpe(f	jet pump
Stützfuss(m	support

T

Tauchpumpe(f, Unterwasserpumpe(f	immersion pump
Tiefbrunnenpumpe(f	deep well pump
Träger(m des Rahmens der Schütze	side frame of gate (leaf)

U

Überdruckventil(n	pressure relief valve
Überlaufleitung(f	overflow line
Überlaufventil(n	overflow valve

...ersetzung(f	reduction gear
...erströmventil(n, Überlaufventil(n	spill valve
...erwurfflansch(m	dismantling flange
...nlaufpumpe(f	rotary pump
...nlaufpumpe(f, Umwälzpumpe(f	circulating pump
...nlaufvakuumpumpe(f	rotary vacuum pump
...nleitungsrohr(n	by-pass pipe
...nterflurleitung(f	underground line
...ntersetzungsgetriebe(n	reduction gear

...akuumhahn(m	vacuum tap
...akuumpumpe(f	vacuum pump
...akuumpumpe-Verdichter-Kombination(f	combined vacuum pump/compressor
...entil(n	valve
...erankerungsschraube(f	anchor bolt
...erbindungsbolzen(m	connecting bolt
...erbindungsgestänge(n	connecting rods
...erbindungshahn(m	connecting cock
...erschlussflansch(m	packing flange
...ersteifungsblech(n	stiffener, stiffening plate
...ertikales Führungsblech(n	vertical side plate, keeper
...ertsteifungsbalken d. Schützentafel	gate beams, cross beams
...orderteil(m	male end
...orfüllventil(n	prefill valve
...orkammer(f	antechamber

W

...ärmepumpe(f	heat pump
...alze(f	roller
...alzenwagen(m	roller train
...alzenwehr(n	roller drum gate
...asserstrahlpumpe(f	water jet pump, water pressure pump

Wechselventil (m, Zweiwegventil (n   two-way valve
Welle (f, Baum (m   shaft, trunnion
Windkessel (m   compressed air chamber

Z
Zahnrad (n   toothed wheel, gear segment
Zahnradpumpe (f   gear pump
Zahnstange (f   rack rail, gate track rack
Zapfwelle (f, Kraftwelle (f   power shaft
Zugring (m   shifting eye, shifting bolt
Zweiweghahn (m   two-way cock
Zwillingspumpe (f   twin pump
Zylinder (m   cylinder

Statics, strength

A

a number of forces(pl	mehrere Kräfte(pl
accidental load	zufällige Last(f
additional load	Zusatzlast, zusätzliche Belastung
angle	Winkel(m
angle of twist	Verdrehwinkel(m
angular girder	geknickter Träger(m
assumed load, design load	angenommene Belastung(f
at rest	in Ruhe(f, ruhend
axial force, direct force	Normalkraft(f

B

beam on two bearings	Balken(m auf zwei Stützen
beam, girder	Träger(m
bearing displacement	Auflagerverschiebung(f
bearing friction	Lagerreibung(f
belt drive	Riementrieb(m
belt velocity	Riemengeschwindigkeit(f
bending	Biegung(f
bending moment	Biegungsmoment(n
bending resistance	Biegungsfestigkeit(f
bending stress	Biegespannung(f
Bernoulli(s) hypothesis	Hypothese(f von Bernoulli
bottom chord, lower boom	Untergurt(m
braking force	Bremskraft(f
breaking load, ultimate -	Bruchlast(f

buckling	Knickung (f
buckling	Knicken (n
buckling load	Knicklast (f
buckling stress	Knickspannung (f
bulging	Beulen (n
bulging resistance	Beulfestigkeit (f

C

calculation of shear, shear design	Schubbemessung (f
cantilever arm	Kragarm (m
cantilever girder	Kragträger (m
center load	zentrische Belastung (f
center of gravity stress	Schwerpunktspannung (f
centre of gravity	Schwerpunkt (m
centre of moments, center of moments	Momentennullpunkt (m
coefficient of elongation	Dehnungskoeffizient (m
coefficient of friction	Reibungszahl (f
combined bending	Biegung mit Normalkraft
component	Komponente (f
composite girder	Verbundträger (m
composite stresses	zusammengesetzte Spannungen (pl
compressed zone, compression zone	Druckzone (f
compressive force	Druckkraft (f
compressive member	Druckglied (n, Druckstab (m
compressive reinforcement, compression reinforcement	Druckarmierung (f
compressive strength	Druckfestigkeit (f
compressive stress	Druckspannung (f
concentrated load	Einzellast (f
concrete stress	Betonspannung (f
condition of equilibrium	Gleichgewichtsbedingung (f
condition of loading	Belastungsfall (m
continuous beam	Durchlaufträger (m
coordinates (pl	Koordinaten (pl
core area	Kernfläche (f
core dimension	Kernweite (f
crack formation	Rissbildung (f
creep	Kriechen (n
creep influence	Kriecheinfluss (m
Cremona method	Cremona-Verfahren (n
Cremona's polygon of forces	Cremonaplan (m
Cross method	Crossverfahren (n
cube crushing stregth, cube compressive strength	Würfeldruckfestigkeit (f

D

deflection	Durchbiegung(f
deformability	Verformungsvermögen(n
deformation	Verformung(f
deformation	Formänderung(f
design, structural design	Bemessung(f
diagonal in compression, compression diagonal	Druckdiagonale(f
diagonal member	Diagonalstab(m
diagram of forces	Kräfteplan(m
distribuited load	verteilte Last(f
driving torque	Antriebsmoment(n
dynamic effect	dynamische Wirkung(f

E

eccentric buckling	exzentrisches Knicken(n
eccentricity	Exzentrizität(f
effectiv length	Knicklänge(f
efficiency	Wirkungsgrad(m
elastic limit	Elastizitätsgrenze(f
elimination method	Eliminationsverfahren(n
equation of kinetics	Arbeitsgleichung(f
equation of moments	Momentengleichung(f
equilibrium	Gleichgewicht(n
equivalent stress	Vergleichsspannung(f
Euler crippling load	Eulersche Knicklast(f
extension	Dehnung(f
extreme (fibre) stress	Randspannung(f

F

fictive slenderness	ideelle Schlankheit(f
fixed end, fixity, constraint	Einspannung(f
fixed girder, built-in beam	eingespannter Träger(m
fixed sheave	feste Rolle(f
fixed, built-in	eingespannt
force	Kraft(f
force polygon	Krafteck(n
force polygone, polygone of forces	Kräftepolygon(n
frame with three hinges	Dreigelenkrahmen(m
frame, framework	Rahmen(m
framework	Fachwerk(n
free sheave	lose Rolle(f
friction force	Reibungskraft(f

G

Gerber girder	Gelenkträger, Gerberträger (m
girder on two supports	Träger (m auf 2 Stützen
graphical solution	graphische Lösung (f
gravitational force	Gewichtskraft (f
group of loads	Lastgruppe (f

H

hanging truss	Hängewerk (n
hog, chamber	Überhöhung (f
Hooke's law	Hookesches Gesetz (n

I

impact force	Anprallkraft (f
in motion	in Bewegung (f
inclined girder	schräger Träger (m
inclined plane	schiefe Ebene (f
influence line	Einflusslinie (f
influence of fatigue	Ermüdungseinfluss (m
initial stress	Anfangsspannung (f
instability	Instabilität (f
integral evaluation	integrale Auswertung (f
intermediate bearing	Zwischenauflager (n
intersection-factor	Querschnittsfaktor (m

L

lattice effect	Fachwerkwirkung (f
lattice girder	Fachwerkträger (m
legal strength	zulässige Beanspruchung (f
length	Länge (f
limiting friction	Gleitgrenze (f
line of application	Wirkungslinie (f
link polygon	Seileck (n
live load, applied load	Nutzlast (f
load distribution	Lastverteilung (f
loading limt	Belastungsgrenze (f
loading, load application	Belastung (f
longitudinal reinforcement, longitudinal steel	
Längsbewehrung (f	
longitudinal tensile force	Längszugkraft (f

M

mathematical	rechnerisch
mechanical work	mechanische Arbeit (f
mode of application	Beanspruchungsart (f

mode of loading	Belastungsart (f
modulus of elasticity	Elastizitätsmodul (m
moment	Moment (n
moment at extremity of member	Stabendmoment (n
moment at support	Stützmoment (n
moment diagram	Momentenfläche (f
moment distribution	Momentenausgleich (m
moment in the span, span moment	Feldmoment (n
moment of friction	Reibungsmoment (n
moment of inertia, second moment	Trägheitsmoment (n
moment theorem	Momentensatz (m

N

neutral axis	neutrale Achse (f, – Faser (f
nominal value	Nennwert (m

O

overturning	Kippen (n
overturning moment	Kippmoment (n

P

parallel forces	parallele Kräfte (pl
partially prestressed	teilweise vorgespannt
path of force	Lastweg (m
path of load	Kraftweg (m
permanent load, dead load	ständige Last (f
permissible extreme stress	zulässige Randspannung (f
permissible stress	zulässige Spannung (f
plate girder, solid girder	Vollwandträger (m
point of application	Angriffspunkt (m
point of intersection	Schnittpunkt (m
preelongation	Vordehnung (f
preliminary dimensioning	Vor-Dimensionierung (f
pressure, compression	Pressung (f
prestress(ed) force	Vorspannkraft (f
prestress(ing)	Vorspannung (f
principal load, main load	Hauptlast (f
principal stress	Hauptspannung (f
prismatic beam compressive strength	Prismendruckfestigkeit (f
proof stress	Streckgrenze (f
proportional limit	Proportionalitätsgrenze (f
pulley block	Flaschenzug (m
punching	Durchstanzen (n

R

radius of inertia	Trägheitsradius(m
redistribution of section forces	Umlagerung(f der Schnittkräfte
reduction of the cross section	Querschnittsschwächung(f
reference point	Bezugspunkt(m
resolution of a force	Kraftzerlegung(f
resultant (force)	Resultierende(f, Mittelkraft(f
resultant force	resultierende Kraft(f
Ritter method	Verfahren(n nach Ritter
rocking pier	Pendelstütze(f
rolling resistance	Rollreibungskraft(f
rope friction	Seilreibung(f
rupture stress, tensile –	Bruchfestigkeit(f

S

safety against rupture	Bruchsicherheit(f
safety coefficient	Sicherheitsgrad(m, Sicherheitsfaktor(m
scale of forces	Kräftemassstab(m
section modulus	Widerstandsmoment(n
section of a beam	Balkenquerschnitt(m
sectional forces	Schnittkräfte(pl
self weight, dead –	Eigengewicht(n
settlement of the support	Auflagersenkung(f
shear	Schub(m
shear force	Schubkraft(f
shear strength	Scherfestigkeit(f
shear stress	Schubspannung(f
shear(ing) force	Querkraft(f
shear(ing) stress	Scherspannung(f
shearing force	Scherkraft(f, Querkraft(f
shrinkage	Schwinden(n
slenderness	Schlankheitsgrad(m
sliding friction	Gleitreibung(f
sloping reinforcement	Schrägbewehrung(f
snow load	Schneelast(f
stability	Standsicherheit(f
stability	Stabilität(f
stability proof	Stabilitätsnachweis(m
static friction	Haftreibung(f
statically determinate	statisch bestimmt
statically indeterminate	statisch unbestimmt
steel stress	Stahlspannung(f
stiffness coefficient	Steifigkeitszahl(f
strength test	Festigkeitsprüfung(f
stress	Spannung(f

stress ratio	Anstrengungs-Verhältnis(n
stress relieving	Entspannung(f
stress-strain diagram	Spannungs-Dehnungs-Diagramm(n
structural analysis, static computation	statische Berechnung(f
superposition	Überlagerung(f, Superposition(f
superposition	Superposition(f, Überlagerung(f
support force	Auflagerkraft(f
support reaction, bearing -	Auflagerreaktion(f

T

tensile force	Zugkraft(f
tensile reinforcement	Zugbewehrung(f
tensile stress	Zugspannung(f
tension flange	Zuggurt(m
tension member, tensile member	Zugglied(n, Zugstab(m
tension(ed) zone, tensile zone	Zugzone(f
theory of elasticity, elastic theorie	Elastizitätstheorie(f
theory of plasticity	Plastizitätstheorie(f
thermidynamic temperature	thermodynamische Temperatur(f
three-cent(e)red arch	Dreigelenkbogen(m
three-moment equation	Clapeyronsche Gleichung(f
top of moments	Momentenspitze(f
torque	Drehmoment(n
torsion	Verdrehung(f, Torsion(f
torsion	Drillung(f
torsion	Torsion(f
torsion strain	Torsionsbeanspruchung(f
torsional moment	Torsionsmoment(n
total load	Totallast(f

U

ultimate stress, tensile stress	Zugfestigkeit(f
undeformed system	unverformtes System(n
undisplaced joint	unverschieblicher Knoten(m
unfavo(u)rable combination of forces	ungünstige Kräftekombination(f
uniformly distributed	gleichmässig verteilt
upper boom	Obergurt(m

W

wind power	Windlast(f
working load	Traglast(f
working load	Gebrauchslast(f

working state   Gebrauchszustand(m

Y
yield stress   Fliessspannung(f

Statik, Festigkeit

A

Anfangsspannung(f	initial stress
angenommene Belastung(f	assumed load, design load
Angriffspunkt(m	point of application
Anprallkraft(f	impact force
Anstrengungs-Verhältnis(n	stress ratio
Antriebsmoment(n	driving torque
Arbeitsgleichung(f	equation of kinetics
Auflagerkraft(f	support force
Auflagerreaktion(f	support reaction, bearing –
Auflagersenkung(f	settlement of the support
Auflagerverschiebung(f	bearing displacement

B

Balken(m auf zwei Stützen	beam on two bearings
Balkenquerschnitt(m	section of a beam
Beanspruchungsart(f	mode of application
Belastung(f	loading, load application
Belastungsart(f	mode of loading
Belastungsfall(m	condition of loading
Belastungsgrenze(f	loading limt
Bemessung(f	design, structural design
Betonspannung(f	concrete stress
Beulen(n	bulging
Beulfestigkeit(f	bulging resistance
Bezugspunkt(m	reference point
Biegespannung(f	bending stress

Biegung mit Normalkraft — combined bending
Biegung (f — bending
Biegungsfestigkeit (f — bending resistance
Biegungsmoment (n — bending moment
Bremskraft (f — braking force
Bruchfestigkeit (f — rupture stress, tensile –
Bruchlast (f — breaking load, ultimate –
Bruchsicherheit (f — safety against rupture

C

Clapeyronsche Gleichung (f — three-moment equation
Cremona-Verfahren (n — Cremona method
Cremonaplan (m — Cremona's polygon of forces
Crossverfahren (n — Cross method

D

Dehnung (f — extension
Dehnungskoeffizient (m — coefficient of elongation
Diagonalstab (m — diagonal member
Drehmoment (n — torque
Dreigelenkbogen (m — three-cent(e)red arch
Dreigelenkrahmen (m — frame with three hinges
Drillung (f — torsion
Druckarmierung (f — compressive reinforcement, compression reinforcement
Druckdiagonale (f — diagonal in compression, compression diagonal
Druckfestigkeit (f — compressive strength
Druckglied (n, Druckstab (m — compressive member
Druckkraft (f — compressive force
Druckspannung (f — compressive stress
Druckzone (f — compressed zone, compression zone
Durchbiegung (f — deflection
Durchlaufträger (m — continuous beam
Durchstanzen (n — punching
dynamische Wirkung (f — dynamic effect

E

Eigengewicht (n — self weight, dead –
Einflusslinie (f — influence line
eingespannt — fixed, built-in
eingespannter Träger (m — fixed girder, built-in beam
Einspannung (f — fixed end, fixity, constraint
Einzellast (f — concentrated load
Elastizitätsgrenze (f — elastic limit

Elastizitätsmodul(m	modulus of elasticity
Elastizitätstheorie(f theorie	theory of elasticity, elastic
Eliminationsverfahren(n	elimination method
Entspannung(f	stress relieving
Ermüdungseinfluss(m	influence of fatigue
Eulersche Knicklast(f	Euler crippling load
exzentrisches Knicken(n	eccentric buckling
Exzentrizität(f	eccentricity

F

Fachwerk(n	framework
Fachwerkträger(m	lattice girder
Fachwerkwirkung(f	lattice effect
Feldmoment(n moment	moment in the span, span
feste Rolle(f	fixed sheave
Festigkeitsprüfung(f	strength test
Flaschenzug(m	pulley block
Fliessspannung(f	yield stress
Formänderung(f	deformation

G

Gebrauchslast(f	working load
Gebrauchszustand(m	working state
geknickter Träger(m	angular girder
Gelenkträger, Gerberträger(m	Gerber girder
Gewichtskraft(f	gravitational force
Gleichgewicht(n	equilibrium
Gleichgewichtsbedingung(f	condition of equilibrium
gleichmässig verteilt	uniformly distributed
Gleitgrenze(f	limiting friction
Gleitreibung(f	sliding friction
graphische Lösung(f	graphical solution

H

Hängewerk(n	hanging truss
Haftreibung(f	static friction
Hauptlast(f	principal load, main load
Hauptspannung(f	principal stress
Hookesches Gesetz(n	Hooke's law
Hypothese(f von Bernoulli	Bernoulli(s) hypothesis

I

ideelle Schlankheit(f	fictive slenderness
in Bewegung(f	in motion

in Ruhe(f, ruhend	at rest
Instabilität(f	instability
integrale Auswertung(f	integral evaluation

K

Kernfläche(f	core area
Kernweite(f	core dimension
Kippen(n	overturning
Kippmoment(n	overturning moment
Knicken(n	buckling
Knicken(n, Knickung(f	buckling
Knicklänge(f	effectiv length
Knicklast(f	buckling load
Knickspannung(f	buckling stress
Komponente(f	component
Koordinaten(pl	coordinates(pl
Kräftemassstab(m	scale of forces
Kräfteplan(m	diagram of forces
Kräftepolygon(n	force polygone, polygone of forces
Kraft(f	force
Krafteck(n	force polygon
Kraftweg(m	path of load
Kraftzerlegung(f	resolution of a force
Kragarm(m	cantilever arm
Kragträger(m	cantilever girder
Kriecheinfluss(m	creep influence
Kriechen(n	creep

L

Länge(f	length
Längsbewehrung(f	longitudinal reinforcement, longitudinal steel
Längszugkraft(f	longitudinal tensile force
Lagerreibung(f	bearing friction
Lastgruppe(f	group of loads
Lastverteilung(f	load distribution
Lastweg(m	path of force
lose Rolle(f	free sheave

M

mechanische Arbeit(f	mechanical work
mehrere Kräfte(pl	a number of forces(pl
Moment(n	moment
Momentenausgleich(m	moment distribution
Momentenfläche(f	moment diagram

Momentengleichung(f — equation of moments
Momentennullpunkt(m — centre of moments, center of moments
Momentensatz(m — moment theorem
Momentenspitze(f — top of moments

N
Nennwert(m — nominal value
neutrale Achse(f, - Faser(f — neutral axis
Normalkraft(f — axial force, direct force
Nutzlast(f — live load, applied load

O
Obergurt(m — upper boom

P
parallele Kräfte(pl — parallel forces
Pendelstütze(f — rocking pier
Plastizitätstheorie(f — theory of plasticity
Pressung(f — pressure, compression
Prismendruckfestigkeit(f — prismatic beam compressive strength
Proportionalitätsgrenze(f — proportional limit

Q
Querkraft(f — shear(ing) force
Querschnittsfaktor(m — intersection-factor
Querschnittsschwächung(f — reduction of the cross section

R
Rahmen(m — frame, framework
Randspannung(f — extreme (fibre) stress
rechnerisch — mathematical
Reibungskraft(f — friction force
Reibungsmoment(n — moment of friction
Reibungszahl(f — coefficient of friction
resultierende Kraft(f — resultant force
Resultierende(f, Mittelkraft(f — resultant (force)
Riemengeschwindigkeit(f — belt velocity
Riementrieb(m — belt drive
Rissbildung(f — crack formation
Rollreibungskraft(f — rolling resistance

S
Scherfestigkeit(f — shear strength

Scherkraft(f, Querkraft(f	shearing force
Scherspannung(f	shear(ing) stress
schiefe Ebene(f	inclined plane
Schlankheitsgrad(m	slenderness
Schneelast(f	snow load
Schnittkräfte(pl	sectional forces
Schnittpunkt(m	point of intersection
Schrägbewehrung(f	sloping reinforcement
schräger Träger(m	inclined girder
Schub(m	shear
Schubbemessung(f	calculation of shear, shear design
Schubkraft(f	shear force
Schubspannung(f	shear stress
Schwerpunkt(m	centre of gravity
Schwerpunktspannung(f	center of gravity stress
Schwinden(n	shrinkage
Seileck(n	link polygon
Seilreibung(f	rope friction
Sicherheitsgrad(m, Sicherheitsfaktor(m	safety coefficient
Spannung(f	stress
Spannungs-Dehnungs-Diagramm(n	stress-strain diagram
Stabendmoment(n	moment at extremity of member
Stabilität(f	stability
Stabilitätsnachweis(m	stability proof
ständige Last(f	permanent load, dead load
Stahlspannung(f	steel stress
Standsicherheit(f	stability
statisch bestimmt	statically determinate
statisch unbestimmt	statically indeterminate
statische Berechnung(f	structural analysis, static computation
Steifigkeitszahl(f	stiffness coefficient
Streckgrenze(f	proof stress
Stützmoment(n	moment at support
Superposition(f, Überlagerung(f	superposition

T

teilweise vorgespannt	partially prestressed
thermodynamische Temperatur(f	thermidynamic temperature
Torsion(f	torsion
Torsionsbeanspruchung(f	torsion strain
Torsionsmoment(n	torsional moment
Totallast(f	total load
Träger(m	beam, girder

Träger(m auf 2 Stützen — girder on two supports
Trägheitsmoment(n moment — moment of inertia, second moment
Trägheitsradius(m — radius of inertia
Traglast(f — working load

U
Überhöhung(f — hog, chamber
Überlagerung(f, Superposition(f — superposition
Umlagerung(f der Schnittkräfte — redistribution of section forces
ungünstige Kräftekombination(f — unfavo(u)rable combination of forces
Untergurt(m — bottom chord, lower boom
unverformtes System(n — undeformed system
unverschieblicher Knoten(m — undisplaced joint

V
Verbundträger(m — composite girder
Verdrehung(f, Torsion(f — torsion
Verdrehwinkel(m — angle of twist
Verfahren(n nach Ritter — Ritter method
Verformung(f — deformation
Verformungsvermögen(n — deformability
Vergleichsspannung(f — equivalent stress
verteilte Last(f — distribuited load
Vollwandträger(m — plate girder, solid girder
Vor-Dimensionierung(f — preliminary dimensioning
Vordehnung(f — preelongation
Vorspannkraft(f — prestress(ed) force
Vorspannung(f — prestress(ing)

W
Widerstandsmoment(n — section modulus
Windlast(f — wind power
Winkel(m — angle
Wirkungsgrad(m — efficiency
Wirkungslinie(f — line of application
Würfeldruckfestigkeit(f — cube crushing stregth, cube compressive strength

Z
zentrische Belastung(f — center load
zufällige Last(f — accidental load

Zugbewehrung (f	tensile reinforcement
Zugfestigkeit (f	ultimate stress, tensile stress
Zugglied (n, Zugstab (m	tension member, tensile member
Zuggurt (m	tension flange
Zugkraft (f	tensile force
Zugspannung (f	tensile stress
Zugzone (f	tension(ed) zone, tensile zone
zulässige Beanspruchung (f	legal strength
zulässige Randspannung (f	permissible extreme stress
zulässige Spannung (f	permissible stress
zusammengesetzte Spannungen (pl	composite stresses
Zusatzlast, zusätzliche Belastung	additional load
Zwischenauflager (n	intermediate bearing

Internal combustion engines

A

accelerator	Beschleunigungsvorrichtung(f
accumulator	Akkumulator(m
adjusting screw	Einstellschraube(f, Leerlauf-Einstellschraube(f
air cleaner	Luftfilter(m
air conductor	Luftschlauch(m
air intake	Luftansaugkrümmer(m
air intake	Lufteintritt(m
air-colled	luftgekühlt
alternator	Wechselstromgenerator(m
ammeter	Amperemesser(m, Amperemeter(n
amperes-hour	Amperestunde(f
anti-freeze	Frostschutzmittel(n
anti-roll bar	Stabilisator(m (-Träger)
anti-rust	Rostschutzmittel(n
armature	Anker(m
automatic cut-out	Regler-Schalter(m
automatic gearbox	automatische Kupplung(f
automatic gearbox	automatisches Getriebe(n
automatic selection	automatische Schaltung(f
auxiliary shaft	Vorlegewelle(f

B

balance weight	Massenausgleich(m, Ausgleichsmasse(f
battery	Batterie(f
battery capacity	Kapazität(f der Batterie(f
bearing shell	Lagerschale(f
belt	Riemen(m
big end bearings	Pleuellager(pl
bleeder screw	Luftablassschraube(f
boiling point	Siedepunkt(m

bolt	Bolzen(m
bonnet	Motorabdeckung(f
bonnet hood	Motorhaube(f
bore	Bohrung(f
bracket	Federbügel(m
brushes	Bürsten(pl
bulb	Birne(f
bush	Bronzelager(n
butterfly valve	Drosselklappe(f
by-pass filter	Abzweigfilter(m

C

cam	Nocke(f
camshaft	Nockenwelle(f
carburation chamber	Mischkammer(f
carburettor	Vergaser(m
carburettor filter	Filter(m des Vergasers
cartridge	Einsatz(m
cells	Zellen(pl
central backbone	Mittelrohr(n
centrifugal filter	Zentrifugal(öl)filter(m
choke tube	Lufttrichter(m
clean oil	sauberes Öl(n
cleaner	Luftreiniger(m(m
clutch	Kupplung(f
clutch pedal	Kupplungspedal(n
coil	Zündspule(f
coil spring	Schraubenfeder(f
cold plugs	kalte Zündkerzen(pl
combustion chamber	Verbrennungskammer(f
combustion chamber	Verbrennungsraum(m
compression ratio	Verdichtungsverhältnis(n
compression valve	Verdichtungsventil(n
condenser	Kondensator(m
connecting body	Anschlussgehäuse(n
connecting rod	Pleuelstange(f
connexions	Briden(pl, Leitungsanschlüsse(pl
contact	Kontakt(m
contact breaker	Unterbrecher(m
contact breaker point	Unterbrecherkontakt(m
cooling fan	Lüfterrad(n

cooling fin	Kühlrippen(pl
cooling rib	Kühlrippe(f
corroded plugs	korrodierte Zündkerzen(pl
corrosion	Oxydation(r
coupling	Muffe(f
cracked plugs	gesprungene Zündkerzen(pl
crankcase	Kurbelgehäuse(n
crankshaft	Kurbelwelle(f
crown gear	Tellerrad(n
cylinder	Zylinder(m
cylinder block	Zylinderblock(m, Motorblock(m
cylinder bore	Zylinderbohrung(f
cylinder head	Zylinderkopf(m
cylinder head cover	Zylinderkopfdeckel(m
cylinder liner	Zylinderbüchse(f
cylinder liner	Zylinderlaufbuchse(f

D

damper	Stossdämpfer(m
de-icers	Entfroster(m
detergent oil	Spülöl(n
diaphragm	Membrane(f
diesel engine	Dieselmotor(m
differential casing	Differentialgehäuse(n
diodes	Dioden(pl
dip-stick	Ölmessstab(m
direct injector	direkte Einspritzdüse(f
dirty oil	verschmutztes Öl(n
dirty plugs	verschmutzte Zündkerzen(pl
disc brakes	Scheibenbremsen(pl
distance(f of electrodes	Elektrodenabstand(m
distilled water	destilliertes Wasser(n
distributer	Verteiler(m
distributer cap	Verteilerscheibe(f
distributor cam	Verteilernocken(m
distributor cap	Verteilerdeckel(m
distributor shaft	Antriebswelle(f
downdraft carburettor	Fallstromvergaser(m
drain plug	Ablassschraube(f (Öl-)
drainage tap	Ablasshahn(m
driven shaft	Abtriebswelle(f
dry liner	trockene Zylinderlaufbuchse(f

dynamo, generator	Lichtmaschine(f

E

earth strap	Masseleitung(g
eccentric pump	Nockenpumpe(f
electric fan	Elektrolüfter(m
electric pump	Elektropumpe(f
electrode	Elektrode(f
electromagnetic control	elektromagnetischer Antrieb(m
electromagnetic engagement	Magnetkupplung(f
engagement	Einrückvorrichtung(f
engin inspection light	Motorraumleuchte(f
engine revs	Motordrehzahl(f
exhaust	Auspuff(m
exhaust pipe	Auspuffrohr(n
external cylinder	äussere Hülse(f

F

fan	Gebläserad(n
fan	Ventilator(m
fan	Ventilatorflügel(m
fan belt	Keilriemen(m
fan belt	Ventilatorriemen(m
fan housing	Gebläsegehäuse(n
fast runnig jet	Hauptdüse(f
fitting, coupling	Befestigungsvorrichtung(f
flexible coupling	Keilnabengelenk(n
flexible coupling	Federkupplung(f
float	Schwimmer(m
float chamber	Schwimmergehäuse(n
float needle	Schwimmernadel(f
flywheel	Schwungrad(n
flywheel starter ring	Starterzahnkranz(m
fog lamps	Nebelscheinwerfer(pl
four-barrel carburettor	Vierfachvergaser(m
four-stroke	Viertakt-
four-way pipe	Vierwegverschraubung(f
freezing point	Gefriertemperatur(f
fuel filter	Kraftstofffilter(m

fuel injection pump	Einspritzpumpe(f
fuel injector	Einspritzdüse(f
fuel pressure line	Druckleitung(f
fuel pump	Kraftstoffpumpe(f
fuel supply pipe	Benzinleitung(f
fuel tank	Brennstofftank(m
fused insulation	Schmelzisolation(f

G

gear	Getriebe(n
gear box ratio	Übersetzungsverhältnis(n
gear lever	Getriebeschalthebel(m
gear pump	Zahnradpumpe(f
gearbox	Getriebegehäuse(n
gears	Zahnräder(pl
gearshift	Schaltgabel(f
gudgeon pin, piston pin	Kolbenbolzen(m

H

hand brake	Handbremse(f
heater plug	Glühkerze(f
heating element	Glühdraht(m, Glühfaden(m
helicoid sector	Schneckensegment(n
hinge	Scharnier(n
holding pin	Haltebolzen(m
honeycomb-type radiator	Lamellenkühler(m
horizontal carburettor	Flachstromvergaser(m
horizontal opposed-piston engine	Boxermotor(m
hot plugs	heisse Zündkerzen(pl
hub	Nabe(f
hydraulic drive	hydraulische Betätigung(f
hydraulic pump	Hydraulikpumpe(f
hydraulic tappets	hydraulische Ventilstössel(pl

I
ignition cable	Zündkabel(n
inclined valve	schräghängendes Ventil(n
indirect injector	indirekte Einspritzdüse(f
ingnition lock, ignition switch	Zündschloss(n, Zündschalter(m
inlet	Ansaugstutzen(m
inlet pipe	Ansaugrohr(n
inlet valve	Einlassventil(n
inlet valve	Saugventil(n
insulating bush	Isolierbuchse(f
internal cylinder	inneres Rohr(n

L
lead	Kabel(n
lever	Druckhebel(m
link	Druckstange(f
lower toggle	unter Nocke(f
lubrication	Schmierung(f

M
magneto	Zündmagnet(m
main bearings	Hauptlager(pl
main shaft	Hauptwelle(f
manifold	Kollektor(m
manual selection	Handschaltung(f
matgnetic field	Magnetfeld(n
measure of voltage	Spannungsmessung(f
mechanical gearbox	mechanisches Getriebe(n
mechanical pump	mechanische (betätigte) Pumpe(f
medium oil	mittleres Öl(n
mesh filter	Siebfilter(m
multigrade oil	Mehrbereichsöl(n

N

needle valve	Nadelventil(n
negative pole	Minuspol(m
neutral	Leergang(m, Leerlauf(m
nuts	Muttern(pl

O

oil cap	Öleinfüllstutzen(m
oil filler	Öleinfüllstutzen(m
oil filter	Ölfilter(m
oil level	Ölstand(m
oil pressure gauge	Öldruckanzeiger(m
oil pressure gauge	Ölstandsanzeiger(m
oil pressure warning light	Öldruck-Kontrollleuchte(f
oil pump	Ölpumpe(f
oil seal, gasket	Dichtring(m, Dichtung(f
oil sump	Ölwanne(f
oil tank	Ölbehälter(m
oil temperature gauge	Öl-Fernthermometer(n
oil-water heat exchanger	Wärmeaustauscher(m
overhead valve	hängendes Ventil(n

P

petrol engine, gasoline –	Benzinmotor(m
petrol gauge	Kraftstoff-Vorratsanzeiger(m
pinion	Antriebsritzel(n
pinion	Ritzel(n
pipes	Leitungen(pl
pipes	Rohrleitungen(pl, Ölleitungen(pl
piston	Kolben(m
piston displacement	Zylinderinhalt(m, Hubraum(m
piston ring	Kolbenring(m
piston rings	Verdichtungsringe(pl
piston stroke	Kolbenhub(m
planetary	Planetenrad(n
plate	Kupplungsscheibe(f
plates	Platten(pl

platinum points	Platinkontakte(pl
play of pedal	Kupplungsspiel(n
plug body	Kerzengehäuse(n
pneumatic pump	pneumatische Pumpe(f
positive pole	Pluspol(m
pressure adjusting valve	Überdruckölventil(n
pressure gauge	Druckmesser(m, Manometer(n
pressure greaser	Druckschmierkopf(m
propan gas engine	Propangasmotor
pulley	Schwungscheibe(f
pump	Hauptbremszylinder(m
pump cylinder	Pumpenzylinder(m

R

rack-and-pinion	Zahnstange(f
radiator cap	Kühlerverschluss(m
radiator cell	Kühlerteilblock(m
radiator connexion	Kühlerschlauch(m
radiator grill	Kühlergrill(m
radiator with vertical tubes	Röhrenkühler(m
raiator	Kühler(m
recirculating ball	Kugelumlauf(m
reduction gear	Untersetzungsgetriebe(n
reflector	Reflektor(m
register nut	Einstellmutter(f
registration pivot	Nachstellbolzen(m
registration pull rod	Nachstellzugstange(f
release spring	Rückzugfeder(f
resistance	Widerstand(m
revolution counter	Drehzahlmesser(m
rim	Tragring(m
rod	Schubstange(f
rod	Kegelradtrieb(m
rod	Stösselstange(f
rotary engine	Rotationskolben-Motor(m
rotor arm	Unterbrecherhebel(m
rotor pump	Laufradpumpe(f
rubber buffer	Gummipuffer(m

S

scraper ring	Ölabstreifring(m
sealed circuit	verplombter Kreislauf(m
sealing ring	Dichtring(m
semi-downdraft carburettor	Halbfallstromvergaser(m
servo-brake	Servobremse(f
shackle	Federlasche(f
shoes	Bremsbacken(m pl
side valve	stehendes Ventil(n
silencer	Schalldämpfer(m
single dry plate	Einscheibentrockenkupplung(f
single-barrel carburettor	Einzelvergaser(m
slip coupling	Schiebemuffe(f
slip joint	Schiebegelenk(n
slow running jet	Leerlaufdüse(f
socket	Anschluss(m, Stromanschluss(m
spark advance control	Zündhebel(m
sparking plug	Zündkerze(f
spray nozzles	Einspritzdüsen(pl
spring retaining collar	Federteller(m
starting handle dog	Andrehklaue(f
starting motor	Anlasser(m
starting motor	Anlasser(m, Starter(m
stationary engine	stationärer Motor(m
stop ring	Anschlagring(m
stroke	Hub(m
summer oil	Sommeröl(n
switch	Einstell-Knopf(m
switch	Unterbrecher(m
synchronized gearbox	Synchrongetriebe(n

T

tachometer	Tachometer(n
tappet clearance	Stösselspiel(n
tappet heads	Stösselkopf(m
terminal nut	Anschlussmutter(f
terminals	Klemmen(pl
thermometer	Thermometer(n
thermostat	Thermostat(m
thick oil	dickflüssiges Öl(n
thin oil	dünnflüssiges Öl(n
three-way pipe	Dreiwegverschraubung(f

throttle, throttle valve	Drossel(f, Drosselklappe(f
thrust bearing	Drucklager(n
thrust spring	Kupplungsdruckfeder(f
timing chain	Steuerkette(f
transmission shaft	Übertragungswelle, Gelenkwelle(f
tread	Lauffläche(f
twin camshaft	doppelt gelagerte Nockenwelle(f
twin-barrel carburettor	Doppelvergaser(m
two leading shoes	selbsttätige Backen(pl
two-stroke petrol (gasoline) engine	Zweitakt-Benzinmotor(m
two-way valve	doppelt wirkendes Ventil(n

U

universal joint	Kardangelenk(n
unsynchronized gear	nicht synchronisierter Gang(m
uper swinging arm	oberer Schwingarm(m
upper toggle	obere Nocke(f

V

V-engine	V-Motor(m
valve	Ventil(n
valve clearance	Ventilspiel(n
valve guide	Ventilführung(f
valve head	Ventilteller(m
valve seat	Ventilsitz(m
valve seat insert	Ventilsitzring(m
valve spring	Ventilfeder(f
valve stem	Ventilschaft(m
vaporizing jet	Düse(f
vertical engine	stehender Motor(m
voltage regulator	Spannungsregler(m

W

warning light	Kontrollleuchte(f
water circuit	Wasserumlauf(m
water pump	Wasserpumpe(f
water temperature gauge	Kühlmittel-Fernthermometer(n
water-cooled	wassergekühlt
wet liner	nasse Zylinderlaufbuchse(f
windings	Wicklung(f, Windungen(pl
windscreen wiper motor	Scheibenwischer-Motor(m
wing nuts	Nachstellmuttern(pl
winter oil	Winteröl(n

**Verbrennungs—
motoren**

A

Ablasshahn(m	drainage tap
Ablassschraube(f (Öl-)	drain plug
Abtriebswelle(f	driven shaft
Abzweigfilter(m	by-pass filter
äussere Hülse(f	external cylinder
Akkumulator(m	accumulator
Amperemesser(m, Amperemeter(n	ammeter
Amperestunde(f	amperes-hour
Andrehklaue(f	starting handle dog
Anker(m	armature
Anlasser(m	starting motor
Anlasser(m, Starter(m	starting motor
Ansaugrohr(n	inlet pipe
Ansaugstutzen(m	inlet
Anschlagring(m	stop ring
Anschluss(m, Stromanschluss(m	socket
Anschlussgehäuse(n	connecting body
Anschlussmutter(f	terminal nut
Antriebsritzel(n	pinion
Antriebswelle(f	distributor shaft
Auspuff(m	exhaust
Auspuffrohr(n	exhaust pipe
automatische Kupplung(f	automatic gearbox
automatische Schaltung(f	automatic selection
automatisches Getriebe(n	automatic gearbox

B

Batterie(f	battery
Befestigungsvorrichtung(f	fitting, coupling
Benzinleitung(f	fuel supply pipe
Benzinmotor(m	petrol engine, gasoline -
Beschleunigungsvorrichtung(f	accelerator

Birne(f	bulb
Bohrung(f	bore
Bolzen(m	bolt
Boxermotor(m engine	horizontal opposed-piston
Bremsbacken(m pl	shoes
Brennstofftank(m	fuel tank
Briden(pl, Leitungsanschlüsse(pl	connexions
Bronzelager(n	bush
Bürsten(pl	brushes

D

destilliertes Wasser(n	distilled water
Dichtring(m	sealing ring
Dichtring(m, Dichtung(f	oil seal, gasket
dickflüssiges Öl(n	thick oil
Dieselmotor(m	diesel engine
Differentialgehäuse(n	differential casing
Dioden(pl	diodes
direkte Einspritzdüse(f	direct injector
doppelt gelagerte Nockenwelle(f	twin camshaft
doppelt wirkendes Ventil(n	two-way valve
Doppelvergaser(m	twin-barrel carburettor
Drehzahlmesser(m	revolution counter
Dreiwegverschraubung(f	three-way pipe
Drossel(f, Drosselklappe(f	throttle, throttle valve
Drosselklappe(f	butterfly valve
Druckhebel(m	lever
Drucklager(n	thrust bearing
Druckleitung(f	fuel pressure line
Druckmesser(m, Manometer(n	pressure gauge
Druckschmierkopf(m	pressure greaser
Druckstange(f	link
dünnflüssiges Öl(n	thin oil
Düse(f	vaporizing jet

E

Einlassventil(n	inlet valve
Einrückvorrichtung(f	engagement

Einsatz(m	cartridge
Einscheibentrockenkupplung(f	single dry plate
Einspritzdüse(f	fuel injector
Einspritzdüsen(pl	spray nozzles
Einspritzpumpe(f	fuel injection pump
Einstell-Knopf(m	switch
Einstellmutter(f	register nut
Einstellschraube(f	adjusting screw
Einstellschraube(f (Leerlauf-)	adjusting screw
Einzelvergaser(m	single-barrel carburettor
Elektrode(f	electrode
Elektrodenabstand(m	distance(f of electrodes
Elektrolüfter(m	electric fan
elektromagnetischer Antrieb(m	electromagnetic control
Elektropumpe(f	electric pump
Entfroster(m	de-icers

F

Fallstromvergaser(m	downdraft carburettor
Federbügel(m	bracket
Federkupplung(f	flexible coupling
Federlasche(f	shackle
Federteller(m	spring retaining collar
Filter(m des Vergasers	carburettor filter
Flachstromvergaser(m	horizontal carburettor
Frostschutzmittel(n	anti-freeze

G

Gebläsegehäuse(n	fan housing
Gebläserad(n	fan
Gefriertemperatur(f	freezing point
gesprungene Zündkerzen(pl	cracked plugs
Getriebe(n	gear
Getriebegehäuse(n	gearbox
Getriebeschalthebel(m	gear lever
Glühdraht(m, Glühfaden(m	heating element
Glühkerze(f	heater plug
Gummipuffer(m	rubber buffer

H

hängendes Ventil(n	overhead valve
Halbfallstromvergaser(m	semi-downdraft carburettor
Haltebolzen(m	holding pin
Handbremse(f	hand brake
Handschaltung(f	manual selection
Hauptbremszylinder(m	pump
Hauptdüse(f	fast runnig jet
Hauptlager(pl	main bearings
Hauptwelle(f	main shaft
heisse Zündkerzen(pl	hot plugs
Hub(m	stroke
Hydraulikpumpe(f	hydraulic pump
hydraulische Betätigung(f	hydraulic drive
hydraulische Ventilstössel(pl	hydraulic tappets

I

indirekte Einspritzdüse(f	indirect injector
inneres Rohr(n	internal cylinder
Isolierbuchse(f	insulating bush

K

Kabel(n	lead
kalte Zündkerzen(pl	cold plugs
Kapazität(f der Batterie(f	battery capacity
Kardangelenk(n	universal joint
Kegelradtrieb(m	rod
Keilnabengelenk(n	flexible coupling
Keilriemen(m	fan belt
Kerzengehäuse(n	plug body
Klemmen(pl	terminals
Kolben(m	piston
Kolbenbolzen(m	gudgeon pin, piston pin
Kolbenhub(m	piston stroke
Kolbenring(m	piston ring
Kollektor(m	manifold
Kondensator(m	condenser

Kontakt(m	contact
Kontrollleuchte(f	warning light
korrodierte Zündkerzen(pl	corroded plugs
Kraftstoff-Vorratsanzeiger(m	petrol gauge
Kraftstofffilter(m	fuel filter
Kraftstoffpumpe(f	fuel pump
Kühler(m	raiator
Kühlergrill(m	radiator grill
Kühlerschlauch(m	radiator connexion
Kühlerteilblock(m	radiator cell
Kühlerverschluss(m	radiator cap
Kühlmittel-Fernthermometer(n	water temperature gauge
Kühlrippe(f	cooling rib
Kühlrippen(pl	cooling fin
Kugelumlauf(m	recirculating ball
Kupplung(f	clutch
Kupplungsdruckfeder(f	thrust spring
Kupplungspedal(n	clutch pedal
Kupplungsscheibe(f	plate
Kupplungsspiel(n	play of pedal
Kurbelgehäuse(n	crankcase
Kurbelwelle(f	crankshaft

L

Lagerschale(f	bearing shell
Lamellenkühler(m	honeycomb-type radiator
Lauffläche(f	tread
Laufradpumpe(f	rotor pump
Leergang(m, Leerlauf(m	neutral
Leerlaufdüse(f	slow running jet
Leitungen(pl	pipes
Lichtmaschine(f	dynamo, generator
Lüfterrad(n	cooling fan
Luftablassschraube(f	bleeder screw
Luftansaugkrümmer(m	air intake
Lufteintritt(m	air intake
Luftfilter(m	air cleaner
luftgekühlt	air-colled
Luftreiniger(m(m	cleaner
Luftschlauch(m	air conductor
Lufttrichter(m	choke tube

M
Magnetfeld(n   matgnetic field
Magnetkupplung(f   electromagnetic engagement
Masseleitung(g   earth strap
Massenausgleich(m, Ausgleichsmasse(f   balance weight
mechanische (betätigte) Pumpe(f   mechanical pump
mechanisches Getriebe(n   mechanical gearbox
Mehrbereichsöl(n   multigrade oil
Membrane(f   diaphragm
Minuspol(m   negative pole
Mischkammer(f   carburation chamber
Mittelrohr(n   central backbone
mittleres Öl(n   medium oil
Motorabdeckung(f   bonnet
Motordrehzahl(f   engine revs
Motorhaube(f   bonnet hood
Motorraumleuchte(f   engin inspection light
Muffe(f   coupling
Muttern(pl   nuts

N
Nabe(f   hub
Nachstellbolzen(m   registration pivot
Nachstellmuttern(pl   wing nuts
Nachstellzugstange(f   registration pull rod
Nadelventil(n   needle valve
nasse Zylinderlaufbuchse(f   wet liner
Nebelscheinwerfer(pl   fog lamps
nicht synchronisierter Gang(m   unsynchronized gear
Nocke(f   cam
Nockenpumpe(f   eccentric pump
Nockenwelle(f   camshaft

O
obere Nocke(f   upper toggle

oberer Schwingarm(m	uper swinging arm
Öl-Fernthermometer(n	oil temperature gauge
Ölabstreifring(m	scraper ring
Ölbehälter(m	oil tank
Öldruck-Kontrollleuchte(f	oil pressure warning light
Öldruckanzeiger(m	oil pressure gauge
Öleinfüllstutzen(m	oil cap
Öleinfüllstutzen(m	oil filler
Ölfilter(m	oil filter
Ölmessstab(m	dip-stick
Ölpumpe(f	oil pump
Ölstand(m	oil level
Ölstandsanzeiger(m	oil pressure gauge
Ölwanne(f	oil sump
Oxydation(f	corrosion

P

Planetenrad(n	planetary
Platinkontakte(pl	platinum points
Platten(pl	plates
Pleuellager(pl	big end bearings
Pleuelstange(f	connecting rod
Pluspol(m	positive pole
pneumatische Pumpe(f	pneumatic pump
Propangasmotor	propan gas engine
Pumpenzylinder(m	pump cylinder

R

Reflektor(m	reflector
Regler-Schalter(m	automatic cut-out
Riemen(m	belt
Ritzel(n	pinion
Röhrenkühler(m	radiator with vertical tubes
Rohrleitungen(pl, Ölleitungen(pl	pipes
Rostschutzmittel(n	anti-rust
Rotationskolben-Motor(m	rotary engine
Rückzugfeder(f	release spring

S

sauberes Öl(n	clean oil
Saugventil(n	inlet valve
Schalldämpfer(m	silencer
Schaltgabel(f	gearshift
Scharnier(n	hinge
Scheibenbremsen(pl	disc brakes
Scheibenwischer-Motor(m	windscreen wiper motor
Schiebegelenk(n	slip joint
Schiebemuffe(f	slip coupling
Schmelzisolation(f	fused insulation
Schmierung(f	lubrication
Schneckensegment(n	helicoid sector
schräghängendes Ventil(n	inclined valve
Schraubenfeder(f	coil spring
Schubstange(f	rod
Schwimmer(m	float
Schwimmergehäuse(n	float chamber
Schwimmernadel(f	float needle
Schwungrad(n	flywheel
Schwungscheibe(f	pulley
selbsttätige Backen(pl	two leading shoes
Servobremse(f	servo-brake
Siebfilter(m	mesh filter
Siedepunkt(m	boiling point
Sommeröl(n	summer oil
Spannungsmessung(f	measure of voltage
Spannungsregler(m	voltage regulator
Spülöl(n	detergent oil
Stabilisator(m (-Träger)	anti-roll bar
Starterzahnkranz(m	flywheel starter ring
stationärer Motor(m	stationary engine
stehender Motor(m	vertical engine
stehendes Ventil(n	side valve
Steuerkette(f	timing chain
Stösselkopf(m	tappet heads
Stösselspiel(n	tappet clearance
Stösselstange(f	rod
Stossdämpfer(m	damper
Synchrongetriebe(n	synchronized gearbox

T

Tachometer(n	tachometer
Tellerrad(n	crown gear
Thermometer(n	thermometer
Thermostat(m	thermostat
Tragring(m	rim
trockene Zylinderlaufbuchse(f	dry liner

U

Überdruckölventil(n	pressure adjusting valve
Übersetzungsverhältnis(n	gear box ratio
Übertragungswelle, Gelenkwelle(f	transmission shaft
unter Nocke(f	lower toggle
Unterbrecher(m	contact breaker
Unterbrecher(m	switch
Unterbrecherhebel(m	rotor arm
Unterbrecherkontakt(m	contact breaker point
Untersetzungsgetriebe(n	reduction gear

V

V-Motor(m	V-engine
Ventil(n	valve
Ventilator(m	fan
Ventilatorflügel(m	fan
Ventilatorriemen(m	fan belt
Ventilfeder(f	valve spring
Ventilführung(f	valve guide
Ventilschaft(m	valve stem
Ventilsitz(m	valve seat
Ventilsitzring(m	valve seat insert
Ventilspiel(n	valve clearance
Ventilteller(m	valve head
Verbrennungskammer(f	combustion chamber
Verbrennungsraum(m	combustion chamber
Verdichtungsringe(pl	piston rings
Verdichtungsventil(n	compression valve
Verdichtungsverhältnis(n	compression ratio

Vergaser (m	carburettor
verplombter Kreislauf (m	sealed circuit
verschmutzte Zündkerzen (pl	dirty plugs
verschmutztes Öl (n	dirty oil
Verteiler (m	distributer
Verteilerdeckel (m	distributor cap
Verteilernocken (m	distributor cam
Verteilerscheibe (f	distributer cap
Vierfachvergaser (m	four-barrel carburettor
Viertakt-	four-stroke
Vierwegverschraubung (f	four-way pipe
Vorlegewelle (f	auxiliary shaft

W

Wärmeaustauscher (m	oil-water heat exchanger
wassergekühlt	water-cooled
Wasserpumpe (f	water pump
Wasserumlauf (m	water circuit
Wechselstromgenerator (m	alternator
Wicklung (f, Windungen (pl	windings
Widerstand (m	resistance
Winteröl (n	winter oil

Z

Zahnradpumpe (f	gear pump
Zahnräder (pl	gears
Zahnstange (f	rack-and-pinion
Zellen (pl	cells
Zentrifugal(öl)filter (m	centrifugal filter
Zündhebel (m	spark advance control
Zündkabel (n	ignition cable
Zündkerze (f	sparking plug
Zündmagnet (m	magneto
Zündschloss (n, Zündschalter (m	ingnition lock, ignition switch
Zündspule (f	coil
Zweitakt-Benzinmotor (m	two-stroke petrol (gasoline) engine

Zylinder (m	cylinder
Zylinderblock (m, Motorblock (m	cylinder block
Zylinderbohrung (f	cylinder bore
Zylinderbüchse (f	cylinder liner
Zylinderinhalt (m, Hubraum (m	piston displacement
Zylinderkopf (m	cylinder head
Zylinderkopfdeckel (m	cylinder head cover
Zylinderlaufbuchse (f	cylinder liner